A WELSH HOUSE AND ITS FAMILY:
THE VAUGHANS OF TRAWSGOED

A WELSH HOUSE AND ITS FAMILY

THE VAUGHANS OF TRAWSGOED

A study of the Vaughan Family and Estate
through seven centuries

Gerald Morgan

With an Afterword by
the Hon. John Vaughan

This book is for
Eleanor and Rowland

First Impression—1997

ISBN 1 85902 472 6

© Gerald Morgan

This book is published with the support of the Arts Council Of Wales.

Printed in Wales by
J. D. Lewis, and Sons Ltd., Gomer Press, Llandysul, Ceredigion

CONTENTS

ILLUSTRATIONS

The author and publisher are grateful to the Earl of Lisburne and the Hon.
Michael Vaughan for permission to use the illustrations on the following
pages: 21, 28, 29, 51, 65, 69, 70, 73, 110, 129, 140, 144, 151, 153, 159, 170,
202, 234, and to the National Library of Wales for illustrations on pp. 165,
166, 173. Other photographs are by the author.

MAPS

ACKNOWLEDGEMENTS

I owe more debts of gratitude than I can easily recall, but my first thanks must go to the present Earl and Countess of Lisburne for their readiness to welcome me to their home, showing me family pictures, records, heirlooms and memorabilia in their possession, and for their willingness to discuss details of the history of the family and its estate. Their support at a Day School held at Plas Trawsgoed in May 1991 was particularly appreciated. Lord Lisburne kindly made albums and other documents available to the National Library of Wales for copying. His son, the Hon. John Vaughan has helped me in discussion, and enabled me to consult family albums, and I am indebted to him for providing an Afterword; Lord Lisburne and his son Michael kindly made it possible for the National Library to photograph pictures from the family collection. The family genealogy of recent generations drawn up by their cousin, Miss Diana Vaughan, was most useful. Some of my enquiries about Llanafan church were kindly answered by the Earl's sister, Lady Honor Llewellyn. All this help was given in a spirit of disinterested generosity. My extra-mural classes, particularly those at Llanfihangel-y-Creuddyn, Cwmystwyth and Llanafan, provided me with many details of local background, and discussion with them has helped clarify my understanding.

Records relating to the family and estate are held principally at the National Library of Wales, but also at the Dyfed Record Office Aberystwyth Branch, the office of the Royal Commission on Historic Monuments and the Public Record Office, Chancery Lane. The staff of all these institutions have been most helpful in every way. I am indebted to Professor Walford Davies, Director of the Department of Extra-Mural Studies at the University College of Wales, Aberystwyth, for his encouragement and support, and to Dr Evan James for many useful suggestions. I owe a special debt to Dr Richard Moore-Colyer, to Dr Stephen Briggs and Miss Caroline Kerkham, who read the typescript and offered a stream of valuable and encouraging comments. I have benefited from discussions with the late Professor Bedwyr Lewis Jones, and with Dr Jill Barber, who supplied me with valuable material from the Llidiardau papers in the National Library. Many others have helped me, including Professor Peter Thomas, Dr Susan Davies, Dr Llinos Beverley Smith, and Dr Anne Knowles of the University of Wales, Aberystwyth, Dr Janet Burton (now of St Davids University College, Lampeter) and the staff of the Dyfed (now Ceredigion) Record Office at Aberystwyth, Mr Peter Lord, Mr Toby Driver, Mrs Ros Laidlaw, Mr Arthur Chater, Emeritus Professor Dafydd Jenkins and Mrs Hazel Stirgess; my apologies to others whose names I have neglected. The staff of the National Library of Wales gave their usual friendly and unstinting help with documents, maps and pictures. I am especially indebted to the Keeper of Maps and Prints, Dr Huw Owen and members of staff, including Mr Paul Joyner and Mr Gareth Hughes. My thanks are also due to Mairwen Prys Jones of Gwasg Gomer, Llandysul, and the Welsh Books Council.

I must confess to my failure to solve a problem of consistency - how to refer to titled members of the family. Constant repetition of `the second Viscount Lisburne', and still worse, `the fourth Viscount and first Earl of Lisburne' who was one man, is irritating, and seems impersonal. Unfortunately, to turn to their personal names can be confusing, since the names Edward, John, Wilmot and Ernest were used for many members of the family. The fourth Viscount and first Earl, Wilmot Vaughan, had a father and a son of the same name; he also had a brother, a grandfather and a son called John Vaughan. I have simply used the forms which seemed to me clearest in the different contexts. I have usually (but not always) ignored the courtesy title of `Lord Vaughan' by which the heirs apparent to the title were traditionally known, and referred to them by their personal names.

I would have liked to include a detailed map of the Trawsgoed estate in Ceredigion. Unfortunately this is a task beyond my capacity. Great estates were not static entities; buying and selling went on continuously, rentals are often incomplete, and farms varied in size from generation to generation. Any map I could produce would be full of inaccuracies. The map on p. 182 shows the parishes in which the family held land.

GERALD MORGAN
Llanafan; Aberystwyth

ABBREVIATIONS

CD = National Library of Wales, Crosswood Deeds

DWB = *The Dictionary of Welsh Biography*, (London, 1959)

NLW = National Library of Wales

NLWJ = *National Library of Wales Journal*

PRO = Public Record Office

THSC = *Transactions of the Honourable Society of Cymmrodorion*

WHR = *Welsh History Review*

FOREWORD

In August 1884 a remarkable scene was enacted on the fine lawns of Trawsgoed mansion. More than five hundred guests, including hundreds of farm tenants on the estate, crowded to celebrate the coming of age of Arthur, Lord Vaughan, eldest son and heir of the fifth Earl of Lisburne. Special trains brought many of the guests, Wheatley and Sons' String Band played melodies of all kinds, huge kettles hanging from tripods boiled vigorously in the open air, and areas were marked off for games and races. The Earl and Countess opened the house to the visitors and showed them round. In the entrance hall they passed beneath portraits of the Earl's father, who had died in 1873, and of Elizabeth Queen of Bohemia (1596-1692). The lower hall to the right held the likeness of Sir William Hooker, seventeenth-century tycoon and Lord Mayor of London; his daughter had married Edward Vaughan of Trawsgoed, and her ample beauty was once praised by Samuel Pepys.[1]

The lower hall and stairway were dominated by a splendid portrait of Wilmot, second Earl of Rochester (1648-1681), courtier, wit, famous poet, rake and hell-raiser. The curious visitor might also have encountered Malet, the Earl of Rochester's daughter, and her husband, the first Viscount Lisburne, not to mention Thomas Wentworth, Earl of Strafford (1593-1641). The walls were virtually hidden by pictures; King William III jostled with a harpist, and the three children of Charles I with an unknown lady in loose drapery. In the dining room, joining together the two themes of British history and Vaughan inheritance, hung a picture of the family's presiding genius, Sir John Vaughan (1603-1674), Lord Chief Justice of the Common Pleas. To him the family largely owed its estate.

Back in the open air, the crowd of visitors assembled on the lawn near a table which supported a massive silver cup, a liqueur stand in the form of three miniature silver barrels, a gold locket with pearl studs, and a finely-bound family Bible. The presentation of these gifts, paid for by the tenants, was made by William Hughes of Morfa Mawr, the largest tenancy on the whole estate. Speeches were followed by feasting in the marquee, and then a long series of toasts, with recitations of the family history and several Welsh poems. The

The coming of age of George Henry Vaughan, 6th earl of Lisburne, 1884.

audience was reminded of the antiquity of the family's roots at Trawsgoed, and of the contribution members of the family had made to local and national history. The occasion was photographed by the house steward, Mr Malins.

The celebration was something more than a feudal survival, more than an acknowledgement by tenants of their loyalty to their landlord. Banners in the marquee celebrated Agriculture, which indeed was the *raison d'etre* of the whole assembly. The Trawsgoed estate, although not a solid block of lands, was a fairly coherent entity; each tenant knew many of his fellow farmers, and all knew Robert Gardiner, the agent, and many of the Earl's other employees. All had a common interest in the well-being of farming and of the Vaughan family, whatever may have been their private criticisms. Some represented families which had held tenancies on the estate for centuries. Only one ominous note appears in the *Cambrian News* account of the event; a speaker referred to the growing impact of American and Dominion wheat on the domestic market, which was depressing farming in Britain. The more percipient in the audience must have suspected that all was not well with the estate, groaning under the burden of debt. But no-one present could have foretold that in seventy years' time, within the lifetime of the tenants' youngest children, the Trawsgoed estate would have been dismantled, the Vaughan family scattered, and the mansion occupied by government administrators, advisers and scientists. The tradition of six centuries was to dissolve more quickly than anyone could have thought possible in 1884. Nor did I foresee when I began this study in 1989 that within seven years the civil servants would have left, and that a private company partly owned by the Vaughan family would reclaim the mansion and gardens.

*   *   *

The Vaughan family and the Trawsgoed estate have a dual historical interest. The first is at the level of local history; the Vaughans were the biggest landowners in Cardiganshire, they provided a number of Members of Parliament, their influence in politics, legal matters and local government was great, and they had an overwhelming impact on the local landscape, and on the lives of many individuals. Their wealth may have been moderate in comparison with the great English aristocratic families, but in Cardiganshire terms they were rich indeed.

The second interest of the Vaughan family is at the national level, both Welsh and British. This is not so much because they provided one significant figure (Sir John Vaughan) in British history, or two other minor figures, but rather because they provide a paradigm of aristocratic fortunes. When other families were rising, the Vaughans rose. When other families yielded to the temptations of gambling, womanising and conspicuous consumption, the Vaughans yielded. When the aristocracy fell into that terminal decline described in such detail by David Cannadine, the Vaughans declined, though not terminally.[2] They are, however, most unusual in being able to trace the family headship back in an unbroken male line for many generations, and although the surviving Trawsgoed archive lacks any large collection of interesting letters, it is so well-packed with deeds, rentals and other documents that it is possible to tell the family's story in some detail, supplemented with material from other sources.

However, the family's fortunes did not always follow the conventional pattern. Intermarriages between Welsh and English landed families were commonplace from the sixteenth century onwards, and many Welsh estates were carried by heiresses to English owners. The Vaughans, however, were able to reverse this trend; four eldest sons married English heiresses, acquiring estates in Somerset, Northumberland, Devon and Middlesex. The Crosswood archive offers little material for the study of these far-flung estates, but a separate archive in the National Library, consisting of a single boxful of letters, throws a good deal of light on the rentals, quarrying and fishing interests of the Northumberland estate in the late eighteenth century.[3]

*   *   *

In their major study, *An Open Elite? England 1540-1880*, dealing with the fortunes of great houses in three English counties, Lawrence and Jeanne Stone list the five elements which make up a great house (in the family sense of the word): the seat or mansion, the expanse of lands, the collection of portraits, heirlooms and documents, the family name with genealogy, and the hereditary title, if any. A great house would also have numerous servants and the best education for the children, but these facilities were shared by wealthy merchants who were not heads of great houses. At first sight one is tempted to try to add other elements, such as the right to shoot game or to a coat-of-arms, but many of the wealthier parish gentry could claim the right to shoot, and the right to a coat-of-arms was never restricted to the aristocracy.

All five elements described by the Stones can be seen in the case of the Vaughan family of Trawsgoed, and it is possible to trace the growth of the estate and family from the status of parish gentry to that of established aristocracy. Their seat had been in their possession since the early fourteenth century, though it almost certainly did not become a large mansion until the seventeenth century; their lands multiplied dramatically in the sixteenth and seventeenth centuries. Heirlooms and documents do not begin to be listed until the eighteenth century, but the archive was certainly in existence before the end of the sixteenth century, while the oldest surviving family painting dates from about 1670, a portrait of Sir John Vaughan, the family's greatest individual member. The family name and genealogy remained stable from the earliest years through to the present day, and the hereditary Lisburne title was acquired in 1695.

The history of the connection between the Vaughan family, Trawsgoed mansion and the Ystwyth valley, as well as the broader family estates beyond, has only been partly explored by historians. This is despite the laying of an essential foundation in 1927 with the publication of Francis Green's invaluable calendar of most of the fine collection of Trawsgoed deeds in the National Library of Wales.[4] The later economic growth and decline of the Trawsgoed estate were examined by J.M.Howells in an important pioneer study, while Sir John Vaughan, the most eminent member of the family, has been the subject of a biographical study; however, the whole story of the family with its estate remains to be told.[5] This book is an attempt to outline that story.

It was not easy to decide how exactly the book should be planned. A straightforward narrative beginning in 1300 and dealing with the family generation by generation would be possible, but it would involve a great deal of repetition of details about the management of the estate. Moreover, the sources vary drastically from period to period in their amplitude and reliability. The result is a series of compromises, based on narrative. Chapter I describes the early growth of the family and estate in a local and national context. Chapter II follows the career of Sir John Vaughan, while chapter III describes the family's most dramatic scandal. Chapters IV and V cover the family from 1741 onwards, but while I have attempted as detailed a coverage as the sources allow up to 1900, it was no part of my self-imposed brief to write the family's recent history in any detail, though it is briefly sketched. Chapter VI outlines the history of the mansion itself, and Chapters VII and VIII deal with various issues to do with the management of the estate and its resources, and are particularly indebted to the work of J.M.Howells. Chapter IX deals with game and shooting, which have been so important in the lives of recent generations of the family and in the management of the estate. It may be objected that more comparisons should be made with other major Welsh and English families and estates; I can only claim that to do so in serious detail would have inflated the book intolerably.

Two caveats should be mentioned. First, the reader must not expect yet another discussion of 'the rise of the gentry' so famously debated by R.H.Tawney, H.R.Trevor-Roper and Lawrence Stone, to name only three of many.[6] If the subject is not exhausted, it is certainly not a prerequisite in a study whose aim is simply to tell a particular story as best the evidence allows, particularly as the evidence for the key period 1500-1550 is so scanty (especially in the cases of those gentry whose families have disappeared by 1600), and the Cardiganshire gentry so limited in space and number.[7]

Second, some readers may feel this study to be uncritical of the rôle of the Vaughans and of the aristocracy in Welsh life, while others may feel that scandal should be left in the decent obscurity of the archives. Any bid to write history must be interpretative, but the agenda underlying this work is a simple one, the attempt to establish what happened, how it happened and who did it. The emphasis throughout is on locating the family within the landscape and society of north Cardiganshire, now Ceredigion, and telling its story.

Such a study would be impossible without the remarkable archive of Trawsgoed deeds and documents in the National Library of Wales, which is one of the richest available for any Welsh estate, recording land transactions, tenancy agreements, family settlements and rentals in great detail. We may divide them roughly into a number of groups, which will be more easily grasped by tabulation:

1. The earliest period, from 1547, records the growth of the original small estate by purchase, mortgage and marriage, and documents of

this kind appear throughout the collection; there are also many documents related to the Cilcennin estate.

2. The Strata Florida grange rentals, leases and related documents, e.g. the disposal of lands to the Herberts of Hafod Uchdryd, the Stedmans of Strata Florida and the Lloyds of Ffosybleiddiaid.

3. Estate rentals, which begin in 1661 and run with many gaps until the sale of the estate in 1947. These include rentals for the Cwmnewidion estate.

4. Family settlements enabling successive owners to settle debts and provide income for dependants, usually by way of annuities, jointures and dowries.

5. Tenancy agreements leasing various properties to farmers.

6. Correspondence about the administration of the estate (disappointingly small, but supplemented by the Lisburne-Northumberland archive in the National Library of Wales).

7. Lead-mining affairs.

8. Some papers of the Montgomery, Somerset, Northumberland, Enfield and Devonshire properties of the family, which are only dealt with briefly in this study.

9. Maps and plans, including three fine volumes of the 1781 maps of Thomas Lewis.

10. Miscellaneous, including tithe matters, timber sales, a few wills, a little personal correspondence, the affairs of General Sir John Vaughan, etc.

Without these collections, and Francis Green's schedules, this work could not have been written.

NOTES

[1]CD II, 2176. This small notebook lists the pictures hanging in the mansion in 1900.

[2]D.Cannadine, *The Decline and Fall of the British Aristocracy* (London, 1990).

[3]NLW Lisburne-Northumberland.

[4]Francis Green, *Calendar of Deeds and Documents, Vol.II, The Crosswood Deeds* (Aberystwyth, 1927). A schedule of additional documents not included in the published volume is available on the shelves of the Gwenogvryn Evans Room in the National Library of Wales. A third tranche of documents is contained in the Roberts and Evans papers now in the National Library, but at the time of writing they are not available for study; it is likely that they relate to the last hundred years and so are not essential to the bulk of this work.

[5]J.M.Howells, 'The Crosswood Estate, its Growth and Economic Development, 1683-1899', University of Wales M.A. thesis, 1956, cited below as Howells, *thesis. The work is summarised in J.M.Howells, 'The Crosswood Estate, 1547-1947', Ceredigion*, III, no.1 (1956), pp. 70-88, cited as Howells, *article*. J.Gwynn Williams, 'Sir John Vaughan, Chief Justice of the Common Pleas', University of Wales M.A. thesis, 1952, cited below as J.Gwynn Williams, *thesis*. The work is summarised in J.Gwynn Williams, 'Sir John Vaughan of Trawscoed, 1603-1674', National Library of Wales Journal, VIII (1953-4), pp.33-48, 121-145, 225-243, cited as J.Gwynn Williams, article. I have used their work extensively, and gladly acknowledge my debt.

[6]Briefly but well summarised in G E Mingay, *The Gentry: the Rise and Fall of a Ruling Class* (Longman, 1976), 50-53.

[7]For a recent broad treatment giving worthy attention to Welsh material, see Felicity Heal and Clive Holmes, *The Gentry in England and Wales 1500-1700* (MacMillan, 1994).

1. PARISH GENTRY

The Trawsgoed estate was once the largest in Cardiganshire, ruling some forty thousand acres from its mansion in the Ystwyth valley south-east of Aberystwyth. When in 1947 Ernest Edmund Vaughan, seventh Earl of Lisburne, sold to their tenants the remaining farms belonging to the Trawsgoed estate, and disposed of Trawsgoed mansion, its park and home farm to the Government, it was the apparent end of a remarkable seven-century relationship between the Vaughan family and the Ystwyth valley, as well as the extinction of a great Welsh estate. However, the influence of the mansion and its family on the immediate neighbourhood is still strong half-a-century later. Local people remember the seventh Earl, who died in 1965, and his first wife, the remarkable Chilean beauty, Maria de Bittencourt (known as Regina), Countess of Lisburne, and recall many acts of individual kindness by the couple. The oldest inhabitants of Llanafan remember the visit of the Prince of Wales in 1923, when a bedroom at the mansion was specially decorated for his one-night stay, and the village school pupils were brought by their teacher to sing 'God Bless the Prince of Wales' beneath the windows. Many local people are the children of former estate employees. A path cut high on Banc Magwr is still known as 'the Lord's Path', by means of which the head of the family could survey his demesne.

A mile away, Llanafan church is full of family memorials in stone and stained glass, and of church furniture given by members of the family, as well as a fine organ. Beneath the church floor lie the remains of many members of the Vaughan family, housed in the Trawsgoed vault. Llanafan School is still The Earl of Lisburne School; the village hall is Neuadd Lisburne. The present Earl and Countess of Lisburne returned to live in the area, having bought back Cruglas farm, Swyddffynnon, and made it their home until 1996. The vicarage in which this book was written used to be the house of the agent for the estate, Robert Gardiner. In its present dining room is a huge safe in which were kept, within living memory, the wages and rents of the estate. In 1991 the present Earl was invited to plant a tree to commemorate the centenary of the mansion's extension, and he chaired a University day-school in the house on the history of the estate and his family. Ownership is greatly reduced, but interest and involvement remain.

*   *   *

The Trawsgoed site had been favoured long ago by previous occupiers. Immediately east of the mansion and garden is a field, bounded by a recent conifer plantation, a wall and the main road. Across this field a low bank is barely visible, running north and then east. This bank, now simply a swelling in the ground, and only obvious to an informed eye, is part of the north-east rampart of a Roman fort whose site actually straddles the present main road. Its very existence had been long forgotten, and only in 1959 was it rediscovered by archaeologists searching for a missing link in the line of forts along Sarn Helen, the Roman road from South Wales to the North. The fort was occupied from approximately 80 A.D. to 120 A.D., either by a thousand auxiliary infantrymen or by a troop of five hundred cavalry. Small excavations provided these dates, while the droughts of 1959 and 1976 gave splendid opportunities for aerial photography to provide details of the fort's plan, since the turf over the banks and streets dried out and bleached more thoroughly than the rest of the site. The classic grid of a Roman fort was revealed—not only to aeroplanes, but to anyone who climbed Y Gaer Fawr, the hill to the south of the river; whence it was again briefly visible during a hot spell in 1990.

More interesting to archaeologists than the well-known grid-plan of yet another Roman fort is the complex of streets outside the fortifications to the west of the Trawsgoed fort. This was the *vicus*, an area for commercial activities and the habitations of camp followers, which has been partially excavated by Dr Jeffrey Davies.[1] The fort was well-sited, commanding a key point in the Ystwyth valley and overlooking the spot at which Sarn Helen crossed the river. The Iron Age hill-forts on either side of the river, Y Gaer Fawr, Llwyn Du, Cefn Blewog, may have already been deserted when the Romans arrived. Roman occupation of the Trawsgoed fort may have been brief in terms of the centuries of Roman presence in Wales, but forty years meant several generations of Roman soldiers, from who knows which part of the Empire, with their economic, social and political presence completely disrupting native life in the locality. Was there any

Trawsgoed park in 1888.

continuity between Roman occupation and later habitation on this spot? Soil erosion by cultivation and weathering may have destroyed the evidence; the favoured nature of the site must have seemed desirable to successive generations of settlers. However, in the fourteenth century it was certainly being farmed by Ieuan Goch of Trawsgoed, whose daughter and heiress Tudo married Adda Fychan, the direct ancestor in the male line of the present Earl of Lisburne. Thus began the connection between the Vaughan family and Trawsgoed.

*   *   *

How did the Trawsgoed estate become the largest in Cardiganshire? What are the origins of the estate and family? We may look first at names. The name *Trawsgoed* is at once simple and baffling. Simple because it plainly means 'the other side of the wood' or 'beyond the wood', and is found (sometimes in partnership with *Is-coed*, 'this side of the wood') in other parts of Wales. But which wood? And if it was 'the other side', from which standpoint are we looking? Are we looking from the south side of the river Ystwyth, perhaps from Trefilan, once an important centre in Ceredigion? Are we, possibly, looking from Llanfihangel-y-Creuddyn, which must have been the administrative centre of the commote of Creuddyn, that early

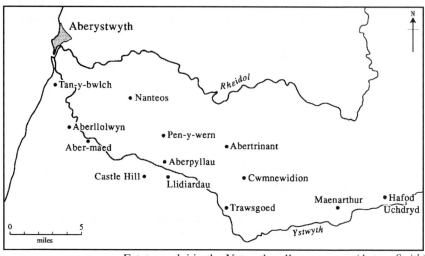

Estate nuclei in the Ystwyth valley.   *(Antony Smith)*

mediaeval lordship lying between the Ystwyth and the Rheidol? In
that case the wood in question may have been the ancient oak wood of
which a fragment is still in place on Banc Magwr, above the farms of
Tan-yr-allt, Berllan-ber and Llannerch-yr-oen, though mostly replaced
by conifers. The present wood along the main road close to the
mansion is a recent creation, entirely absent from the map of 1771,
and was probably planted between 1800 and 1830 to give privacy,
game-shelter and to disguise the brick-pits once worked there. No
matching Is-coed is known in the area. The meaningless English
translation, Crosswood, seems to have been first used in the eighteenth
century; the second half of that century was a period when the
Vaughan family came closest to losing their Welsh roots, since they
spent long periods in London or on their English estates in Devon and
Northumberland. I have preferred the original Welsh name in this
book except where the English form is demanded by sources.

The Ystwyth valley was the setting for the foundation and early
growth of the Trawsgoed estate. The river flows from its bleak and
boggy source south-eastwards for a while, then turns sharply south-
west down the long Ystwyth fault through Cwmystwyth, past Hafod
Uchdryd, dropping into a spectacular gorge below Pont-rhyd-y-groes
and emerging into a broader valley below Llanafan bridge. Thence it

leaves the great geological fault and takes a less hurried path to the sea. The upper reaches of the river were once surrounded on both sides by lands belonging to the Cwmystwyth grange of the monastery of Strata Florida. These lands had been the gift of Rhys ap Gruffydd, the Lord Rhys (d.1197), to the monks, and we shall see that together with seven other Cardiganshire granges belonging to the monastery, they eventually passed into the hands of the Vaughans of Trawsgoed.

In its lower reaches the river passed not only Trawsgoed, but a chain of smaller estates, some still well-remembered (one indeed, the Castle Hill estate, is still functioning) and others lost even in local memory. To the north of the river were the estates of Cwmnewidion and Aberpyllu, with Nanteos and Abertrinant on tributary streams. To the south of the river were Llidiardau, Castle Hill, Aber-mad, Aberllolwyn and Tan-y-bwlch. Not all these estates flourished at the same time, but by the sixteenth century several were in the hands of families whose genealogies survive, tracing their ancestry back to patriarchal figures of the twelfth and thirteenth centuries: Gwaithfoed, Llawdden and Collwyn ap Tangno.

Who were these families? Some were certainly the descendants of free Welsh tribesmen whose genealogies had once been guarantees of their land-holding status, people who had survived more than two centuries of disruption, social and administrative upheaval, warfare and rebellion between 1060 and 1300. Others may have been the parvenus of the Middle Ages, men who by obtaining Crown office and by taking advantage of the frequent disruptions of local society by events such as the Edwardian Conquest, the Black Death and Owain Glyn Dŵr's rebellion, were able to establish themselves as landowners. Certainly no members of these groups traced descent from the original princely family of Deheubarth, whose north Ceredigion branch had become extinct in the early fourteenth century through the deliberate policy of Edward I.

These families may have gained favours from the royal administration which took over the lands of North Cardiganshire from the Welsh princes in 1277, perhaps as rewards for holding offices such as those we know were held by the early Vaughans. From field names it is possible to show that even these little proto-estates had themselves grown by taking over smallholdings and cottages in the vicinity of the original mansion house. For example, the large farm of Glennydd (opposite Llanilar) included a field called Llety Powell ('Powell's

house or lodging'), obviously separate in origin. The Wenallt
(Llanafan) farm map of 1781 shows the higher land of the farm as
'Tyddyn y Bedw' (Birch Farm); it too must once have been a separate
settlement. Both Glennydd and Wenallt were in their turn swallowed
by Trawsgoed. The growth of estates was like the functioning of a
food-chain of predators.[2]

Toward the end of the Middle Ages, Trawsgoed was simply a small
landholding in the Vale of Ystwyth, and the first of the Vaughan
family connected with it was Adda Fychan.[3] Adda Fychan claimed
descent from Collwyn ap Tangno of Gwynedd and his wife Winifred
or Gwenfrewi, she being a descendant of Hywel Dda, the tenth-
century Welsh king. Collwyn ap Tangno is a man of whom we know
virtually nothing, yet he was certainly an historical figure, a mediaeval
patriarch, connected with Meirionnydd, from whom a number of
Welsh families claimed descent.[4] The early family descent from father
to son was believed to run thus:

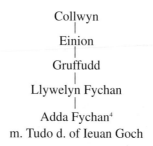

Collwyn
|
Einion
|
Gruffudd
|
Llywelyn Fychan
|
Adda Fychan[4]
m. Tudo d. of Ieuan Goch

Adda Fychan's father Llywelyn Fychan was a juror in Ultra Aeron
(north Cardiganshire) in 1292, which helps locate Adda's marriage to
Tudo, heiress of Trawsgoed, early in the fourteenth century. This
marriage would have brought his wife's Trawsgoed property, perhaps
originally only a few dozen acres, into the family. Nothing can be
known of the house they occupied on the site, but it may have been a
hall-house of wood, plaster and thatch, or possibly a substantial earth-
walled building with thatched roof, supported by crucks.

Then, until the middle of the sixteenth century, all we have is a list
of names in direct male descent in the genealogy, with some of these
names appearing in government records as holders of Crown offices,
or in connection with legal proceedings. Adda ap Llywelyn Fychan is
well documented, thanks to the work of Ralph Griffiths, whose
research I paraphrase, I hope adequately, in the next two paragraphs.[6]

In 1331 Adda ap Llywelyn Fychan had stood as pledge for one Ieuan ap Llywelyn Fychan when Ieuan was accused of murder. In the same year Adda was beadle or administrative officer of Creuddyn, the first rung on the ladder of posts which he subsequently climbed. In 1344 he was escheator of South Wales (i.e. Carmarthenshire and Cardiganshire), holding office for at least two years. His job was to administer and sell estates which had become forfeit to the Crown, either through treason or lack of heirs. In 1344-48 he paid £40 for the right of bestowal of minor offices in the county, and would have recouped this large payment from those on whom he bestowed appointments. In 1346 he had to account to the Black Prince's Council for the lands of Ieuan ap Madog Fychan, which had been forfeited. Before 1348 he was deputy steward of the county, and although he was ordered to be removed from office because Edward I had excluded Welshmen from holding office in Wales, the order was ineffectual, and he continued to act in the post, surviving the dreadful visitation of the Black Death in 1349-50. He was overseas in 1355, presumably on royal service in France, when he was appointed attorney to the constable of Cardigan Castle. He was obviously a most active figure among the minor Welsh dignitaries scrambling for places under royal patronage, and must have been a key figure in the family's history.

After that it is difficult to connect Professor Griffiths's lists of office-holders with men named in the Vaughan genealogy. This may of course be due to genealogical problems; the descent is not entirely certain, but probably ran as follows:[7]

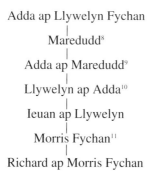

Adda ap Llywelyn Fychan
|
Maredudd[8]
|
Adda ap Maredudd[9]
|
Llywelyn ap Adda[10]
|
Ieuan ap Llywelyn
|
Morris Fychan[11]
|
Richard ap Morris Fychan

Maredudd ab Adda and his son Adda ap Maredudd were certainly office-holders under the Crown, and the son was probably head of the family at the time of the Glyn Dŵr rebellion in 1400 which shook all Wales to the core. In his turn Llywelyn ab Adda and his son Ieuan also held office during the fifteenth century, while Ieuan's son Morris Fychan may have been steward of the county of Cardigan under Lord Ferrers in the sixteenth century.[12]

These bare dates and and confusing names of obscure office-holders may seem no more than dry facts in dusty manuscripts, and I have tried to banish the details to end-notes, but they show a family of some local importance, able and willing to bid for office, trusted by the Crown's representatives. They were what would later come to be called parish gentry, small freeholders of land, anxious to maintain and if possible improve their family fortunes. Whether they were involved in Glyn Dŵr's Rebellion of 1400-12, when the royal administration of Cardiganshire virtually collapsed and hardly any taxes were paid for a whole generation, it is impossible to say; we can only draw limited conclusions from such sparse information. One may guess from their very survival that if they did at any time support Glyn Dŵr, it was only while it was politic to do so, and they must have emerged from the debacle on the Crown side, having either remained loyal or returned penitent to the fold. Then, like other gentry families, they had to survive the Wars of the Roses, which however seem to have left the Aberystwyth area comparatively unscathed.

Cardiganshire is regarded by the only Welsh historian of the Wars of the Roses, H.T.Evans, as having been Lancastrian in sympathy, and the constableship of its castle was a key office held for a time by Jasper Tudor. However, under the rule of Edward IV and Richard III the key figure in south-west Wales was Walter Devereux, Lord Ferrars, who died fighting for Richard III against Henry Tudor at Bosworth in 1485. Would Morris Fychan, who was probably head of the Trawsgoed family at the time, have dared to join Henry's followers as they marched north through Cardiganshire? It seems unlikely, but there is no evidence either way.[13]

The differences between the small Trawsgoed estate of the period up to 1630 and the later estate were more than a matter of acreage. The early estate was compact; its lands were confined to the parishes of Llanafan and Llanfihangel-y-Creuddyn, with an overflow into Llanbadarn Fawr along its southern edge, and a plot in the town of Aberystwyth. This compactness contrasts with the later sprawl across twenty-two parishes. The family would themselves have farmed the land closest to the little mansion, renting the rest as a handful of farms in the middle Ystwyth valley. The lands would have been divided into small patches and strips, separated by earth balks, dead-hedges (a primitive form of fencing), or by hurdles erected to protect a patch of corn or hay. These lands were largely intermingled, so that no farmer held a single block. That this was the case is clear from the survival of such patches in the late eighteenth-century maps of the estate farms prepared by Thomas Lewis, now in the National Library of Wales, particularly the map of Ysbyty Ystwyth; one farm consisted of eight entirely separate fields and strips. The rents that the landowner collected were at least in part rents in kind and services rather than in cash; in their turn they had to pay taxes, which went to the officers of the Principality of Wales and effectively to the Crown, and tithes, which for Cardiganshire north of the Ystwyth were almost entirely owned by the abbey of Vale Royal at Chester.

As well as holding and farming their lands, and occasionally serving in Crown offices, the male members of the Vaughan lineage seem to have married well. From the time of Tudo, wife of Adda Fychan, we know the names and lineages of all the wives of the direct heirs. Each wife was the daughter of a free man boasting a genealogy of at least four generations, giving him gentry status in Welsh eyes. Gwerful wife of Adda ap Maredudd was a descendant of Llywelyn Caplan and co-heiress of her father Llywelyn Goch, while Morris Fychan's second wife, whose name is lost, was daughter and co-heiress of another Llywelyn Goch of Glynaeron. However there is no record of lands in the Aeron valley belonging to the Vaughans at this time.

The chaos of much of the fifteenth century was the forerunner of a period of drastic change throughout Wales. The accession of the Tudors in 1485 was followed by a series of major developments—the Acts of Union of 1536 and 1542, the introduction to Wales of the office of Justice of the Peace, the closure of the monasteries in the 1530s, and the development of a money economy. The Act of Union meant that legal distinctions between the Principality and the Marcher Lordships, between Welsh and English, disappeared. For the first time Welshmen could sit in the House of Commons, representing the new Welsh constituencies created by the Act. The Courts of Great Sessions were established to administer justice in Wales, but the London courts such as Star Chamber and Chancery were also available.

Ambitious Welshmen could take advantage of these new circumstances to create large estates or even business interests, as well as themselves taking up careers in the law. The office of Justice of the Peace was a key to local political power, since magistrates did far more than deal with petty crime; they actually directed local government. The closure of the monasteries in 1535-39 brought a huge amount of land onto the market as the Crown first leased and then sold the enormous monastic estates, so that the wealthy and ambitious could gain new holdings, thus securing both future income and influence. At first these lands were held either by consortia of English businessmen or by great families such as the Devereuxs, and their purchase was beyond the reach of freeholders in remote Cardiganshire, but conditions would change and families would grow.

These were certainly dynamic times in Wales. Older estates which had already emerged from the breakdown of the Welsh clan-land system could expand, or if the family line failed or produced an incompetent heir, disappear. New estates were created, some of them based not on freehold tenure but on the buying-in of leases. Thus the Herbert family from Llangurig crossed into Cwmystwyth in the mid-sixteenth century and started buying up farm leases from the original tenants of Strata Florida abbey, whose 99-year leases had been granted by the last abbots. Though not thereby becoming freeholders, the Herberts were forming the nucleus of what eventually became the

Trawsgoed mansion in 1888, rear view.

Front view of Trawsgoed mansion, 1888.

Hafod estate. Some of the small estates in the valley quickly fell on hard times; the Aberpyllu estate across the river Ystwyth from Llanilar, worth £150 a year in 1590, disappeared completely during the course of the early 17th century, for want of heirs. The two successor farms, Pyllau Uchaf and Pyllau Isaf, were eventually absorbed into separate estates: Pyllau Isaf went with Glanystwyth to the Hafod estate before being exchanged into the hands of the Vaughans of Trawsgoed in the nineteenth century, while Pyllau Uchaf belonged to Nanteos.

Could we visit the Ystwyth valley as it was in 1547, we might not be able to see any reason why the Trawsgoed family, rather than any other, should within a hundred years become the greatest landowners in the county. They certainly had interesting names in their genealogy—King Hywel Dda of course, and Llywelyn Caplan of the family which produced Dafydd ap Gwilym, for example. But a genealogy, however distinguished, is no guarantee of future success, and for several generations the descendants of Adda Fychan do not seem to have owned much more than 'the *plas* at Trawsgoed', a messuage called Tir Dafydd Benllwyd, and some unnamed lands in the parish of Llanfihangel-y-Creuddyn.[14] We may obviously suppose that Tir Dafydd Benllwyd had been bought from the descendants of a Dafydd Benllwyd, showing an earlier process of growth; it may possibly have been the land immediately to the south-west of the mansion site, between it and Abermagwr. As for the lands in the parish of Llanfihangel-y-Creuddyn, this may have been what is now Lodge Farm, which for centuries formed the home farm of the estate. The only clue is the location of the parish boundary between Llanafan and Llanfihangel-y-Creuddyn. It runs right athwart the grounds of Trawsgoed, between the mansion and the home farm, suggesting that perhaps these were originally separately owned, or at least that they were separate holdings.

That Trawsgoed was not an exceptional holding is suggested by the 1544 Lay Subsidy roll. This major unpublished document lists hundreds of names of landholders in north Cardiganshire (the list for the south is mangled and incomplete) who contributed to royal funds. The richest men in the county paid up to 13s 4d per head for lands or goods, at a rate of one penny in the pound for property worth between one and four pounds, and twopence in the pound above that. Thirty-one men and women from Llanafan paid the subsidy, including

Richard ap Morris Fychan of Trawsgoed, but while he paid fourpence, David ap Howell and Jenkin Llywelyn of Llanafan each paid a shilling, and the rest of the men of the parish paid fourpence, threepence, twopence or a single penny—Richard's half-brother Thomas paid twopence. There was therefore no major landholder in Llanafan in the early sixteenth century, and the family was still very small beer.[15] The simplified genealogy for the period runs as follows:

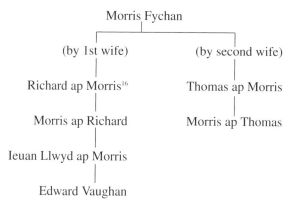

```
                      Morris Fychan
          ┌──────────────────┴──────────────────┐
      (by 1st wife)                        (by second wife)
          |                                       |
    Richard ap Morris[16]                  Thomas ap Morris
          |                                       |
    Morris ap Richard                      Morris ap Thomas
          |
    Ieuan Llwyd ap Morris
          |
     Edward Vaughan
```

In 1547 Richard ap Morris took an important step on the family's behalf. He arranged a marriage between his son Morris and a local heiress, Elliw daughter of Howell ap Jenkin, probably of Llanilar. Howell had died, leaving his daughter and lands in the care of trustees, who undertook the negotiations on her behalf; the two young people probably had little or no say in the matter. The legal document drawn up to settle the lands of the two families on the bride and groom survives, and it is the first document we have directly related to the estate. It mentions the lands already described above, and the lands brought to the marriage by Elliw.[17] There were nine farms altogether, which must have more than doubled the size of the estate. The parishes in which they lay are not named in the document, and only three of the farms, Brenan, Cerrig-yr-wyn and Llwynrhingyll, are identifiable by name today, but it is safe to assume that the others were also in or near the Ystwyth valley.

Richard ap Morris and his son Morris ap Richard are the first heads of the Vaughan family of whom we know more than the barest details. As the genealogy shows, Richard had a half-brother, Thomas ap Morris Fychan, who was dealing in land in 1542,[18] and it must be the latter's son, Morris ap Thomas, who appears to have disputed ownership of the Trawsgoed estate with his cousin, Morris ap Richard.[19] The matter was put before an arbitrator, John Pryse of Gogerddan, the foremost man in north Cardiganshire, and in 1566 he confirmed Morris ap Richard in his ownership of twenty-six land-holdings and three mills.[20]

Morris was certainly an ambitious man; in 1547 his father was content to describe himself and his son by the title 'gentleman', but by 1565 Morris ap Richard is referred to as 'esquire', a big social step in a class-conscious society, even though it was not a formal title. In the ten years following his marriage, according to the surviving Crosswood deeds, Morris ap Richard only acquired one additional holding, called Tir Deio Pengrych, in the parish of Llanfihangel in 1551, and again this place-name is lost to us. His father Richard was still alive, and he acquired three more holdings in Llanfihangel-y-Creuddyn in 1555. One of the three was Tyddyn Abermagwr, the others are not named. In 1558 Morris ap Richard bought a share in the tenancy of Esgairgelynen in Cwmystwyth, part of the lands of Strata Florida, whose fuller story we shall soon encounter. This was a considerable step, since Esgairgelynen is some miles from Trawsgoed.[21] But if Morris ap Richard was not purchasing much land in the 1550s, he was accumulating capital by granting tenements in perpetuity for cash and rents, money which he would soon put to active use.

Unfortunately Morris ap Richard remains a shadowy figure in the historical record. We know more about many contemporary Cardiganshire gentlemen, some of it not to their credit, because their wills survive or because they became involved in litigation. For example, Rhys ap Dafydd ap Jenkin of nearby Aberpyllu, an apparently respectable figure who was twice high sheriff of the county before his death in 1589, was father of four illegitimate children by three different women; but then illegitimate children appear frequently in the gentry wills and genealogies of the time. Thomas Jones of Llanbadarn, a justice of the peace and an important figure in the county before his death in 1627, was accused before the Court of Star Chamber of forging land deeds. Richard Pryse of Gogerddan (d. 1623) was accused of levying illegal taxes, misappropriating ammunition and armour and corrupt impressing of soldiers, reminiscent of Shakespeare's Justice Shallow. David Lloyd J.P. of Aber-mad (d.1630) and his sons were frequently before the same court both as defendants accused of assaults, riot, marching up and down the streets of Aberystwyth on market days, assault in Llanbadarn churchyard, bribery and illegal imprisonment, and as plaintiffs they accused others of similar misdemeanours. Welsh gentry life was colourful, not to say violent, and litigious in the extreme, but Morris ap Richard of Trawsgoed avoided such disputes. Many of those Star Chamber cases were probably prosecuted more in the hope of bankrupting a competing or quarrelsome neighbour than in the disinterested pursuit of justice, and they were usually met with vigorous counter-accusation.[22]

However, one bloody event stands out painfully from the family's otherwise apparently regular course of life. A single document preserved in the records of the Cardiganshire Court of Great Sessions for 1565 points unequivocally at Richard ap Morris Fychan of Llanafan, gentleman, as apparently responsible for a brutal murder. Nor is this a report of slander, but a coroner's inquest verdict.

On 28 May, 1565, Ieuan Lloyd ap Lewis of Llanychaearn, esquire, had gone to Llanafan in an attempt to restore peace in a conflict 'between subjects and their liege lords'. It is uncertain whether Ieuan was a justice of the peace, but as an esquire he would certainly have felt himself involved in any disturbance in the Ystwyth valley. At about 6 p.m. Richard ap Morris Fychan of Llanafan, gentleman, had attacked Ieuan Lloyd with a sharp weapon, giving him a blow on the head, which knocked him down, and another blow, causing a wound seven inches long. Ieuan had been carried home grievously wounded, and died on 6 June. An inquest was held the following day (most unusually), and the blame placed on Richard ap Morris, who in the meantime had fled.[23]

A coroner's verdict is of course not a trial verdict. However, the violent death of a man of the rank of esquire, which was a serious even though unofficial title in the sixteenth century, and an accusation made against a gentleman, would not have been taken lightly. Unfortunately, there are no more court documents until 1580. Unfortunately, too, we cannot be entirely certain about Richard ap Morris Fychan. As will be seen below, the Richard who arranged the marriage of 1547 seems to have gradually handed over the running of the estate to his son Morris, but a deed of 1563 shows him to be still active two years before the murder of Ieuan Lloyd. However, Welsh naming habits confuse the issue painfully; Richard's son Morris had a number of children by his

wife Elliw: Ieuan (the eldest), Gwenllian, Morgan, Elizabeth, Jenkin—
and Richard, who would, like his grandfather, have been called
Richard ap Morris Fychan.[24] However, he could not have been more
than eighteen years old, and was probably younger, at the time of the
murder. It seems likely then that it was Richard senior, though well
advanced in years, who must have stood accused of the killing, and
fled. There must have been a hue and cry after him, and sheriffs in
other counties must have been asked to search for him. However, in
the absence of any further records for fourteen years there is no means
of knowing what happened, and it certainly did not affect his well-
established son Morris in his promotion of the Trawsgoed estate.
Indeed, the very next inquest in the records was conducted by him as
coroner.

As we have seen, it is not possible to decide exactly what lands
Richard ap Morris of Trawsgoed already owned in 1547 before he and
his son Morris set out to acquire more by marriage and purchase in the
following years. But the settlement of the dispute of 1566 left Morris
ap Richard with what was probably the most extensive single estate in
the Ystwyth Valley; the Aberpyllau estate worth £150 a year still
existed at this time, but some of its land was outside the valley.[25] By
this time, if not before, Morris would have derived his income mainly
from rents, and only to a lesser degree from farming land in his own
occupation. From 1560 onwards Morris ap Richard had been actively
buying more land; new holdings in Llanafan and Llanfihangel-y-
Creuddyn were joined to the estate.[26] Morris's father Richard was still
alive at this time, and obtained some rights on part of the extensive
lands of Cwmnewidion, though the rest remained a separate estate
until 1786.[27]

In 1568 Morris made an interesting purchase, the ancient demesne
of Maenarthur near Pontrhydygroes, whose earlier history seems lost
to detection; it was not part of the Strata Florida granges, and was
perhaps another independent estate like Aberpyllau, but smaller.[28] This
acquisition is reflected in a folk-tale still current in the locality; it tells
that the ladies who owned Maenarthur (or in another version,
Maenarthur Cottage) were tricked by the Lord of Trawsgoed, who
coveted their property. They were invited to a meal at Trawsgoed and
were well entertained, but on their return home Trawsgoed servants
arrived, demanding to search their horses' accoutrements, in which
they 'found' silverware from the mansion. The ladies were taken back

to Trawsgoed, where they were offered the choice between surrendering their rights and recourse to the courts—where the sentence for theft could have been hanging. This is obviously a folktale, with similarities to that of Benjamin in the Book of Genesis, but it reflects a truth, that there was deep distrust by the peasantry of the aristocracy, whom they believed to be capable of the blackest depths of skulduggery; similar tales are told of Herbert Lloyd of Peterwell and Morgan Herbert of Hafod. Interestingly, another local folk-tale purports to explain how it came about that the farm of Ty'n-y-rhyd (now Pengrogwynion) was lost to the Vaughans, supposedly its original owners. The tale claims that a head of the family, 'Lord Lisburne', was gambling in a tavern with 'Squire Pryse' of Gogerddan. One bet centred on a race between two flies on a table; Lisburne lost the bet and the farm. The factual truth of the tale is unproven either way, though it certainly reflects another truth—that aristocrats were willing to make the craziest bets. The two tales make an illuminating contrast with the widespread latterday folk-opinion of the great estates as having been beneficial sources of employment, charity and social cohesion, an opinion still held locally about the Vaughan family.[29]

Apart from theft and gambling of the kind suggested by the folk-tales, but not proveable in the case of Trawsgoed, there were more respectable ways of accumulating land—purchase, marriage, inheritance and mortgage. Marriage to an heiress was obviously important: Adda Fychan, his descendants Richard Fychan and Morris Fychan all married heiresses[30]. Morris ap Richard did not rest on this achievement, however, but purchased land vigorously; in 1571 he bought Llety Synod and Tyddyn-y-waun-un-fuwch (Llwynwnwch today), bordering on Fron-goch. There was a final brief burst of buying in 1585 and 1586 before Morris's death at some unknown date before 1602. Morris ap Richard was the true first founder of the Trawsgoed estate known to us, though his father Richard seems to have been a canny operator too, marrying his eldest son to a landed heiress, and continuing himself to acquire land, nearly always within convenient reach of Trawsgoed.

Morris ap Richard survived for almost forty years after his marriage in 1547, and left a considerably increased estate to his heir. How did he manage to build it up so successfully? Much of the detail is lost to us, and we certainly cannot depend on the folktales of Maenarthur or

Ty'n-y-rhyd as a historical source. Many of his acquisitions were
made through mortgage, lending money on the security of land, and
taking over the land when the mortagor failed. Presumably he financed
his operations by using income from tenancies, minor offices and just
possibly by borrowing, though that was very expensive. In addition to
his purchases of land, there is a single example of Morris investing in
church property, the tithes of Lledrod parish. A Maurice Vaughan was
named Justice of the Peace in 1575, but was omitted in the lists of
1577 and several subsequent years. A Maurice Vaughan is listed again
for 1592, and remained on the subsequent lists until 1605 and was
then reinstated in 1607 (when Morris Vaughan of Trawsgoed was
certainly dead) and the name appears again in 1612, 1615 and 1618;
this is almost certainly Morris Vaughan of Glanleri.[31] Whether the
earlier references are to Morris ap Richard is uncertain.

Despite Morris ap Richard's success and longevity, he was certainly
not the most eminent man in North Cardiganshire. The Joneses of
Llanbadarn and of Nanteos (unrelated families) were wealthier; the
Powells, too, were in process of expansion, having moved from their
ancestral home in Ysbyty Cynfyn to Llechwedd Dyrys, opposite
Nanteos, on which they cast covetous eyes while buying land in and
around Aberystwyth. Outstanding were the Pryses of Gogerddan. In
the Lay Subsidy of 1613, Morris's grandson Edward Vaughan of
Trawsgoed paid £1, while Sir Richard Pryse paid £2.13.4. Even half a
century later, by which time the Vaughans had increased their estate
considerably, Sir John Vaughan's house at Trawsgoed had eight
hearths, while Sir Richard Pryse, Baronet, had sixteen at Gogerddan.[32]
Early members of the Pryse dynasty were praised by the poets, who
hardly seem to have visited the minor gentry of the Ystwyth Valley,
with only two known exceptions.[33] Richard ap Rhys of Gogerddan was
J.P., Custos Rotulorum (keeper of the rolls) of the county and member
of the Council of Wales and the Marches, and his son John Pryse was
an M.P. between 1553 and 1583, High Sheriff of the county in 1570
and of Merioneth in 1580. In the next generation Richard Pryse was
M.P. between 1584 and 1622, and was knighted in 1603, while
Richard's grandson Richard was also an M.P., and was made a baronet
in 1641. From Richard ap Rhys onwards for several generations the
Pryses were lawyers, as the Vaughans later became for several
generations. The evidence clearly shows how the Pryses outranked the
Vaughans at this time. Indeed, although the Vaughans eventually

acquired more land than the Pryses, and a peerage, the Pryses usually held political primacy in the county.

The 1613 and 1627 Lay Subsidies give the sums paid by various heads of wealthy Cardiganshire families, offering a crude and sometimes inaccurate scale of comparison:[34]

1613	Richard Pryse (Gogerddan)	53s 3d
	Morgan Herbert (Cwmystwyth)	32s
	Edward Vaughan (Trawsgoed)	20s
	John Stedman (Ystrad Fflur)	20s
	Thomas Pryse (Glan-frêd)	20s
1627	Edward Vaughan (Trawsgoed)	24s
	Dame Gwenllian Pryse (Gogerddan)	24s
	David Lloyd (Aber-mad)	24s
	Thomas Pryse (Glan-frêd)	24s
	Edward Jones (Nanteos)	12s
	Hugh David Vaughan (Cwmnewidion)	8s
	William Herbert (Cwmystwyth)	8s

We should not conclude from this, however, that Trawsgoed's wealth had grown to equal Gogerddan's, but it was presumably greater than that of Nanteos by 1627.

We know little of Morris ap Richard and his wife Elliw as parents, though they produced four sons and seven daughters, most of whom reaching maturity. Morris arranged typical marriages for them; for example, one son and one daughter married into the important Lloyd family of Ffosybleiddiaid, Swyddffynnon, while another married David Vaughan of Cwmnewidion, no relation. Morris's eldest son and heir, Ieuan or Evan Llwyd ap Morris is a shadowy figure, named only once in the Trawsgoed archive, and otherwise only known as witness to a local will, and in the genealogies. He spent the long years waiting for his inheritance by marrying three times, twice to women from Montgomeryshire and once to a widow. Only the first marriage produced children, four sons and two daughters. Both Morris and Ieuan were dead by 1601, when Ieuan's eldest son Edward, who firmly adopted the surname Vaughan, was head of the family. Where Edward Vaughan went to school is a mystery, but he was sent by his father to complete his education at the Inns of Court in London; he was admitted to the Inner Temple in 1600, being then 'late of Clements Inn'. Oxford and Cambridge were the first goals of the sons of wealthy gentry, with a subsequent move to the Inns of Court, but there is no record of Edward Vaughan at either of the universities.

One of Edward Vaughan's earliest transactions is also one of the most interesting, since it involved the destiny of his only surviving younger brother. We have no details of how his ancestors provided for younger sons. Their best hope was to marry heiresses, but many had to content themselves with a humbler fate. In 1601, for example, Edward Vaughan signed an indenture binding his younger brother Morgan Vaughan as an apprentice to Myles Puller, draper of Salop, but this seems to have been exceptional in the family's history.[35]

In that same year of 1601 Edward married Lettis or Letitia Stedman of Strata Florida. This was an important marriage, and though Lettis was not an heiress, and presumably did not bring land to her husband, she did bring £300 of useful cash or credit, and an alliance with a well-connected family.[36] The Stedmans had acquired the site of Strata Florida and the monastic lands in the vicinity, but they did not own the Strata Florida granges, those great swathes of land with which the monks had been endowed by the Lord Rhys. The Stedman-Vaughan connection was obviously a valuable one for both families; the Stedmans were also related by marriage to the Pryses of Gogerddan and the Lloyds of Llan-llyr. Edward Vaughan was rising in the world. In addition to his family concerns, 1601 saw Edward Vaughan protesting to the authorities in London that he could not carry out his work as collector of the Lay Subsidy of that year, because Cardiganshire was too impoverished an area to yield the sum demanded.[37]

Edward Vaughan was the next great builder of the estate after his grandfather Morris. His marriage settlement of 1601 lists, apart from mills, forty-six properties, double the number mentioned forty years earlier.[38] Edward certainly seems to have been a combative, perhaps ruthless, character. In 1602 arbitrators chosen from among the local gentry settled a dispute between him and his grandmother Elliw, who must have been nearly eighty years of age. The arbitrators laid down that Edward should pay his grandmother four pounds a year for life, and that she should hold the Maenarthur grist mill and cottage.[39] Perhaps here, hidden beyond recognition, is the kernel of the Maenarthur folk-tale cited above. Edward also came into conflict with his tenants over his Cwmystwyth mills, by insisting that they should grind all their grain at his mills, while they argued that they need only use these mills for grain actually grown on their lands and not any additional grain they might purchase.[40]

As well as increasing his rents and income from his mills, Edward Vaughan made some effort to involve himself in the exploitation of the lead underlying the lands of Cwmystwyth. In 1618 he, with Sir Richard Price of Gogerddan and Thomas Jones of Llanbadarn, was alleged to have stopped the working of the mines at Cwmystwyth on behalf of their commercial allies, and in 1631 his claim to mine lead on his own land gave rise to a parish boundary dispute.[41] These are the first mentions of the Vaughans in connection with the lead-mining industry, which was to bring the family much wealth in later generations.

The settlement of 1566 between Morris ap Richard, Edward's grandfather, and Morris ap Thomas ap Morris of Llanilar must have been recalled in 1608, when John Vaughan ap Morris Thomas of Llanilar seems finally to have been forced to abandon his father's claim to Trawsgoed and the estate following the failure of another lawsuit.[42] Meanwhile, like his grandfather, Edward Vaughan seems to have played cautiously for a while after his marriage, but between 1611 and 1626 he acquired no fewer than fifty-one additional properties or shares of properties, thus doubling the size of the estate since his marriage.[43] Edward Vaughan, like his grandfather Morris, bought land within convenient reach of Trawsgoed, consolidating the estate in the six parishes of Llanafan, Ysbyty Ystwyth, Gwnnws, Llanilar, Llanbadarn and Llanfihangel-y-Creuddyn, so that the upper and middle regions of the Ystwyth valley came more and more under his control.

The earliest surviving plate in Llanafan church may bear mute witness to Edward Vaughan's activities. A silver chalice and paten bear the date 1633, the year of William Laud's consecration as Archbishop of Canterbury, and they match the designs most favoured by Laud's ecclesiastical reforms. They may well have been given to the church by Edward Vaughan. An even earlier piece belonging to the church is an extraordinary silver dish decorated with ten warriors and fighting winged monsters, and with an patterned boss in coloured enamel. This, too, may have been given as early as the seventeenth century.[44]

Edward Vaughan's relationship with the Stedmans of Strata Florida was unusually close. Not only had he married Lettis Stedman in 1601;

in 1624, now a widower, he married Anne Stedman,[45] widow of John Stedman and daughter of Sir Thomas Jones of Abermarlais, one of the leading men of south-west Wales, while at the same time his son and heir John Vaughan married Jane, the eldest daughter of Anne and the late John Stedman. Additionally, John Vaughan's sister, another Jane, married the younger John Stedman of Strata Florida. This marriage ensured that Jane's valuable marriage portion, worth a thousand pounds, along with confirmation of the Stedman ownership of some former Strata Florida lands, went to the Stedmans. Finally, Henry Vaughan, John Vaughan's younger brother, married Mary Stedman, Jane Stedman's sister. As has been pointed out by T.I.Davies, Mary was already Henry Vaughan's step-sister, sister-in-law and second cousin.[46]

Henry profited mightily by his Stedman marriage; the Stedmans had acquired Cilcennin demesne and estate, and by his marriage to the Cilcennin co-heiress he became its squire.[47] The four Stedman-Vaughan marriages within so short a time are an extreme example of the intensity with which gentry families pursued marital advantage. We know nothing of the social life of either Vaughans or Stedmans at this time, but heads of gentry families, their wives and some of their adult children would attend the Court of Great Sessions at its half-yearly week-long meetings in Cardigan, the most important social occasions in the county, and family alliances would certainly be mooted and clinched at these rallies of the powerful.

Edward Vaughan's name appears in the lists of Justices of the Peace from 1604 onwards, and he was high sheriff of the county in 1618/9. Unfortunately his name remains on the lists of Justices until 1638; unfortunately, because he died in 1635. Whether Edward Vaughan J.P. is Edward Vaughan of Trawsgoed is therefore a little doubtful, but as the latter was one of the county's major and most active landowners, the two must surely be the same man, and the name presumably survived posthumously in the J.P. lists through an oversight. No other Edward Vaughan was prominent in Cardiganshire at this time.

Although the county's Quarter Sessions records for this period have been lost, Edward Vaughan's name appears in the records of the Court of Great Sessions. A stray record in the family archive shows him sitting with John Stedman and others in the case of three women who had thrown one John Lewis of Lledrod out of his house.[48] Contemporary wills show that Edward Vaughan played the part expected of prominent local figures. His name occurs frequently as a tutor or guardian for legal infants, and as a witness. For example, in 1607 he witnessed the will of David Lloyd ap Harry of Llanfihangel-y-Creuddyn.[49] Two years later David's son Richard lay on his deathbed, and named Edward Vaughan as guardian of his young children. Vaughan also helped the executor by jointly undertaking the usual bond or guarantee of honest administration. In 1608 Hugh Prichard of Cwmnewidion left his daughters in the tutelage of Richard Pryse of Gogerddan, Edward Vaughan of Trawsgoed, and four other men. Occasionally Edward was a direct beneficiary; in 1619 Rice Griffith of Llanfihangel-y-Creuddyn left:

> To Edward Vaughan Esq. my Land Lord on yoke of oxen whereof the on is coloured pale blacke and thother coale black without any white spots.

This was almost certainly a heriot or payment to the landlord to guarantee the succession of the dying man's son to the tenancy. Several later wills show the Vaughans as the recipients of more substantial bequests. In 1687 Edward Vaughan's grandson, another Edward, acquired Maesdwyffrwd and five other farms from their childless owner Henry Lloyd who claimed a distant relationship, and in 1703 Edward's son John was bequeathed the Llanilar farm of Hendre Rhys by John Price of Rhandir, Llangwyryfon, who was also childless, Price insisting in his will that his surviving relatives should 'pay all possible respect duly and service to my Lord and family in all things fair and lawful', and requiring also that the Vaughans should have first refusal on any sale of his other lands.

In 1630 came the most remarkable of all the family's acquisitions of land. Edward's son John Vaughan, already a successful lawyer and member of parliament, negotiated the purchase of eight Cardiganshire granges of Strata Florida lands from a group of London businessmen acting for Robert Devereux, Earl of Essex, whose family had held the land for several generations. It was a good time to buy; John Vaughan's legal income would sustain the family, and the ninety-nine-year leases which the last abbots had negotiated with their tenants were falling in rapidly. Suddenly the Trawsgoed estate was much the largest in Cardiganshire, although much of it was poor mountain land.

Nominally at least, the purchase totalled some thirty thousand acres, and its price was £4,300, of which £3,000 was a mortgage advanced by the Earl of Essex, with a rent-charge of £300 a year; the balance of £1,300 was to be paid in cash.[50] There was also a Crown rent of £112 a year to collect and pay over, as well as triennial *commorthas*. J.M. Howells believed that in 1630 the ancient estate yielded £418.18.8 per annum, while the Strata Florida granges produced £713.0.9., a total of £1,131.19.5.[51]

A grange, in this context, was an administratively distinct area of land belonging to a monastery. Since some of the Strata Florida granges were contiguous, it is difficult to know the origin of the divisions between them. The Blaenaeron, Mefenydd, Pennardd, and Cwmystwyth granges formed a single block of land centred on the monastery; their internal bounderies may go back to the pre-monastic period, and presumably had some administrative convenience for the monastery.[52] Certainly the Trawsgoed rentals retained the distinction between these granges until the end of the 18th century. Of the other granges, the northernmost was known variously as Doverchen (an anglicized form of the Welsh *Y Dywarchen*, literally a piece of turf) or as Tirymyneich (monks' land); it stretched eastward from what is now Penrhyncoch. Morfa Mawr lies on the coast just south of Llan-non; Anhuniog (usually spelt Haminiog), is the hinterland of Aberarth, and Hafod-wen lies between Betws Bledrws and Ystrad Aeron. For the Vaughans it was a dramatic development. Suddenly their estate spread beyond the Ystwyth valley to new parishes—Ystrad Meurig, Caron, Llanddewibrefi, Lledrod, Dihewid, Silian, Llansanffraid and Llanfihangel Ystrad Aeron. At the same time many additional properties in Llanfihangel-y-Creuddyn, Gwnnws and Llanbadarn Fawr came under their sway.

The acquisition of the eight granges did not, however, mean that all the lands once belonging to Strata Florida became the entirely personal property of the Vaughans. The monastery's demesne lands were not part of the deal; they had much earlier become the property of the Stedman family, and on the death of Richard Stedman in 1747, along with other lands acquired by the Stedmans, the abbey property became the Abbey Estate of the Powell family of Nanteos. As has been shown, the Vaughan and Stedman family were joined in a series of marriage alliances, and following the monastic land-purchase, John Vaughan sold a number of tenements to John Stedman for a thousand pounds.[53]

In 1632 an important Chancery suit between John Vaughan of

Trawsgoed and Morgan Herbert, tenant of Hafod Uchdryd, was settled by arbitration. As we have already seen, the Herbert family had acquired by purchase a number of leases in Cwmystwyth which had been granted in the 1520s and 1530s by the abbots of Strata Florida. These leases formed the family estate of Morgan Herbert of Hafod Uchdryd and his father William, who had married Margaret Vaughan, sister of John Vaughan. These lands, the nucleus of the Hafod estate, were now assured to the Herberts in exchange for a down payment to the Vaughans of £300, and the annual payment of £22 chief rent due to the Crown.[54]

The process of selling to tenants continued during the 1640s, the largest sale being a grant of 1648 to Oliver Lloyd of Ffosybleiddiaid, the sitting tenant. The deed names fifteen properties or parts of properties, the nucleus of the Ffosybleiddiaid estate.[55] It will be remembered that Morris Vaughan had, two generations earlier, married a son and a daughter into the Lloyd clan. In 1651 John Vaughan sold Mynachty (Llanbadarn Trefeglwys) with two other farms and Pennant mill to Gaynor Gwyn, widow; this formed the nucleus of the later Mynachty estate.

The possession of the Strata Florida lands was not free of obligations. When it sold land, the Crown retained the right to a rent even when they became the freehold property of purchasers, and this was payable (though without any inflationary increase) for centuries, until finally the Vaughans bought out the Crown's right to this 'chief rent'. Centuries later the Crown would lay claim to the wastes, used by generations of farmers as sheepwalks without boundaries or documentary evidence of ownership, causing disputes which were still in process of settlement in the early 1990s. Previous owners of the granges had already sold or leased some land; Hugh Vaughan of Cwmnewidion had acquired the important farm of Pentre Briwnant in Cwmystwyth, but that did not include the mineral rights. Along with the title to the abbey lands, John Vaughan claimed the right to levy the triennial Welsh tax *comortha* for the Crown, presumably making a profit as he did so although the tax had been proclaimed illegal.

Despite the burdens and complications of the Strata Florida purchase, John Vaughan was still acquiring new lands during the late 1630s, particularly those close to Trawsgoed which had not yet been acquired by the family. He must also have been repaying his mortgage to the Devereux family, either from rents, sales or from his earnings as a lawyer. The latter source may explain how he was able to pay Sir John Lewis of Abernant Bychan £755 for nine tenements and mill-shares in Llanilar, Llanafan and Llanfihangel.[56]

John Vaughan himself, to judge from the Crosswood deeds, seems to have delegated some responsibility to his brothers Henry, Edward and Morris. Henry's career is briefly outlined below; Edward lived at Maenarthur, and was a J.P. by 1654; Morris's name appears as signatory to a number of land transactions.[57] It is interesting to contrast these younger brothers, who had been enabled to become squires in their own right or who served the family interest by helping to administer the estate, with the fate of their uncle Morgan Vaughan who as we have seen had been apprenticed to a Shrewsbury draper. There were two other brothers, Walter and James, and sisters Jane, Margaret, Dorothy, Ann and Mary, whose history is obscure.

Although John Vaughan was obviously in charge of the estate from 1630 onwards, his father Edward did not die until 1635; he may have been incapacitated by illness from taking any serious part in the running of affairs in his last years, though he did effect a lease shortly before his death.[58] His will, the first surviving Vaughan will, was proved at Carmarthen on 27 October, 1635, by his younger son Morris Vaughan.[59] He asked to be buried in Llanafan church, and left twenty shillings to St David's Cathedral; the usual gift from yeomen and minor gentry at this time was between four and twelve pence. Significantly, the will bequeathed to John Vaughan all the remaining real estate 'not formerly estated upon him', reinforcing the impression that John was already in control of most of the estate. Glennydd farm and mill were bequeathed to the youngest of his sons, Edward, 'until he be paid £400 by my son John Vaughan', a usual method of ensuring some security to a younger son. Cash provision of £100 each was made for Morris and Henry Vaughan, and the income of the rectories of Llanfihangel-y-Creuddyn and Llanafan[60] and the prebend of Lledrod was to dower his daughters Jane and Margaret, Ann and Mary having presumably married already.[61]

It is worth digressing for a moment to look at Henry Vaughan, the most successful or fortunate of John Vaughan's younger brothers. He had acquired the Cilcennin estate, between the rivers Aeron and Wyre, in the right of his marriage to its co-heiress, Mary Stedman. She, of course, was sister to Jane, the wife of John Vaughan; the two brothers had married two sisters. John also granted him lands in the same area

from the Strata Florida granges of Hafodwen and Anhuniog. The size
of the Cilcennin estate may be judged from a magnificent Trawsgoed
deed of 1680, drawn up years after Henry's death between his three
married daughters and a syndicate of three trustees responsible for its
division between the heiresses.[62] It included at least seventy-one farms
and pieces of land of varied acreages, thirteen houses and a mill. It
included property in parishes stretching from Llanarth to Aberystwyth,
and must have seemed at the time almost as impressive as the
Trawsgoed estate. Its heart was the Cilcennin demesne and the
surrounding area; Henry also owned a number of the remarkable
mediaeval strips of land surviving to this day at Llan-non.[63]

Henry Vaughan became a J.P., and in both 1642 (under the King)
and 1654 (under the Commonwealth) was Sheriff of the county. An
anonymous contemporary source, discussed in the next chapter with
reference to John Vaughan, described him as:

> Harry Vaughan, anything for money, a proselyte and favorite to all the
> changes of tymes; a sheriff for his late Majesty, afterwards for
> Cromwell; justice of the peace under each, tyrant in power,
> mischievous by deceit; his motto—Qui nescit dissimulare, nescit
> vivere.[64]

Henry Vaughan died in 1666, and there must have been confusion over
his inheritance. Having three married daughters, he had prepared a
draft will leaving his estate to his grandson Vaughan Price, son of Sir
Matthew Price of Newtown, with remainder to Vaughan Price's heirs,
who were to take the name of Vaughan. However, the will was not
proved; letters of administration were granted to the widow Mary
Vaughan. The document includes her oath that her husband had died
intestate. Inevitably therefore the estate was divided between the three
daughters by the document of 1680; the gap of time between
Vaughan's death and the settlement should not surprise anyone
familiar with the law's delays. It transpired, however, that part of the
estate reverted to the Vaughans of Trawsgoed, and this caused some
confusion in the next century.

With John Vaughan's succession to the family estates after his
father's death in 1635, we have come to the most important individual
figure in the Vaughan family history, and the first whose biography
can, and has, been written, by Prof. J. Gwynn Williams. We have
already seen that, almost certainly as a result of his London contacts,

legal prowess and earning power, he was able to multiply the Trawsgoed estate several times over in a single transaction. His story is retold in the next chapter.

NOTES

[1]J.F.Davies: 'Excavations at Trawscoed Roman Fort, Dyfed', *Bulletin of the Board of Celtic Studies*, XXXI (1984), pp.259-292.

[2]The processes which enabled landowners to increase their estates and establish themselves as gentry have been much discussed, but the once acrimonious scholarly debate has now subsided. See Felicity Heal and Clive Holmes, *The Gentry in England and Wales* 1500-1700 (MacMillan, 1994). The basic discussion for Wales is still H.A.Lloyd's *The Gentry of South-west Wales 1540-1640* (U.W.P. 1968), with the addition of Philip Jenkins, *The Making of a Ruling Class: the Glamorgan Gentry 1640-1790* (Cambridge, 1983).

[3]Fychan was later anglicised as Vaughan; although Welsh bychan means small, as a personal name it was originally used like American Junior, to distinguish between a father and son of the same given name.

[4]Collwyn is the traditional spelling, though Gollwyn is preferred by the great modern genealogist P.C.Bartrum. The genealogies given in the text are taken from the Vaughan family pedigree, but I have compared it with Bartrum's work in his *Welsh Genealogies A.D. 300-1400*, II (Cardiff, 1974), esp. pp. 301, 323. The link with Collwyn ap Tangno must be, as Bartrum indicates, defective, since there are not enough generations between Tangno and Adda. Whether this means, as some sceptical historians might feel, that the genealogy is spurious, must remain an open question. The family pedigree, a splendid scarlet-bound manuscript volume on vellum, was drawn up by York Herald of Arms in 1921 and is in the Earl of Lisburne's ownership; a copy has recently been made by the National Library of Wales. It is henceforth referred to as *Pedigree*.

[5]*Pedigree* gives simply Adda ap Llewelyn Fychan ap Griffith. Alcwyn Evans gives an extra generation, so that Adda Fychan is the son of Adda and grandson of Llywelyn Fychan. An Adda Fychan ab Adda was reeve of Llanbadarn (i.e. Aberystwyth) from 1376 till 1386, and beadle of Creuddyn in 1396/7. Lewis Dwnn connected Adda with Llanddwy (between Abermagwr and New Cross), although the property is not historically associated with Trawsgoed.

[6]R.A.Griffiths, *The Principality of Wales in the Later Middle Ages*, I (Cardiff, 1972), esp. pp.211-12.

[7]Cf. Francis Jones, 'The Old Families of South-West Wales', *Ceredigion*, IV, 1, (1960), esp. p.9. He does not cite his sources, but F.J. is a highly reliable authority, and is confirmed by *Pedigree*.

[8]A Maredudd ab Adda was constable of Genau'r-glyn in 1357-59, and of Mefenydd in 1360-61.

[9]Adda ap Maredudd ab Adda was constable of Mefenydd in 1389/90, beadle of

Creuddyn in 1391/4, escheator of Cardiganshire in 1395, and reeve of Creuddyn in 1397-98.

[10]Adda ap Meredith's son Llywelyn was beadle of Creuddyn in 1434/5 and of Mefenydd in 1457/8. Llywelyn's son Ieuan may be that Ieuan ap Llywelyn who was beadle of Creuddyn in 1518/20.

[11]Unless a generation is missing from all the genealogies, the use of the surname Fychan suggest a genuine surname rather than the 'Junior' form.

[12]That is, according to Pedigree. But Ralph Griffiths' lists of office-holders do not include him.

[13]H.T.Evans, *Wales and the Wars of the Roses* (Cambridge, 1915; new edition 1995).

[14]CD II,4.

[15]PRO. E179/263/32. I am grateful to Dr Evan James for the loan of his microfilm of this document. Lay subsidies were occasional taxes on lands and/or goods by which the sovereign could raise money for a particular purpose. Landholders were often expert at cheating the tax-collector, and the figures are not wholly to be relied upon.

[16]Richard had two other sons, Hugh ap Richard and David Lloyd ap Richard.

[17]CD II,4.

[18]Cwrtmawr Deed 736. He released two farms, both in Llanbadarn Fawr, to John ap Ieuan Goch and Maurice ap Jenkin ap Ieuan Goch. He is named in the Lay Subsidy roll for 1542, and according to the Lisburne Pedigree, he married Gwen daughter of Rhys ap David ap Jenkin of Aberpyllu.

[19]This dispute between the cousins in 1566 deserves further comment. It may be, as Professor J.Gwynn Williams suggests, that Thomas ap Morris was claiming cyfran, a share of ancestral lands under Welsh law. If so, it is interesting to recall that arbitration was an approved method of adjudication in Welsh law, although the last formal powers of Welsh law had been swept away even from the Marcher Lordships by the Acts of 1536 and 1543. Morris ap Thomas lost his claim, but at least he may not have been burdened by the enormous costs of court procedures. Morris's father Thomas, brother of Richard and son of Morris, appears in the Lay Subsidy list of 1542, and had himself married an heiress. But the litigation of 1566 is puzzling in view of the evidence of the 1547 marriage settlement, where Morris ap Thomas ap Morris was one of the parties to settling the lands on Morris ap Richard.

[20]NLW CD I, 47.

[21]See F.Green, *The Crosswood Deeds, passim,* for these and subsequent references.

[22]See Ifan ab Owen Edwards (ed.), *A Catalogue of Star Chamber Proceedings relating to Wales,* (Cardiff, 1929). Accusations made in the Star Chamber may often have been highly exaggerated.

[23]NLW WALES 4/883/5/24.

[24]Lewis Dwnn, *Heraldic Visitations of Wales,* I (Llandovery, 1846) p.50.

[25]In the parishes of Llanfihangel-y-Creuddyn, Llanilar, Rhosdïe, Llanbadarn Fawr, Aberystwyth, Llanfihangel Genau'r Glyn and Llancynfelyn, according to the will of Rees David ap Jenkin, PRO 1592 39 Harrington.

[26]CD I, 24, 26, 29, 30, 37. In Llanafan, Tyddyn-y-Nant, Tyddyn-y-Fron and Tyddyn-bach, (the first two names survive as Ty'n-nant and Ty'n-fron), Tyddyn-y-wern and Tyddyn Ieuan ap Phillip; in Llanfihangel-y-Creuddyn, Tyddyn Llewelyn Tew ap Deio.

[27]BM Egerton Charter 287 of 14.3.1563/4.

[28]For Aberpyllau see also PRO Chancery C.2 Elizabeth T8/40 1/1/1602-3.

[29]I am grateful to Mr D.Hopkins of Maenarthur and the late Matthew Evans of Ysbyty Ystwyth for telling me these folk-tales, which have not been previously published, and which Mr Robin Gwyndaf kindly tells me are not known to St Fagans. Ty'n-y-rhyd does not figure in the Old Schedule of Gogerddan Deeds in N.L.W.

[30]Heiresses do not figure after Morris Fychan until John Vaughan the first viscount, who had married the daughter of the Earl of Rochester; the third and fourth viscounts also married heiresses.

[31]For the Cardiganshire J.P.s see J.R.S.Phillips, *The Justices of the Peace in Wales and Monmouthshire 1541 to 1689*, (Cardiff, 1975), pp. 185-203.

[32]Lay Subsidy: PRO E/179/219/84. Hearth Tax: PRO E179 219/94. My thanks to Dr Evan James for copies of his transcripts of both documents.

[33]Lewis Dwnn to Morgan Herbert of Trawsgoed (before 1589), NLW MS 5270, 197a; Rhisiart Phylip to Dafydd Llwyd ab Ifan of Aber-mad, NLW Peniarth MS 117, 393; see Hywel D. Roberts, 'Noddwyr y Beirdd yn Sir Aberteifi', University of Wales M.A. thesis, 1969.

[34]PRO E179/219/84 and E179/219/87. For the difficulties of using the Lay Subsidy rolls see H.A.Lloyd, *The Gentry of South-west Wales, 1540-1640* (Cardiff, 1968), pp. 25-6.

[35]CD I,140.

[36]She gave her husband five sons and five daughters.

[37]G.Dyfnallt Owen, *Wales in the Reign of James I* (London, 1988), p. 166.

[38]CD I, 147.

[39]CD I, 147.

[40]H.A.Lloyd, *op.cit*, pp.68-69.

[41]*Ibid.*, pp. 83, 79.

[42]CD I, 59.

[43]It is difficult to agree with Professor J.Gwynn Williams, (*NLWJ*, VIII, p.227) that 'there are no traces of large scale purchases during Edward Vaughan's control of the Trawscoed estate'.

[44]J.T.Evans, *The Church Plate of Cardiganshire* (Stow-on-the-Wold, 1914), pp. 33-35.

[45]She is named as Agnes Vaughan in Edward Vaughan's will of 1635; see CD II, 48.

[46]T.I.Davies, 'The Vale of Aeron in the Making', *Ceredigion* III, 3 (1958) p.205.

[47]Numerous documents in the Crosswood archive refer to Cilcennin and its associated lands before Henry Vaughan's marriage; the estate deserves a more detailed treatment than can be offered in this book.

[48]CD I.297. Dr Susan Davies has shown me that Francis Green, in a rare lapse, dated this document incorrectly in The Crosswood Deeds, attributing it to 1654 instead of 1627, the correct date.

[49]All wills referred to are available in the National Library of Wales Church in Wales probate records for the Archdeaconry of Cardigan, and are there listed by year, name and parish.

[50]The rent-charge was eventually sold by Frances Duchess of Somerset (nèe Devereux) to a consortium including Sir William Hooker, Sir John Vaughan's wealthy son-in-law, who presumably wrote it off; there is no further trace of it in the archive. CD II, 126.

[51] J.M.Howells, op.cit., p.22. No rentals survive for this period, but the figures seem very reasonable.

[52] See D.H.Williams, *Atlas of Cistercian Lands in Wales*, (Cardiff, 1990), pp.56-7, 96.

[53] CD.II.59

[54] Late in the 18th century Thomas Johnes was still paying £22 chief rent for the Hafod estate to Trawsgoed, although he held by freehold.

[55] CD I, 266

[56] CD I, 266

[57] CD I, 297.

[58] CD I, 258

[59] CD I, 257 and II, 48.

[60] The reference to rectories is odd; Llanfihangel-y-Creuddyn and Llanafan were never rectories with control of tithes, but were vicarages, the tithe income of which went to the owners, at this time the Palmer family.

[61] A puzzling twist is provided by the survival of the will of Anne Vaughan, widow, of Maenarthur, made in 1650. Maenarthur was the property of Trawsgoed, so this could be the widow of Edward Vaughan senior, his second wife whom he had married in 1624. Anne bequeathed all her goods to her only son Edward Vaughan, gentleman. Is this the same Edward to whom Glennydd was conditionally bequeathed? It seems likely, since among the witnesses to the will were John Vaughan and Jane Vaughan. The word only means that Edward must have been a son of Edward senior's second marriage, and half-brother to John Vaughan.

[62] They were Mary, wife of Morgan Herbert of Hafod Uchdryd (she d.1677), Jane wife of Sir Matthew Price of Newtown and then of Sir Basil Price of Park Hall, Warwickshire, and Anne Vaughan, wife of Thomas Lloyd of Llanllawddog (Pedigree, p.4).

[63] CD I, 483.

[64] Cited in J.R.Phillips, *A List of the Sheriffs of Cardiganshire* (1868), p.16. The motto translates as 'he who knows not how to dissimulate knows not how to live'.

[65] For the draft will, CD I, 375; for the letters of administration, NLW Church in Wales Probate records, Henry Vaughan, Cilcennin, 1665/6. By the draft, a thousand pounds was willed to another grandson Henry Herbert (second son of Morgan Herbert of Hafod Uchdryd) and eight hundred pounds to his grandson Henry Lloyd, son of Thomas Lloyd of Llanllawddog.

II. 'OLD, GOOD MR VAUGHAN'

John Vaughan certainly had the most brilliant career of any member of the Vaughan family.[1] It was his success, both personal, political and financial, that raised the Vaughans of Trawsgoed above the common run of Welsh gentry families, enabling them eventually, though not in his lifetime, to reach the titled aristocracy. He is also the first Vaughan whose career we can trace in some detail, and whose character has been described for us by contemporaries, though they do not always agree among themselves. He was certainly a controversial character, and although a moderate in politics, cannot have been the easiest of men to get on with, though his close friends were devoted to him. Born in 1603, John Vaughan was sent to King's School, Worcester, from 1613 to 1618, then (aged fifteen) to Christ Church, Oxford, and in 1621 to study law at the Inner Temple in London. He was called to the Bar in 1630. As well as the Law, he enjoyed poetry and mathematics, and was described as 'a man of great parts of nature, and very well adorned by arts and books.' At Oxford he was almost certainly tutored by his uncle Jenkyn Vaughan, Fellow of All Souls; at the Inner Temple he made the culturally and legally valuable acquaintance of the great scholar, lawyer and politician John Selden, and was 'so much cherished by Mr Selden that he grew to be of entire trust and friendship with him.' Selden is said to have discerned in him:-

> a ready Wit and sound Judgement, (and) did studiously afford him Occasion of making a right use of two such excellent Ingredients, and frequently admitted him to the Converse of himself and other worthy Persons . . .

This friendship opened the door to learned and political Jacobean society, that of Edward Hyde (Lord Clarendon), Ben Jonson, Thomas Carew, Thomas Hobbes, Charles Cotton and Sir Kenelm Digby, a brilliant circle of Stuart poets, scholars and savants. It may be assumed that he spent a good deal of time working in the lawcourts, but virtually nothing is known of his legal career during the pre-Civil War period. However, it is safe to say that he anticipates the opinion of Sir Lewis Namier on the legal profession in the eighteenth century:-

The legal profession was the most democratic of all those concerned with matters of state; for there naturally was no way of rising at the Bar except by ability and hard work, and seldom, if ever, were men raised to the Woolsack or the Bench who had not distinguished themselves at the Bar.[2]

As for parliament, men could choose to seek a seat, as people do today, for a variety of reasons. One reason, true of several of the later Vaughan MPs, was again well put by Namier:

What mattered to them (i.e. the country gentlemen) was not so much membership of the House, as the primacy in their own 'country' attested by their being chosen to represent their county or some respectable borough.[3]

This may well have been true of other early members for the county and borough seats of Cardigan, but it was not true of John Vaughan, who was more energetic and able than the common run of MPs. Of

John Selden (1584-1654), lawyer, politician and mentor of Sir John Vaughan. Unattributed.

course the Vaughan family had not yet acquired the Strata Florida granges, and was not yet equal in wealth and influence to the Pryses of Gogerddan. It was a greater distinction to represent a county seat than a borough, and the Cardiganshire seat since the beginning of Welsh representation in 1536 had usually been held by one of the Gogerddan family—John Pryse (1553-5, 1563-84), his eldest son Richard Pryse (1584-5, 1588-9, 1593, 1601, 1614, 1621-2), his second son Thomas Pryse (1597), his son-in-law Sir John Lewis (1604-11) and his grandson-in-law James Lewis (1626, 1628-9, 1640, 1656-8).

It is worth reviewing briefly the political background to the Vaughan involvement in politics.[4] The Act of Union of 1536 had ended the isolation of Cardiganshire and the Principality of Wales, previously cut off by the Marcher Lordships from contact with England. Henceforth Wales had parliamentary representation, and like most of the Welsh counties, Cardiganshire had one county member and one borough member. There was grumbling dispute in Cardiganshire as to which towns might take part in the election of the borough member. Voting, if there was a ballot, took place in Cardigan, and Aberystwyth and Lampeter were always involved. At first Trefilan, Adpar and Tregaron also took part, but gradually dropped out. The borough voters were the burgesses, whose numbers could be increased at the whim of the masters of the borough councils, while in the county electorate registered freeholders (including long-term tenants) had the vote. The borough councils were usually controlled by nominees of the local grandee—Pryse of Gogerddan in Aberystwyth, Phillips of the Priory in Cardigan, and the Lloyds in Lampeter. Ownership of the Priory estate eventually passed to Gogerddan in 1693, giving the Pryses an even stronger power base in the county. Tregaron, until it lost its right to participate in 1730, was controlled by Nanteos.

Given the Gogerddan dominance in the county, John Vaughan had to be content with nomination for the Cardigan Boroughs and not the more esteemed county seat in the election of 1628, when the estate (probably still worth less than £600 a year) was as yet in his father's hands. However, that Parliament was soon suspended by Charles I, and was followed by eleven years of the king's personal rule. In March 1629 Vaughan's mentor John Selden was imprisoned by the king, and detained until May 1631; during his time in Parliament Selden had been critical of the king, and had helped in the attempted impeachment of the royal favourite, the Duke of Buckingham.[5] John Vaughan presumably returned to the Bar; in 1637 he was appointed deputy steward of the manors of Mefenydd and Creuddyn. In the same year he bought a swathe of lands in the parish of Llanilar and the neighbouring parishes from Sir John Lewis and his son James Lewis, of Abernant Bychan. He stood again in 1640 for the borough seat, and was re-elected to the Short Parliament of 1640 and to the Long Parliament which began sitting in the same year.

It is not appropriate here to elaborate on all Vaughan's numerous parliamentary activities, so well summarised by J. Gwynn Williams. However, it helps us understand the man to know that he disapproved of the king's arbitrary use of imprisonment against his opponents (the thought of John Selden's incarceration must have been often in his mind), and that he criticised the king's levying of Ship Money, the tax by which Charles I sought to avoid the necessity of summoning parliament to finance his dictatorial rule; in this Vaughan was at one with a majority of unwilling taxpayers. Vaughan was a moderate critic of royalty, one who did not wish to see either revolutionary disruption or royal absolutism, and he therefore defended Parliament's limitations of royal prerogative, limitations which were so obnoxious to the monarch. Interestingly too, Vaughan was put on a House committee to investigate the disputed election for Caernarfon, since it was felt necessary to have a Welsh member on the committee. As a lawyer, he is known to have practised in the court of Star Chamber, which would certainly have been financially profitable for him, and he took an interest in the affairs of fellow-Welshmen. Vaughan was a Welsh-speaker himself, as we know not only from his interest in the Laws of Hywel Dda and the Book of Llandaf, but from contemporary witness.[6] He was also one of three men appointed to settle the translation of the 1662 Prayer Book into Welsh.

Membership of the Parliament of 1640 was a position fraught with difficulties after the years of Charles I's personal rule, especially perhaps for a man who was a monarchist but not an absolutist. The eleven years between Parliaments had produced a bitter harvest. There was anger among many MPs and in the country at arbitrary rule and taxation, especially the notorious Ship Money. The king's divine right to rule still commanded some respect, so he was not the first object of attack, which instead fell on his ministers, Archbishop Laud and the Earl of Strafford. Vaughan sat on House committees for abolishing the

Courts of Star Chamber and High Commission; the former at least had probably provided him with fat fees in earlier times, but such a tool of royal autocracy was doomed. He was involved in preparing the charges against Archbishop Laud and in drafting the Triennial Bill, intended to make it impossible for the monarch ever again to rule without summoning regular parliaments.

However, John Vaughan was a man of the middle way, unwilling to go to the extremes of Pym and Hampden in attainting and executing the King's once-powerful minister the Earl of Strafford (whose portrait remains in family ownership). When the rift between king and Parliament was becoming intolerable to moderates, Vaughan left London (in 1642), but instead of joining Charles at Nottingham he retired to Trawsgoed, and though declaring for the king, he did not attend the Oxford Parliament, despite being summoned thither. He protested his loyalty to the monarch, and in 1643 wrote to Morgan Herbert of Hafod Uchdryd lamenting the fall of Tenby to the Parliamentary forces. Interestingly enough, although he is best defined as a moderate royalist, his great friend John Selden was rather a moderate Parliamentarian, but the dire divisions of political life did not affect their mutual esteem, which remained intact until Selden's death in 1654. The best evidence of this is the fulsome Latin dedication to Vaughan of Selden's last published work, *Vindiciae Maris Clausi.*

John Vaughan's political stance in the Civil Wars is not entirely clear. A vicious attack was made on him in a pamphlet apparently published after the Restoration:-

> One that will upon fits, talke loud for Monarchy, but scrupulous to wet his finger to advance it. He served Burgess for Cardigan in the Long Parliament; but quitted it upon Strafford's tryal; named by his Majesty one of the Commissioners to attend the treaty in the Isle of Wight, but refused it; personally advised Cromwell to put the Crown on his owne head; purchased Mevenith, one of his late Majesty's Manors within the County of Cardigan; personally assisted the taking of Aberystwyth, a garrison then kept for his late Majesty. These services kept him from sequestration; bore offices in the late several governments. He is of good parts, but puts too high a value on them; insolently proud and matchlessly pernicious; by lending £800 to Col. Philip Jones and other favourites of the late tymes, procured the command of the County he liveth in, to continue in his friends and descendants to this day.[7]

This is from a well-known text which describes a number of leading

Cardiganshire gentlemen. It is often quoted in part, yet bearing marks of self-contradiction as well as considerable malice. In part it seems to have been written while Vaughan was alive (e.g. the word 'liveth'), yet the reference to his descendants commanding the county he lived in suggests he was dead at the time of writing. 'Pernicious' is a description no-one else ever used of Vaughan. He is generally credited with having retired during the Commonwealth period *pour cultiver son jardin*, but in 1657 along with his brother Henry of Cilcennin and nearly all the leading gentry of the county, he was named under the Protectorate as a Commissioner for Cardiganshire, in order to raise money for the government.[8] There is no evidence to show that he took part in the siege of Aberystwyth in 1646; it does however appear that John Jones of Nanteos, previously a royalist, did so, and the same pressures probably caused John Vaughan to trim his sails too. As for the suggestion that he advised Cromwell to assume the Crown, this could be malice, or simply reflect what many men thought who saw the need for political stability, and no valid alternative. The accusation against John Vaughan which is most directly supported by other witnesses is that of pride.

Edward Vaughan, Sir John's son, edited his father's papers in 1677 (a beautifully printed volume), prefacing it with a brief memoir, which states categorically that he spent the Civil War and Commonwealth period at home in retirement, maintaining that 'it was the Duty of an honest Man to decline as far as in him lay, owning Jurisdictions that derived their Authority from any Power, but their lawful Prince.'[9] We do have three letters from Vaughan's hand written in the spring of 1644. The first, to Morgan Herbert of Hafod Uchdryd, has already been mentioned, and shows his royalist inclinations. The second and third are to Colonel Herbert Price.[10] The third letter describes his own activity in the face of the threat to Cardiganshire:

> Here will no great good be done until some force appears. I prepare what may be, having these some days fixed the trained band of this quarter, who are altogether undisciplined in the nature of a garrison, where they are diligently exercised, and will become of use signifying nothing before. I collect what volunteers I can to arm with the arms in my power as dragoons, and what horse can be prepared; but these will come in presently upon your appearance and summons.

Vaughan was to claim later that his house at Trawsgoed had been ravaged by Parliamentary forces in the spring of 1645; whether it was this that led to the rebuilding of the mansion it is impossible to tell. In 1648 Vaughan's estate was threatened with confiscation; it is not known how he survived this threat. All we have is his statement of 1660 that he compounded for his estate, and he certainly sold £300 pounds' worth of property in 1648. Thenceforward he seems to have survived unscathed, and largely uninvolved in public affairs until the Restoration of the monarchy in 1660.[11] Scant clues do exist pointing to his local activities; in 1649 John Stedman of Ystrad Fflur named John Vaughan as executor of his will, and in the same year Morgan Herbert of Cwmystwyth named John Vaughan in his will as a creditor for £250. This suggests that most of the price of £300 due to Vaughan for Hafod in 1630-2 had not yet been paid. In 1656 Lewis ap Rees of Llanfihangel-y-Creuddyn left John Vaughan two oxen as a heriot or inheritance fee for his son's entry into the family tenancy.

From 1654 Vaughan was busy as one of the executors of his friend John Selden, who died in that year. The four executors were also the principal legatees, and shared Selden's vast fortune of £40,000 between them, perhaps the single largest cash perquisite ever to land in the lap of the Vaughan family. Selden's possessions included a famous library, most of which was given by the executors to the Bodleian Library at Oxford (hence Selden End in the Old Library). Robert Vaughan of Hengwrt, the industrious collector of Welsh manuscripts, wrote to John Vaughan begging the loan of the Book of Llandaf, one of Selden's possessions, so that he could copy it, and offering to make a copy for John Vaughan to keep. The volume was already in the Bodleian, but Vaughan borrowed it, brought it to Trawsgoed and lent it to Robert Vaughan, who felt:

> bound to remember this Gentleman not only for his worth, as being an eminent Lawyer, and every way a most accomplished Gentleman, but also for his singular civility to mee, in encouraging my studies, and lending me the ancient M.S. booke of Llandaffe to transcribe.

The volume did not return to the Bodleian, however, but remained at Trawsgoed until it passed to the Davies family of Gwysaney, following an inter-family marriage;[12] Vaughan was perfectly entitled by the terms of Selden's will to keep the book. One of his grandsons was named Selden Vaughan, obviously in pious memory of an influential and valued family friend.

Sir John Vaughan (1603-1674), Chief Justice of the Common Pleas.
Artist unknown, wrongly attributed to Vanderbanck.

Despite John Vaughan's involvement with the legal profession, Parliament and London society during the years 1628-1640, he did not neglect the Trawsgoed estate. We have already seen that he, rather than his father, was responsible for the purchase of the eight Strata Florida granges, the most ambitious single acquisition in the estate's history. It must have been a considerable burden at first; Vaughan had to pay the Earl of Essex £1,300 down, and £300 a year, as well as a Crown rent of £112 a year. Although the total price of £4,300 should have been paid off by 1640, the £300 a year payment was still a charge on the Trawsgoed estate in 1670, when it—the annual payment—was sold by its then owner, the dowager Duchess of Somerset, to Sir William Turner and Sir William Hooker, aldermen of the City of London, and Richard Herbert of Ceri, Montgomeryshire.[13] There are no further references to this £300-a-year rent charge, perhaps because the wealthy Sir William Hooker had married his daughter Letitia to John Vaughan's eldest son, Edward Vaughan, and may possibly have paid off the debt.

With the Restoration of 1660 Vaughan's star shone again. He immediately began to gain new appointments: steward of the lordships, manors and lands of Mefennydd, Creuddyn, Haminiog, Caerwedros and Perfedd, and deputy Lord Lieutenant of Cardiganshire. Politically he was cautious at first, not seeking election to Parliament in 1660, though he did so in 1661, this time for the county seat, in which, remarkably, he replaced Sir Richard Pryse, of Gogerddan, who had held non-parliamentary office under the Commonwealth, and who had taken the seat in 1660. At first John Vaughan refused offers of a judgeship, preferring to return to practise at the bar, and then to work in the House of Commons as a member of the Cavalier parliament which began sitting in 1661.

In Parliament Vaughan soon became a leading figure and influential speaker, involved in a wide range of business. He served on 259 committees and chaired fourteen of them. He strongly favoured free trade, criticising monopolies. He was a loyal churchman and monarchist, but was also loyal to the legislation he had supported in 1640-42. When in 1664 Charles II's supporters moved to repeal the Triennial Act, Vaughan attacked them vigorously, denouncing it as 'a mear cheate', and asking whether other Acts of the Long Parliament, such as the abolition of Star Chamber, would also be repealed. A summary of the speech has survived:

> Is surprised at the haste with which it (i.e. repeal) proceeds; cannot see anything in the bill which demands its repeal; refutes objections; details the miseries caused by the non-sitting of Parliaments; refers to the mischievous decision of the judges on ship money, in the late reign; thinks this bill does not sufficiently provide for the certainty of Parliaments, and moves that it be laid aside, and another brought in, removing such clauses in the Bill for Triennial Parliaments as are not thought respectful enough to the King.[14]

The argument against the Act was that it was derogatory to the king's prerogative; Vaughan hit back with drastic logic in his pungent style:

> I dare boldly assert that there is noe Law but takes either from the King's prerogative or the People's Liberty.

Samuel Pepys at least was impressed:

> The great matter today in the House hath been that Mr Vaughan, the Great Speaker is this day come to town and hath declared himself in a speech of an hour and half with great reason and eloquence against the repealing of the Bill for Triennial Parliaments; but with no success. (March 8th 1664)

Vaughan reminded his listeners that the courts had been quite inadequate as defenders of liberty against an overreaching sovereign in the 1630s, even though there had been some good judges; only Parliament could offer real security.

Vaughan lost the day, but showed himself again to be a defender of parliamentary freedom and a fine orator. Pepys provides comment from a valuable source in his diary for 3 July 1666:

> Mr Finch one of the Commissioners of Excise and I fell to discourse of the parliament and the great men there; and among others Mr Vaughan, whom he reports as a man of excellent judgement and learning, but most passionate and opinionate. He hath done himself the most wrong (tho he values it not) that is, the displeasure of the King in his standing so long against the breaking of the Act for a Triennial parliament, but yet [I] do believe him to be a most loyall gentleman.

However, as a loyal Anglican Vaughan obviously approved the 1662 expulsion from their parish livings of two thousand clerical appointees of the Commonwealth regime, and the return of the bishops to the House of Lords. This support might be thought to have pleased the Court and Church party, but Vaughan also opposed Charles II's efforts to extend toleration to Roman Catholics and Dissenters, fearing that this would undermine established order. In 1664 he opposed a grant of £2,500,000 for the king to war against the Dutch; with good-humoured irony, the Commons first voted him down and then elected him chairman of the committee appointed to levy the grant.

In 1667 Vaughan was a leading speaker for the impeachment of the Earl of Clarendon, Charles II's former companion in exile, now his first minister, but of whom the king had tired. Vaughan's main charge against Clarendon was that he was a menace to Parliamentary liberty. A letter from John Lloyd to Sir Richard Wynne tells of Vaughan's address to the Commons:

> Mr Vaughan's speech .. knocked him quite downe I do believe never to rise in the Horizon at least. Mr. Sergt. Maynard had spoken well and long for him [i.e. Clarendon] but was smartly reflected on by Vaughan who sayd he wondered any man that pretended to understand law should dare to offer for law (to that house) which was not soe.

Clarendon himself gives us a valuable sketch of John Vaughan from his law-student days onwards, written when the great minister was in exile partly as a result of Vaughan's campaign against him:

> Sir John Vaughan was then a student of the Law in the Inner Temple, but at time[s] indulged more to the politer learning, and was, in truth, a man of great parts of nature, and very well adorned by arts and books; and so much cherished by Mr Selden, that he grew to be of entire trust and friendship with him, and to that owed the best part of his reputation, for he was of so magisterial and supercilious a behaviour, that all Mr Selden's instructions, and authority, and example, could not file off that roughness of his nature so as to make him very grateful. He looked most into those parts of the Law which disposed him to least reverence to the Crown, and most to popular authority, yet without inclination to any change in government; and therefore, before the beginning of the Civil War, and when he clearly discerned the approached to it in Parliament, (of which he was a Member,) he withdrew himself into the fastnesses of his own Country, South Wales, where he enjoyed a secure, and as near an innocent life as the iniquity of that time would permit; and upon the return of King Charles the Second, he appeared under the character of a Man who had preserved his loyalty entire,and was esteemed accordingly by all that party. His friend Mr Hyde [i.e. Clarendon himself, writing in the third person] who was then become Lord High Chancellor of England, renewed his old kindness and friendship towards him, and was desirous to gratify him in all the ways he could, and earnestly pressed him to put on his gown again, and take upon him the office of a Judge; but he excused himself upon his long discontinuance, (having not worn his gown, and wholly discontinued the profession from the year 1640, full twenty years,) and upon his age, and expressly refused to receive any

promotion; but continued all the professions of respect and gratitude imaginable to the Chancellor, till it was in his power to manifest the contrary, to his prejudice, which he did with circumstances very uncommendable.[15]

With Clarendon's exile achieved, Vaughan was now a major influence in parliament. He was involved in suppression of highwaymen, in a new public accounts bill, and chaired a committee on freedom of speech in parliament. He became involved in an attempt to impeach another over-mighty subject, the Duke of Ormond, Lord Lieutenant of Ireland. Vaughan had a particularly Welsh interest in opposing Ormond, who was attempting to improve the Irish cattle trade, then as now a cause of grievance to Welsh farmers. However, the impeachment failed. But Vaughan was no head-hunter; when the Earl of Sandwich was in trouble in 1668 for distributing naval booty without due process, Vaughan defended him, thus mightily pleasing Sandwich's loyal servant, Samuel Pepys. Vaughan was well-known to Samuel Pepys as 'old, good Mr Vaughan', a description not written for public consumption, and which with other Pepysian references, tends to counterbalance the previously-quoted and anonymous description of him as 'insolently proud and matchlessly pernicious'.[16]

Some of Vaughan's parliamentary involvement was in Welsh matters. He was ordered, along with two others, to peruse the existing statutes and to bring in a proviso to ensure a translation of the 1662 Book of Common Prayer into Welsh, which was published in 1664. He defended his native Cardiganshire against overmuch taxation, trying to get the burden shifted to North Wales, which he thought to be unduly favoured, and was eventually successful.

Vaughan certainly had a pithy style. Commenting on the abuses of the Hearth Tax, he told the House to prosecute corrupt officials and not make new laws, 'for multiplying of laws . . . is but multiplying of riddles,' a lesson modern parliaments have not learnt. When a law was passed specifically allowing a charge of treason to be brought on the word of two witnesses, Vaughan caustically remarked that thenceforth he would take good care not to dismiss two servants at the same time. He knew how essential it is for the laws to be written clearly:

> When a Law is given to any people, it is necessary that it be conceiv'd and publish'd in words which may be understood, for without that the Law cannot be obey'd; and a Law that cannot be obeyed, is no Law.[17]

When it was proposed to enfranchise Durham, which had no M.P., Vaughan spoke against the motion with a kind of cranky sarcasm:

> it was not necessary to increase the numbers of Members, the House not having room sufficient to contain those Members that were already elected, and that multitude of Members retarded business . . . The northern parts are sufficiently provided already.[18]

Vaughan was knighted at the palace of Whitehall on 30 May, 1668,[19] and was appointed Chief Justice of the Common Pleas, over the heads of the Attorney General and Solicitor General of the day; the post was considered to be worth about four thousand pounds a year, and he held it until his death in 1674.[20] The post incidentally involved him in acting as Deputy Speaker of the House of Lords; in 1669 he became a Privy Councillor.[21] It is in a sense surprising that Vaughan, who had been such a leader of the moderate country party against the court absolutists, should have been thus promoted to the Bench; however, he was being promoted out of the House of Commons, and could thus no longer take an active lead in politics. Nevertheless, when important cases came before his court, he was able to show his mettle.

This is most obvious in his historic verdict in Bushell's Case in 1671. Two Quakers, William Penn and William Mead, were charged with unlawful assembly for open-air preaching. The jury in the case found them not guilty, and the authorities vented their rage on the jurors by fining them each forty marks (1 mark = 13s4d). Jury-member Bushell refused to pay, was imprisoned, and brought a writ of *habeas corpus* in the Court of Common Pleas. Vaughan found in his favour, ruling against the punishment of juries for bringing in verdicts contrary to the wishes of the authorities. This was a vital blow for the freedom of the individual against the Crown, and is still an essential principle of liberty. Juries, not judges, are the arbiters of fact, and cannot be fined or imprisoned even for giving perverse verdicts. This, however, is only the most memorable of Vaughan's many judgements and enormous industry in legal affairs. Of particular interest for Wales is the last of his Reports, whose completion was frustrated by his death; it dealt with the powers of the London courts in Wales, which had its own Courts of Great Sessions. He argued that London courts had no right of final process in Wales. Vaughan knew the legal history of medieval Wales very well, and his knowledge is displayed in his surviving notes, in which he argued against the extension of the powers of London courts in Wales.

Lawrence Stone comments on the impetus a legal career could give to the rise of an individual and his family, describing lawyers as 'those rapacious beneficiaries of the age'.[22] Vaughan must be presumed to have enriched himself greatly both during his earlier period at the Bar and after the Restoration; he continued to buy land during those periods, and it would seem that for some periods at least his son Edward was managing affairs at home while his father was busy in London. One of Vaughan's largest purchases was made late in life, that of the Gwernioge estate in Montgomeryshire, bought in 1671 and yielding £371 per annum in rent.

Sir John Vaughan died suddenly in Serjeant's Inn in Chancery Lane on 10 December 1674. His funeral was a splendid one, attended by the Lord Keeper and the Lord Privy Seal, the Earl of Carbery and the Bishop of Rochester, as well as an impressive array of judges and parliamentarians, led by the King's Serjeants and the Attorney and Solicitor Generals. The sermon at the Inner Temple Church was preached by Edward Stillingfleet, later a notable Bishop of Worcester. Sir John's body was buried in the Temple Church, London, with a splendid Latin inscription to commemorate him:

Hic Situs est
Johannes Vaughanus
Eques Auratus Capital Justiciar, de Com
Banco filius Edwardi Vaughan de Trowscoed
in Agro Dimetarum Ar, & Leticiae Uxoris
Ijus filiae Johannis Stedman de Strata
Florida in eodem Com. Ar. unus
e quatuor praedocti Seldeni
Executoribus Ei Stabili amicitia
Studiorumq Communiore
a tirocino Intimus
et praecarus
Natus erat xiiii die Sept. An^O
Dni 1603 & denatus x^O die
Decembri, An^O Dni 1674
Qui juxta hoc marmor
Depositus adventu
Christi propitiu
Expectat
Multum deploratus.

Unfortunately this memorial was completely destroyed by German bombs in 1941.

Sir John Vaughan was a great parliamentarian and a remarkable lawyer, who believed in constitutional monarchy and sought to reconcile the rule of law with the liberty of the individual. It was because he saw Dissenters and Roman Catholics as a threat to the rule of law that he approved of restrictions placed on them; nevertheless, when they appeared in his court he treated them with scrupulous fairness. Vaughan cherished the status of the House of Commons, defending it against the Lords and the overreach of monarchs. He may have made himself wealthy by his practice at the Bar, but as parliamentarian and judge he was untainted by the bribery and corruption of the times, and was enormously respected, not only by Pepys and Selden, by Thomas Hobbes and Matthew Hale, but by fellow parliamentarians and lawyers. Some found him over-proud and difficult, but 'No man in this House hath more honour for him than I,' said Sir Thomas Littleton; Sir Robert Howard said that he could not 'express himself more, than every person here thinks, of Mr. Vaughan's worth.' When Lord Keeper Finch addressed Vaughan's successor in the office of Chief Justice of the Common Pleas, he said that Vaughan's death had 'deprived the King of an excellent servant, this court of a learned Chief Justice and the whole kingdom of a very useful magistrate.'

More critical views of Vaughan as a parliamentarian have been propounded, for example in the official history of Parliament:

> [He was a] good orator . . . his name is associated with some useful legal reforms, but he was not a particularly far-sighted politican . . . his abandonment of precedent in the proceedings against Clarendon savours too much of political expediency. Most of the compromises at which he aimed proved untenable in the fairly short run. He was far more successful as a judge.[23]

It is worth observing that Sir John Vaughan was a man who made the best use of his talents. A lesser man could have been satisfied living at home on his rents or have concentrated on preserving and extending his estate; instead, Vaughan took up an advantageous career and put his ambition and great abilities to work.

*   *   *

Edward Vaughan, like his father, was at the Inner Temple (1653) and was called to the Bar, but does not seem to have practised. During the 1660s he spent time in London, but also did a good deal of administering of the Trawsgoed estate on his father's behalf. He was M.P. for the county seat from 1669 until his death, and was briefly a Lord of the Admiralty in 1679-80. He is never cited in the general histories of the period, but was in fact a vigorous though not extreme member of the Country party, taking much the same line as his father had done in favouring the middle path of government. He served on

Edward Vaughan (d.1683), son of Sir John Vaughan.
Wrongly attributed to Vanderbanck.

140 committees and made 220 recorded speeches. He was energetic against popery, and fiercely opposed the Declaration of Indulgence by which Charles II sought to ease the lives of Catholics and Dissenters. Such opposition was of course inspired, at least in part, by fear of a Catholic succession to the throne:

> When the King may dispence with any law it must be manifestly for the good of the subject. If it does injury to the subject it is illegal . . . if this Declaration signifies anything, the Church of England signifies nothing . . . This prerogative is illegal.[24]

He had something of the trenchant style of his father; in opposing royal prerogative, he argued:

> The King has power of war and peace, but not otherwise than by law. If to raise money, you [addressing the Speaker] may go out of your chair and we home.[25]

In 1677 he opposed the building of twenty warships, concerned at the King's repeated requests for more money; this must have infuriated Pepys. He was involved in the impeachment of the Earl of Danby, then Lord Treasurer, and in the investigations of the Popish Plot.

Bishop Burnet described Edward Vaughan as 'a man of great integrity, had much welch pride, and did great service.'[26] Despite his Welsh pride, he was the first of the Vaughans to marry out of Wales; his wife was Letitia Hooker, daughter of a foolish but wealthy London alderman. Samuel Pepys briefly describes a visit to the Hooker family in 1666, when Letitia was sick in childbed, noting that her mother was 'a most beautiful, fat woman.'[27] The marriage would certainly have been an arrangement by the parents of the couple for their mutual advantage. The Hooker dowry would have been welcome to the Vaughan interest, the Vaughan descent, estate and status to the Hooker interest. To secure this marriage, which took place in the year 1665, William Hooker had promised a dowry of £2,050, while a jointure of £300 a year was settled on Letitia. Edward only survived his father by ten years, dying in 1684, aged about 48, and he was buried at Ludlow, where his Latin memorial is fulsome in his praise. Ludlow was of course the meeting-place of the Council for Wales and the Marches, and was then the nearest Wales had to a capital, though of course it is in England.

Edward Vaughan's English marriage calls in question the status of the Welsh language in the family. He was himself the son of Welsh-speaking parents (it seems fair to presume that the Stedmans had become thoroughly Welsh); unfortunately we do not know for certain where his children were raised. If at Trawsgoed, as seems likely, they would almost certainly have been wet-nursed by local women, a process which, reinforced by the close attendance of servants, may well have ensured the survival of Welsh on their tongues as a second language. This is guesswork, however.

Edward's son John, who became the first Viscount Lisburne in 1695, was still a minor in 1684, and did not stand for Parliament in his father's place (though in the election of 1701 Lewis Pryse of Gogerddan took the county seat when still under age). The Trawsgoed deeds show that the widow Letitia managed the estate until March 1688, when her son's name begins to appear jointly with hers. There is no need to suppose that her management was in name only; there is as we shall see other evidence of female involvement in managing the estate. She finally disappears from the record in 1691. Edward Vaughan's will of 1683 in the Public Record Office shows how wealthy the family had become. He increased the settlement on Letitia from £300 a year to £400; he proposed leaving £3,500 as a marriage portion to his daughter Letitia (money owed by Sir Hugh Owens); £2,200 to his daughter Jane; £1500 to his daughter Elizabeth and £1,700 to his daughter Bridget.[28] His son Selden Vaughan was to receive:

> all my gold in the custody of my brother in law William Hooker Esquire which gold is sealed up with my seale in Two Leather purses the one containeing Nine hundred broad peeces or thereabouts the other Two hundred guineyes or thereabouts.

The family's steady upward progress was sealed with the marriage in 1692 of John Vaughan to Malet Wilmot, daughter and co-heiress of the second Earl of Rochester the famous rake and poet, and his elevation to an Irish peerage as Viscount Lisburne and Baron Fethers in 1695. Who negotiated this marriage? John's father Edward was dead. There are other mysteries in connection with the peerage: why should the Lisburne title have been chosen, and why should John Vaughan have been ennobled at all?

There had been one Lisburne peerage already. Adam Loftus, member of a prominent Irish family, was raised to the Irish peerage with the Lisburne title in 1686 by James II, soon after he had succeeded to the throne. However, despite James's favours to him, Loftus refused to follow the king in war and exile, but turned his coat and raised a regiment, Lord Lisburne's regiment, to fight for William and Mary in Ireland. There, at the siege of Limerick in September 1691, he was slain. Childless, his peerage died with him.

It is difficult to decide exactly why John Vaughan was given a peerage, nor why the Lisburne title should have been revived so swiftly after its demise. J.M.Howells marshalls the arguments judiciously: it may have been for Vaughan's service to his county, or a belated recognition of his grandfather's achievements. A later generation of the family made a plausible suggestion, perhaps preserving valid family tradition, that it was 'for signal services rendered by him at the Revolution' (of 1688).[29] This could perhaps be the case; there is a silent witness in the possession of the family to this day, a state portrait of William III, which according to its title-plate was given by the king to Vaughan. The picture shows the armoured king against a Dutch background, suggesting a pre-1688 painting conveniently at hand as a royal gift. It must surely be associated in some way with the bestowal of the peerage, but for what reason is still obscure. However, Howells' most interesting argument, citing Sir Lewis Namier in his support, is that peerages were not at this period bestowed for particular services, but on men who had reached a certain social level. Presumably the Lisburne title was chosen simply in order to disinfect its tainted memory. Adam Loftus had supported the Catholic cause, while John Vaughan was loyal to the Revolution of 1688.

It was certainly the opinion of the editors of *The Complete Peerage* that the peerage was a direct consequence of the marriage of John Vaughan to the daughter of the Earl of Rochester, since it had brought him within a magic circle of expectation. Malet Vaughan's sister had married the Earl of Sandwich, so something had to be done for Malet's husband. Lawrence Stone offers general support for this understanding of the bestowal of such peerages:

> Family after family rose up in the world by the simple device of piling estate upon estate by the judicious choice of brides . . . In the circumstances of the day, such entrepreneurial activity usually resulted in the granting of a title.[30]

John Vaughan (1669-1721), 1st viscount Lisburne. Unattributed.

King William III, attributed to Nettscher, presented by the king to
John Vaughan 1st viscount Lisburne.

While accepting the force of this argument, I feel equally the witness of the state portrait, that some service or friendship was perhaps being recognised. Dr Peter Thomas suggests that Lord Carbery of Golden Grove (1640-1713), who was Custos Rotulorum and an English peer, may have helped John Vaughan in matters of patronage; he was certainly accused by Lewis Pryse of Gogerddan of 'perverting Crown influence to assist Lord Lisburne and his Whig friends'.[31] Another slight clue is to be found in the manuscripts of the House of Lords; in 1692 the Exchequer was paying a pension of £150 to a John Vaughan, who may possibly have been our man, though again there is no explanation for the pension other than royal favour.[32]

The life of John Vaughan the first Viscount is frustratingly obscure both before and after 1695. Only occasional snippets emerge, like his subscription to Edward Lhuyd's *Archaeologia Britannica* of 1708. His marriage is a teasing subject; his wife Malet (who had been given her maternal grandfather's surname as her Christian name) was a very good catch in the terms of the marriage market. Her father, the Earl of Rochester, had been one of Charles II's favourites; he was notorious for his bouts of low living and for his disrespectful attitude to the king, but he could always charm his way back into favour. He was also one of the great poets of the period; his satires are savage but telling, though some are so scabrous that they remained out of print for nearly three centuries. Rochester had three daughters and a son, but the son, the third Earl, died childless, and the sisters inherited. Portraits of their father and of their brother are in the Lisburne collection. Two portraits of Malet also survive in the family collection; one is a delightful betrothal portrait of her as a shepherdess, the other a portrait of a sadder and wiser married woman, though there is no evidence to show that her marriage was particularly unhappy. The ceremony took place at St Giles's-in-the-fields in August, 1692, and she died in January 1709, having borne three sons and three daughters.

As for Vaughan himself, ennobled three years after his marriage, only a minimum of correspondence appears to have survived. For example, in 1705 he wrote from Trawsgoed to Robert Harley, Queen Anne's Principal Secretary, to complain that some non-jurors (supporters of James II) had been made Justices of the Peace in Cardiganshire following the death of King William III, and asking for a new Commission for the county.[33] In 1706 he wrote again to Harley complaining of attacks by his political enemies.[34] He was obviously on terms with the highest in the land, and repaid the Crown with loyalty; as lord lieutenant of Cardiganshire at the time of the 1715 Jacobite rebellion, when Lewis Pryse of Gogerddan was a leading Welsh Stuart sympathiser, Lisburne sought the deployment of regular troops to preserve the peace.[35] A few letters to his sister Bridget survive from the period 1714-16, referring obliquely to the death of his second wife Elizabeth in 1716, and to his alienation from his eldest son.[36]

By this time it is possible to identify party interests in politics, though the word party should not be taken as equivalent to a modern political party. Rather perhaps we should speak of interests, sometimes identified as Whig and Tory, though nothing is yet hard and fast. The Tories were the Court party, usually supporting the Stuart monarchs, while the Whigs were the country opposition. After Queen Anne's death in 1714 the Tories tended to be identified as Jacobites and the Whigs as Hanoverians; in Cardiganshire Gogerddan and Nanteos usually headed the Tory interest and Trawsgoed the Whig interest. After being twice defeated in elections for the county seat in the Commons, first in 1689 by the Gogerddan candidate John Lewis of Coedmore, then in 1690 by Sir Carbery Pryse of Gogerddan, John Vaughan gained the seat in 1694 without contest, since Pryse had died. However he had to stand down in 1698 in favour of John Lewis, and did not seek election again. In both his unsuccessful challenges, 1689 and 1690, he petitioned the House against the result. This was a usual course of action, and hardly surprising in view of the frequent shenanigans at contested elections, but Vaughan seems to have had some right on his side, and only lost his second petition by one vote.

By good luck the election poll book for the contest of January 1689 survives.[37] The voters are listed by townships under the names of the two candidates, according to whom they had supported. The document is most revealing. The majority of parishes voted *en bloc* for one candidate or the other. Since the Gogerddan interest supported John Lewis, it is hardly surprising that the voters north of the Rheidol were solidly for him, though there was a small area, including Cyfoeth-y-brenin and the town of Aberystwyth, where Vaughan picked up a few votes. The Ystwyth valley and Mefenydd were equally solid for Vaughan, as were the great majority of Caron voters. South of the Aeron the Moyddyn area was almost equally divided between the two men, while the lower Teifi valley and the Cardigan area were solidly for Lewis. Lewis eventually won by 374 votes to 362.

Lady Malet Wilmot, daughter of the Earl of Rochester, (d. 1708),
wife of the first viscount Lisburne.

Despite John Vaughan's political setbacks, he commanded
sufficient wealth and land, and such valuable social connections,
especially his peerage, that it seemed that nothing would hinder the
family's further elevation to the ultimate goal, namely an English
peerage, with a seat in the House of Lords. Unfortunately, as the cliché

has it, a chain is only as strong as its weakest link. While John Vaughan, first Viscount Lisburne, was adequate to his situation, his son John by Malet was to prove that weak link, so weak that he almost brought utter ruin to the Trawsgoed estate. That sounds dramatic, and may be an overstatement of one man's responsibility. The family's very wealth and status were potential sources of weakness. Much of Edward Vaughan's wealth had gone to dower his daughters and benefit his younger sons, and while he had qualified and worked as a lawyer, the first viscount Lisburne his son could not be expected to labour; he must live of his own. This respectable behaviour was to prove as damaging drain on the resources of some wealthy families as the occasional appearance of a ne'erdowell heir. Aristocratic status demanded extravagant expenditure, conspicuous consumption— another drain on landed estates. Massive debt was to become commonplace among the aristocracy and gentry, and the gentry of Cardiganshire were more vulnerable than most, given the comparative poverty of their land-base.

NOTES

[1]I have depended greatly though not exclusively on the work of Professor J.Gwynn Williams; see Foreword, note 5. I am responsible for any errors of fact or interpretation.

[2]Namier, *The Structure of Politics at the Accession of George III*, (London, 2nd edn, 1957), p. 42.

[3]Ibid. p.5.

[4]For general background see G.E.Mingay, *English Landed Society in the Eighteenth Century*, (London, 1963); F.M.L.Thompson, *English Landed Society in the Nineteenth Century*, (London, 1963); Lawrence and Jeanne C.F. Stone, *An Open Elite? England 1540-1880*, (Oxford, 1984); D.W.Howell, *Patriarchs and Parasites: the gentry of south-west Wales in the eighteenth century*, (Cardiff, 1986).

[5]For Selden's life see Sir Frederick Pollock (ed), *The Table Talk of John Selden*, (London, 1927).

[6]W. Notestein (ed.): *The Journal of Sir Simonds d'Ewes*, (New Haven, 1923) p.455.

[7]As printed in John Hughes, *A history of the parliamentary representation of the county of Cardigan*, (Aberystwyth, 1849), p.13; taken by him from the *Cambrian Register* of 1795.

[8]Lucy E.Ll.Theakston & John Davies, *Some Family Records & Pedigrees of the Lloyd Family of Allt yr Odyn . . .*, (Oxford, 1912), appendix, p.xxv.

[9]Edward Vaughan (ed.), *The Reports of Sir John Vaughan, Lord Chief Justice of the Court of Common Pleas* (London, 1677)

[10]See J.R.Phillips, *Memoirs of the Civil War in Wales and the Marches*, (London, 1874), Vol. II, pp.154-7.

[11]For Vaughan and Trawsgoed in the Civil War, see J.R.Phillips, *loc.cit.*, Vol. I, p.342, and the Cambrian Quarterly, I, p.61.

[12]Letitia, Sir John's granddaughter, married Robert Davies of Gwysaney, Flintshire.

[13]CD II, 126.

[14]Mary Green (ed), *Calendar of State Papers Domestic: Charles II, 1661-1662*, (London, 1861), p.330.

[15]Cited in John Hughes, *op.cit.*, pp.13-14.

[16]John Vaughan figures frequently in Pepys's Diary (references are to Robert Latham (ed.), *The Shorter Pepys*, (Penguin, 1987); he opposed the financing of the Navy in 1664 (p.446); in 1666 he is described as 'the great Vaughan' in a parliamentary context (p.644); in 1667 Pepys recorded a rumour that Vaughan was about to become a privy councillor (p.790); in 1667 he is 'old good Mr Vaughan' (p.815); in 1668 Vaughan commented to the Duke of Albemarle of Pepys's speech at the Bar of the House of Commons 'that he had sat 26 years in Parliament and never heard such a speech there before' (p.886); in 1668 Pepys was glad of Vaughan's appointment as Lord Chief Justice (p.913).

[17]Reports, p.305.

[18]Basil D. Henning (ed.), *The History of the House of Commons, 1660-1690*, (London, 1983), p.630.

[19]Thus *Pedigree*. Samuel Meyricke, *A History of Cardiganshire* (Brecon, 3rd edn. 1910) p.341, followed by J.Gwynn Williams, gives the date as 1668, which is certainly correct.

[20]However, in a letter to his servant Evan Jones (NLW MS 4955), Sir John Vaughan authorised Jones to receive £250 'att his Maties Receipt of the Excheqr . . . for my ffee or sallary for this present Michaelmas Terme'.

[21]H.M.C. *The Manuscripts of the Marquess of Ormonde*, New series, V (ed.F.Elrington Ball), p.58.

[22]L. Stone, *The Crisis of the Aristocracy*, Oxford (1967), p.90.

[23]Henning, op.cit., p.630.

[24]Ibid., p.624.

[25]Ibid., p.625.

[26]Cited in NLW 12,359, F13.

[27]Robert Latham (ed.), *The Shorter Pepys*, (London, 1987), p.583. Letitia died at Trawsgoed in 1716; will dated 17.2.1709 proved 2 May 1717, P.C.C. 104 Whitfield. She bore her husband two sons, John and Selden (will 10.10.1700, proved 25.1.1701, P.C.C. 11 Dyer), and six daughters.

[28]These large dowries reflect not only the Vaughans' increased wealth, but the considerable inflation in dowries generally, which outstripped the increased cost of living in the 17th century.

[29]CD II, 293. This is Wilmot the third Viscount in 1760 petitioning the King for a seat in parliament.

[30]Stone, *The Crisis of the Aristocracy*, p.91.

[31]See Peter Thomas, 'County Elections in Eighteenth-Century Cardiganshire', *Ceredigion*, XI, no.3 (1991), p.242.

[32]H.M.C. *The Manuscripts of the House of Lords 1692-3* (ed. E.F.Taylor & F.Skene), p.168.

[33]L.K.J.Glassey, *Politics and the appointment of Justices of the Peace 1685-1720*, (Oxford, 1979), pp.176-77. Non-jurors were those who refused to swear loyalty to the new monarchy of William and Mary.

[34]H.M.C. *The Manuscripts of the Duke of Portland*, Vol. IV (ed. S.C.Lomas), pp.275, 283.

[35]Romney Sedgwick (ed), *The History of Parliament: the House of Commons 1715-1754*, II, (London, 1970), p.493.

[36]Shropshire Record Office 1536/2/1-10.

[37]NLW Nanteos MSS Box 20, unscheduled.

III. SCANDAL

Scandal in English and Welsh history is most commonly associated with the courts of Charles II and the Prince Regent, but the monarchs who separate those two very different figures nevertheless saw many individual scandals among their subjects.[1] One such was the case of the Trawsgoed inheritance. A drunken, clandestine wedding and accusations of infidelity and of bastardy, heavily laced with squalid gossip, eventually led to a sensational dénouement in court. None of these events was unique, of course, and the general background has been vividly set out by Lawrence Stone, whose work has illuminated my understanding of the story set out in this chapter.[2] Essentially, this was a world where a man could indulge his sexual whims without fear of any worse retribution than an attack of gonorrhoea, while a woman was expected to live chastely, and to suffer severely should she err. These were times when it was extremely easy to get married casually, and almost impossible to remedy the mistake. Match together a weak, self-indulgent man and a strong-willed woman in such circumstances, and the conflict was bound to be dramatic, and to be worth retelling.

John Vaughan, son of Edward Vaughan and grandson of Sir John Vaughan, continued to add to the family estate, and as we have seen, he gained an Irish peerage in 1695 before his death in 1721. His eldest son, also John, seems to have begun accumulating debts before his father's death and his own succession to the estate and title in 1721. In 1718 the estate owed a total of £5,750 to a London barrister, Thomas Jones. In the same year the Vaughan lands in Montgomeryshire and Somerset were sold for £26,000.[3] The Llidiardau papers in the National Library give details of a few of the second viscount's later debts. For example, in 1729 he owed £600 to Thomas Powell of Nanteos; he owed Martha Hunt of Bewdley, widow, the sum of £1,525 (due on a mortgage to her late husband), and in 1736 one Richard Banks was pursuing a claim against him.[4]

John Vaughan was born of his father's first marriage in 1692 to Malet, daughter of the notorious rake Wilmot, second Earl of Rochester. Because repetitions of the names Edward, John and Wilmot can cause some confusion in following the remarkable story which follows, a simplified genealogical chart may help:[5]

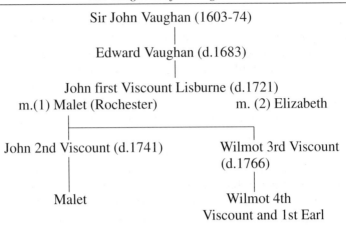

Sir John Vaughan (1603-74)
|
Edward Vaughan (d.1683)
|
John first Viscount Lisburne (d.1721)
m.(1) Malet (Rochester)   m. (2) Elizabeth
┌──────────────────────┐
John 2nd Viscount (d.1741)   Wilmot 3rd Viscount
| (d.1766)
| |
Malet   Wilmot 4th
                               Viscount and 1st Earl

In 1716 John Vaughan the second Viscount had married Anne Bennet, daughter of Sir John Bennet.[6] She was some seven years older than her husband, and no documents survive in the Trawsgoed archive to show whether a jointure was settled on her. In any case, she died childless in 1723. Widowhood did not apparently weigh heavily upon John Vaughan, as we shall see. His brother Wilmot admitted, many years later, that John Vaughan was 'very negligent and careless and indolent in the management of his affairs and in exorting and supporting his right to the family estates.'[7] How careless he was becomes clear from his behaviour immediately before and during his second marriage. Thanks to surviving documents relating to the subsequent lawsuit Lisburne versus Vaughan,[8] John Vaughan emerges from the shadows into a fairly lurid light in Montgomeryshire at Christmastide, 1724/5, amid a host of relatives, neighbours and servants, both his and those of others. He had a number of acquaintances in the Caersws area, with whom he probably remained familiar since his usual road to London was via Llanidloes and Shrewsbury. We must meet some of the characters involved.

Apart from John Vaughan the second Viscount, thirty-year-old widower, owner of a mortgaged estate, heavy drinker, a gambler and very certainly involved with a number of mistresses, the most important character in the Christmas drama is 21-year-old Dorothy Hill, daughter of Captain Richard Hill, an Irish army officer on half-pay.[9] Richard Hill himself is interesting enough to deserve a brief diversion. He was the third son of the Dean of Kilkenny. As a youth he joined the original Lord Lisburne's Regiment in the war of 1689-91, and distinguished himself at the siege of Londonderry in 1689, for which he was rewarded with a Dublin legal sinecure. He then fought in two campaigns in Flanders, and returning to Britain in 1692, he killed one Mr Montford in a duel, and left the country for Newfoundland. On his return he settled in mid-Wales, on the Henblas[10] property of the Glynne family (the Glynnes of Glyn Tryweryn) to whom he acted as agent, and married into the family, his wife being Dorothy Glynne (d.1731). In 1704 Hill sought Queen Anne's pardon for the death of Mr Montford, with the support of the Duke of Marlborough. What is baffling is that he claims he was only sixteen when he fought the duel in 1692, meaning that he was thirteen at the siege of Londonderry with Lord Lisburne's Regiment, which is hard to believe.[11]

Richard and Dorothy Hill had at least two daughters, Dorothy (b.1704) and Cordelia, and possibly a third whose name I cannot discover.[12] John Vaughan must already have made Dorothy's acquaintance, since Cordelia Hill, at least before 1729 and probably several years earlier, had married the Trawsgoed agent, David Lloyd of Breinog in the Aeron Valley.[13] David Lloyd is an typical example of a small squire who worked as agent for a greater. Years later, Bridget Jones described the Christmas of 1724 to the lawyers. The Viscount was staying in one of the mansions of the Severn Valley between Newtown and Llanidloes. His drinking habits are vividly portrayed; Bridget Jones's husband took him to the house of one Valentine Hughes, where they:

> drank very plentifully and were very gay and frolicksome, burning their Hats and Wigs.[14]

More respectable activities were also in train:

> Sir John Pryce then of Newtown in the county of Mountgomery Bart had a meeting of several Musitians as well as Vocal Musick to celebrate the Nativity of our saviour and Invited several Ladys and Gents to partake thereof . . .

Viscount Lisburne and Bridget Jones's husband attended this occasion, and apparently Lady Pryce:

> observing some familiarity between the said late Viscount and the said Miss Hill and never Imagining that the said late Viscount had the least

Intention of making her his Lady as she was a person so much Inferior to him in point of Quality and Fortune

tried to arrange to send Miss Hill home 'lest any mischief might ensue'. So:

After coming from Church in the morning on Christmas day aforesaid the said Miss(es) Hills came and breakfasted at this deponent's house and were the same morning sent home to their ffather's house.[15]

Later, apparently on the same day, Captain Hill arrived at the house of Valentine Hughes and invited the Viscount to come to Henblas, where he drank well and spent the night, awaking in some confusion, not knowing where he was and seeking to leave immediately. Captain Hill being unable to persuade him to stay sent for Dorothy; consequently:

(he) was prevailed upon to stay to Breakfast there and having ordered his horses to be got ready and brought to the Door after Breakfast the said Mr Hill followed him to the Door with some spirituous Liquors which they then drank . . .

Dorothy then persuaded him to stay for dinner, after which:

(he) was plyed with liquor by the said Mr Hill and much Intoxicated and was so kept there till sometime in the night when a marriage was brought about.

Bridget Jones's account is certainly telescoped; she gives the impression that the marriage took place on Boxing Day, but in fact it occurred on January 10th, 1725, and the ceremony was performed by the Vicar of Llandinam, John Gilsley. Letitia Vaughan, the Viscount's sister, claimed that a friend of the Viscount, one Captain John Morris of Carrog:-

being with his Lordship at Henblas . . . and observing his Lordship to be very hot and intoxicated with liquor and fearing he was determined to marry the said Dorothy which would be very detrimental to him he rode away as fast as he could to Wythen Jones Esq (a Llanidloes attorney) to send him to Henblas to prevent it if possible, and that the said Wythen Jones made all the speed he could there and ventured his Life in so doing it being then a very deep Snow and the Waters very much out but before said Jones arrived there being the next day . . . the Marriage was over.[16]

Many of the witnesses claimed that Captain Hill had no money to give his daughter a dowry, but it appears that he sold his Dublin sinecure in order to give each of the girls a thousand pounds.[17] Captain Hill and Dorothy had certainly brought off a coup; whatever the Viscount's weaknesses, he was a remarkable catch in terms of that ruthless mechanism, the contemporary marriage market.

Witnesses differ on the development of the marriage after the sobered Viscount returned with his wife to Crosswood. He certainly made one important provision for her; a document of jointure, settling on her an income from the Trawsgoed estate of £400 a year in the event of his death.[18] Some witnesses say that they behaved well towards each other for the first two years, though Dorothy herself claimed that she had miscarried through the Viscount's rough treatment of her. In 1727, however, she gave birth to a daughter, named Malet for the Viscount's mother.

Not only did the Viscount become a father in 1727; in September of that year he defeated Thomas Powell of Nanteos for the county parliamentary seat. He was, of course, not entitled to sit in the House of Lords, since his title was an Irish one, and he was refused admission to the Irish House of Lords because his father had not enrolled his patent. He went to London, and played a minor role in the House of Commons, voting for the Whig government on the Excise Bill in 1733 and the repeal of the Septennial Act in 1734. On his first visit to London following his election he stayed away from home for two whole years, not once returning to visit his wife and baby daughter, nor do they seem to have left Wales. This absence is unexplained by the witnesses, and can hardly have been justified by pressure of parliamentary business; it can perhaps only be understood in the context of a world where a husband could do virtually what he pleased without much fear of the consequences.

The Viscount might have stayed away longer still, but the Vicar of Llanfihangel-y-Creuddyn, the Reverend Peregrine Stokes, wrote to him in the summer of 1729 to express his concern about Dorothy Vaughan's behaviour; the letter itself, unfortunately, does not survive. Lawrence Stone suggests that it was most often the servants who were first aware of wifely adultery, but that they were reluctant to inform the husband directly, for fear of dismissal.[19] Dorothy had supposedly been misconducting herself with the Viscount's agent, David Lloyd—her brother-in-law! This was at a time when a man was legally barred from marrying his deceased wife's sister on the grounds that it was incestuous. According to the Viscount's sister Letitia Vaughan, the Viscount set out from London in June, but did not arrive at Trawsgoed for three months![20] This, according to Letitia, was because he spent some time in Montgomeryshire on the way. If she is right (there is no evidence one way or the other) it suggests that the Viscount was remarkably complaisant, and certainly his own moral position gave him no right to be otherwise. Apart from the lengthy depositions she made in the case of Lisburne vs. Vaughan, Letitia Vaughan remains an obscure figure, except that she was born about 1704, lived at least part of her life near Shrewsbury, and was a very broad-minded lady; an anonymous lawyer scribbled on one of the documents in the case that, being unmarried, she was the mother of twins. She was still a spinster in 1753. When Letitia joined the Viscount for his trip to Trawsgoed she had in her service one Mrs Phillips, his current mistress. His position, returning as he was to reproach his wife with her supposed misconduct, was compromised even by the double standards of the day.

Letitia Vaughan describes at length the Viscount's return to Trawsgoed. We should picture the mansion not in its present, classical garb of the late 18th century, but having a more complex, gabled appearance dimly preserved in the map of 1756 now in the National Library of Wales. A later survey describes the house as:-

> a large old irregular Stone Building covered with Slate, (which) consists of 2 Handsome Parlours, a large Hall, which may be converted into a dining Parlour and Passages, a good Kitchen with Scullery Larders Etc to which adjoins a House Keepers Parlour and Closset on the Ground floor, over which are 6 good Lodging rooms, 2 dressing rooms and Clossets; and over them Garrets. At one end whereof adjoins at present 2 other small Parlours with 2 rooms over them much decay'd and ruinous and therefore should be taken down.[21]

According to the witnesses (all on Vaughan's side) the Viscount was circumspect in his approach to his wife. Letitia claims that:

> he ordered a Bed to be made for him in the Tapestry Room at one end of the house and a Bed for the Deponent (i.e. Letitia Vaughan) in the next Room to it and the said Viscountess lay at the other end of the House.[22]

The Viscount asked his wife to clear herself of the accusation that she had conducted herself improperly with her brother-in-law David Lloyd, who had left Trawsgoed by this time; Dorothy's response was that 'she did not care what anybody said of her, and went out of the room'. The two remained at loggerheads for some weeks before Dorothy announced that she wanted to return to her father's house at Henblas, threatening that she would go on foot if the Viscount did not assist her. He provided horses, and she left Trawsgoed never to return, and abaondoning her little daughter Malet. Whatever her feelings, she made a serious mistake in thus leaving Trawsgoed without actually having been thrown out, since as the deserting party she was liable to be divorced, could not claim alimony, and would not be entitled to her jointure until her husband's death.[23] Nor could she claim guardianship of Malet; unless a wronged husband agreed otherwise, he was automatically guardian of his young children.

John Vaughan was therefore the injured party, and as such could choose one of several courses of action. The age of duelling between injured husband and wife's lover was past,[24] and the consistory courts of the Church were discredited.[25] He could either seek a divorce through a personal act of Parliament, or a private separation, or else he could simply refuse any further recognition of his estranged wife. He does seem to have contemplated divorce (see below), but the procedure was extremely expensive, and anyway he had no apparent desire to remarry. Any form of acknowledgement of his wife's existence, such as would be necessary in the case of an agreed legal separation, was anathema. An agreed separation might involved his wife having the care of his daughter, might even have involved him in paying some form of allowance to her, and as long as he lived, he could deny her both by refusing any settlement.

Eventually, after John Vaughan's death, legal proceedings became inevitable in order to determine who should inherit the Trawsgoed estate. In the enquiries made later by the lawyers for evidence in the case of Lisburne vs. Vaughan (which was only to be settled in 1754), many of the depositions made by servants and others are somewhat unsatisfactory; partly through the passage of time, partly because some important witnesses were no longer alive. Much is tittle-tattle, gossip and hearsay. We have vivid glimpses of the servants in this world of the squirearchy; men with names like Marmaduke Copsey, reared at Trawsgoed, who could share his master's bedroom, while a maid could share her mistress's bed. This is a far cry both from the nineteenth century world of invisible servants and from the twentieth century's morbid suspicions of such behaviour.

The lawyers questioned both Dorothy and David Lloyd, who denied adultery; servants claimed that he had been seen going in and out of her chamber, and that they had romped in the hay during the harvest. Cordelia, first wife of David Lloyd and sister of Dorothy, had died at some date before evidence was collected. Dorothy's Montgomeryshire cousin, Catherine Clunn, surprisingly gave evidence in support of Viscount Lisburne. She claimed that when she and Cordelia had been at Trawsgoed before the Viscount's return, she had seen:-

> some familiarities . . . and liberties and Freedoms taken by him (i.e. David Lloyd) with her (i.e. Dorothy) too great for an Agent to take with his Lady.

Thomas Doughton, footman at Trawsgoed, deposed that:-

> 'twas a common saying in the Family that it was hard that one Man should supply two Sisters.[27]

Wythen Jones the Llanidloes attorney believed, or at least deposed, that:-

> the said David Lloyd and the said Lady Lisburn were Indecently familiar with Each other and that the Reverend Mr Stoakes then Chaplain to the said Viscount Lisburn and who is since dead gave his Lordship an account by Letter.[28]

David Lloyd claimed that he had left the Viscount's service before the confrontation of Michaelmas, though apparently because of a dispute over accounts; he maintained that he had remained on good terms with his former employer. He denied 'any Indecent Behaviour between him and Lady Lisburne, or that any reflections were made on his conduct, or that Lord Lisburne had heard of it.' Interestingly, a National Library of Wales map of Grogwynion in 1741 shows the little holding of Llwyncogau as being the property of David Lloyd—only two miles from Trawsgoed mansion.

We know nothing of Dorothy between 1729 and 1732, though it seems that during that time David Lloyd and his wife Cordelia were living near Henblas, while Dorothy was with her father. She was accused of being extremely familiar with her cousin Edward Glynne of Glynne, her mother's nephew, so much so that some witnesses were prepared to claim that she had compromised herself with him; there is talk of creaking doors and empty rooms in the middle of the night.[29] John Lloyd, the agent at Glynne, who had married into the Glynne family, deposed that Edward Glynne had actually admitted to him that he had got the Viscountess with child, and that Edward Glynne had accompanied him to Wrexham to arrange a place for Dorothy to lie in; this last evidence is full of convincing detail.[30] In Dorothy's support however her maid Mary Martin testified not only to the suggestive behaviour of the Viscount with Mrs Phillips during the journey to Crosswood ('she frequently sat on the said late Viscount's Lap in the Chaise on their way down from London') but also to Dorothy's good behaviour at Henblas, whither she had accompanied her Ladyship for seven months during 1729/30:-

> during which time she generally lay in the same Bed with her Ladyship and that her Ladyship during all that time behaved in a decent and Virtuous manner.[31]

However, during the early months of 1733 it became the talk of the neighbourhood that Dorothy was pregnant. After quarrelling with her father she left his house in high dudgeon and called at nearby Berth Eirin, the home of Doctor Stafford Rice, wanting to borrow a horse to ride to Glynne, since her father was angry with her. The doctor described how Captain Hill came to his house to enquire about his daughter. Hill asked whether the Doctor believed that Dorothy was with child, to which the Doctor replied that this was what was generally believed:-

> Richard Hill wept very much and in great sorrow and concern said Damn it I fear it is so.[32]

Hill asked the Doctor's wife to go to Dorothy to persuade her to return to Henblas, or if she would not, to live with her sister at Glascoed, where he would build an apartment for her. Mrs Rice performed the errand, but found Dorothy intransigent:-

> (she) refused to accept of such an offer but said she would go abroad and take her pleasure and did not chuse to live with her ffather for she had been Confined long enough with him and saith she then observed the said Viscountess was with child.[33]

One of the accusations made against Dorothy during the investigations for the case of Lisburne v. Vaughan was that she had attempted to conceal her pregnancy. To what purpose she might have done this it is difficult to imagine, but her cousin Catherine Clunn claimed that when she had reproached Dorothy with being pregnant, Dorothy had shown her linen stained with menstrual blood. Later, Catherine testified, Dorothy's cousin Mary Glynne admitted that she had used chicken and duck heads from the kitchen to achieve this effect.[34] Catherine Clunn also claimed that Edward Glynne had given Dorothy twenty guineas towards her lying-in. Glynne absolutely denied this, and any intimacy with Dorothy.[35] It was of course necessary for both David Lloyd and Edward Glynne to deny adultery with Dorothy in order that she might maintain the legitimacy of her child.

When her delivery was near, Dorothy left the Severn valley for Bunbury, in Cheshire, accompanied by Mary Glynne. A baby boy was born on July 19th, 1733, and baptised with the name Edward Vaughan on July 23rd.[36] Dorothy was to claim in her evidence that, when told that the baby was a boy, she had immediately exclaimed that Viscount Lisburne now had an heir. But the question of the baby's paternity is not so easily solved, nor that of the two other children subsequently born to Dorothy, both of whom appear to have died in infancy. Catherine Clunn, like John Lloyd, claimed that Edward Glynne had actually admitted paternity. There is no significance in the baby's name Edward, since this had been previously borne by a number of men in the Vaughan family, and Dorothy would have chosen it in order to help establish the child's legitimate descent. There is significance in the ambiguous wording of the baptism entry as copied in 1733:-

> Edward son of Dorothy wife to Lord Viscount Lisbon Baptised in Bunbury psh July 23 1733.

Baptism entries usually state the child to be the son or daughter of X by his wife Y.

The matter of Edward's status was, of course, crucial. Edward Glynne and David Lloyd both denied misconduct; any admission would have ruined Edward Vaughan's argument in the lawsuit, Lisburne v. Vaughan, which followed the second Viscount's death. Dorothy naturally claimed that her husband the Viscount was the child's father.[37] Strictly speaking she was right; she was, in law, still the wife of the Viscount, and therefore she could claim that her child was automatically legitimate, unless her husband could prove that he could not have had access to her during the previous nine months.[38] However, in the process of collecting evidence in the case of Lisburne v. Vaughan she was pressed for proof, but her lawyers were unable to produce witnesses who could swear that the Viscount had actually been under her roof. They did discover one William Taylor of Aberystwyth, who claimed to have heard the Viscount say that he had a son called Edward, but in view of the Viscount's recorded behaviour, this seems unlikely. Dorothy's supporters could show easily enough that he had passed through the Severn valley during 1732, and had stayed nearby, but there was no evidence of meetings. Thomas Evans, a Montgomershire servant, recalled that he had rung the bells of Llanwnog church in 1732 on the occasion of a visit by the Viscount, who had sent him a pan of ale for his trouble, and that he knew the Viscount well 'having often gone out Sporting with him and shoed his Horses and Cleaned his Pistols.' Only Dorothy herself, in the vaguest language, claimed that 'he came to her at Henblas by night and had intercourse with her'.

One particularly dubious witness was a John Pritchard, once servant to Captain Hill, who claimed that Dorothy had misconducted herself both with David Lloyd and with Edward Glynne. He was paid a pension of seven shillings a week by Wilmot Vaughan who succeeded to his brother's title and estate, and it was claimed that Pritchard had once said, 'Damme! they would never be where they are, but for me,' and to have died penitent.[39] The Viscount, however, always claimed that the breach between him and his wife was absolute, and he actually asked Wythen Jones in 1733 to collect evidence with a view to a divorce (hence the certified copy of the baptism entry), but was unable to meet the enormous expense. Charles Richards of Penglais attempted to reconcile the pair, but in vain. When at an unnamed time after 1729, Beata Jones, wife of Wythen Jones, was at Trawscoed, Dorothy had come to Cwmnewidion, about a mile away, in hope to see her little daughter Malet at the least. However, said Mrs Jones, this:-

> put his Lordship and the whole House in great Confusion and his Lordship ordered all the Doors thereof to be shut and barrd and sent threatening Messages to Mrs Lloyd [of Cwmnewidion] for receiving her.[40]

It was her opinion that Edward Glynne was 'generally reputed to be the Father' of Edward Vaughan, and David Lloyd of Dorothy's other children who died in infancy.[41]

On an even more dramatic occasion, again undated, John Vaughan summoned a number of his friends, along with the Reverend Jenkin Jenkins of Llanafan, to Trawsgoed. He required the curate to celebrate Holy Communion, partook of the bread and wine, and then swore an oath on the Bible that he was not the father of Edward Vaughan or any other of Dorothy's children except Malet. His oath was taken by Thomas Powell of Nanteos, J.P., in the presence of the curate, Stafford Price and Thomas Parry, squire of Llidiardau. In the meantime Vaughan was living by his old lights; we also know from the diary of the first Earl of Egremont that he was still visiting London; the Earl invited him to a meeting of Irish peers on the subject of the Princess Royal's wedding, but he did not attend.[42]

John Vaughan also visited Ireland, for what reason does not appear. According to Winifred Pritchard, a Trawsgoed laundrymaid, the Viscount had an Irish mistress called Mrs Roach:-

> after the said Mrs Roach had lived with his Lordship some Considerable Time his Lordship went with her to Dublin where the said Mrs Roach Robb'd his Lordship of all his Plate and Valuable effects and ran away after which his Lordship brought one Mrs Savage with him from Dublin who Eat Drank and lived with him like a wife to his death.[43]

We shall see that Mrs Roach and Mrs Savage were not his only mistresses during this period, though by 1740, when his health must have been failing, Mrs Savage was resident and obvious in charge at Trawsgoed, along with her son John Vaughan, fathered by the Viscount. In the meantime Dorothy appears to have been living with David Lloyd and his second wife Bridget at Henblas, Captain Hill having returned to Ireland.

In May 1740 the Viscount made a first will, which needs to be given in some detail:[44]

> My body I recommend to be buryed in my Ffamily Vault in the parish Church of Llanavan between the Hours of Eight and Twelve of the Clock in the Night time by the Assistance of my own Servants and the neighbouring Gentlemen ffreeholders whose ffamilyes have bore a due Regard to the Memory of my Great Grandfather Sir John Vaughan and his Successors.

He obviously did not expect much respect for himself. He left to his brother Captain Wilmot Vaughan all his lands in Great Britain, and the title of Lord Viscount Lisburne. Following the family settlement made in 1720,[45] there was no question of Malet inheriting the estate, which was in tail male. This document, rather than the Viscount's will, was the basis for Wilmot's claim to the estate and title. The will left:-

> to Mrs Anne Savage now in my service all my other reale Chattell or personall estate or tenements in the Kingdom of Ireland and also the profits of the lease of part of Crycklas and also the Bed, Bedding, tables, Chairs, Scrutore[46] and other furniture whatever of my Bedchamber.

There is no evidence whatsover that the Viscount had any real estate in Ireland. He also left £100 for Anne Savage and for the maintenance of his natural son by her, John Vaughan, for three years, with another £100 after three more years, and £300 to John at the age of 17, with reversion to his mother should he have died by then. (He may perhaps have done so, since there is no further trace of him). Moreover, Anne Savage 'shall be peaceably and quietly permitted to possess take and enjoy her Cloathes, Rings, Wearing Apparell, ffurniture Household and every Thing that is her own in my House at Crosswood.'

To his two natural daughters Mary and Jane (no surnames given) the Viscount left ten pounds each 'to sett them out Apprentices', with three pounds each per annum during their apprenticeships, 'Jane to have her Cattle and Stock from the Demesne.' To his servant Thomas Jones he left all his clothes except linen and laced clothes; to six other servants he left a suit of mourning each. To his Thomas Parry of Aberystwyth (and of Llidiardau), Attorney-at-Law, he left his law books, his best gold watch and fifty pounds; to 'my worthy neighbour the Reverent Mr Jenkin Jenkins All my Books of Divinity' (these were probably in mint condition), with the rest of his books to young John. Lewis Parry, his friend and neighbour of Penuwch, was to receive ten pounds, with two pounds annually to 'my trusty servant Anne Jones Gardenweeder Woman', and three pounds annually to Mrs Mary Rogers 'now in my service'. Ten pounds was to be given by the hand of the Reverend Jenkins to the poor of Llanfihangel-y-Creuddyn and Llanafan. Finally, £3000 was to go to his daughter Malet provided she did not cross her guardian, namely her uncle Wilmot the heir and executor and guardian of 'all my children legitimate and illegitimate.'

If she were, for example, to marry contrary to her uncle's advice, she would receive only £500, the rest going to Wilmot.[47]

Almost everything changed when the Viscount made a second will in January 1741, only a month before his death.[48] Anne Savage, now described as being of St John's Parish, Dublin, is to receive eight hundred pounds towards raising her son John. Mary Rogers and Anne Jones, widow, both of Llanafan, are to receive twenty pounds each, and Thomas Jones of Aber-mad and Thomas Evans of Llandeilo are each to receive fifty pounds. Anne Savage is to have the choice of his wearing apparel for her son John, and must divide the rest of his clothes 'among Morgan David Lewis my present keeper, John his son and such other of my Servants as she shall think proper and deserving.' Mary, daughter of Gwenllian Savage of Llanafan, and Jane, daughter of Elizabeth Dudrick of Llanafan, (sic, probably for Dudlick, still a well-known name in the locality), are each to receive sixty pounds. They were obviously the Viscount's illegitimate daughters. All the rest of his property and goods are to go to his brother Wilmot, executor; should he refuse the executorship, Sir Herbert Lloyd of Peterwell is to be executor.

Out go the references to his daughter Malet (though she was otherwise provided for), to Thomas and Lewis Parry, the Reverend Jenkin Jenkins, the poor of the parishes, his servant Thomas Jones, and his books. Why bring in Thomas Johnes of Aber-mad and Sir Herbert Lloyd of Peterwell, those notorious rascals, at the expense of comparatively respectable local figures? Between the two wills it is clear that he had at least three mistresses at Trawsgoed who bore him children: Ann Savage of Dublin, Gwenllian Savage of Llanafan (can their shared surname be a coincidence?) and Elizabeth Dudlyke, and probably Mary Rogers and Anne Jones as well.

Another baffling feature of the last will is that, though proved at Carmarthen, it is not referred to in the legal papers relating to the case of Lisburne versus Vaughan, though admittedly Wilmot Vaughan's claim to the estate was based on the family settlement of 1720, and not on a will. The typescript schedule of additional Crosswood papers in the National Library notes that there was with the first will a letter describing the circumstances of its discovery, but the letter has disappeared.

The second Viscount's death naturally changed the scene drastically. Dorothy, now dowager viscountess Lisburne, immediately acted; she sent letters to all the tenants demanding that they pay their rents to her son Edward. But Wilmot Vaughan, the dead man's brother and new viscount Lisburne, had occupied Trawsgoed, and he sent out handwritten notices to all the tenants:-

> Whereas a paper is dispersed among you Insinuating that the Estate of my late Brother Lord Viscount Lisburn Deceased is discended upon a pretended Son of his and requireing you to pay your Accrewing Rents to the pretended Mother of such Child Now these are to give you Notice that my said late Brothers Estate and Title are discended upon and now vested in me as I am his Brother and legall Heir under diverse of my ffamily Settlements. And that no pretended Child or Children or pretended wife or wives of my said late Brother have any Right thereto And that I will Evidence and Support my Title and your Occupations against any such illegale Clayments and will protect and Indempnifye you against all Proceedings tending to impeach or Disturb my Just Right you are therefore to Continue my Tenants and duly to pay your Accrewing Rents to me who am
> Your reall Friend
> Lisburn

One copy of this document bears the words 'To Mr David Lloyd these'. Wilmot was not mealy-mouthed. In 1743, writing to the lawyers involved in Dorothy's suit for her jointure and without too much care for accuracy or self-contradiction, he says:

> you know the History of the Ladies life, How that she played the whore at his Lordships house in the country when he was in Parliament and had two or three Bastards by his Steward in his absence, how that she went immediately after his Lordships returne into the country to her fathers house and never returned again to Crosswood but lived in Adultery with Glyn the reputed father of ye Bastard.[49]

Dorothy Vaughan had two problems. The first was to ensure her jointure of £400 a year from the hostile Wilmot, whose notice to the tenants insinuated that she was not even his late brother's legitimate wife. The second was to claim the inheritance for her son Edward Vaughan. She seems to have taken them in that order. The Plas Llangoedmore papers recite the story of her jointure, which we need not repeat in detail. Suffice it to say that Wilmot was forced to acknowledge her marriage; the courts decided that she was entitled to her jointure with arrears, but Wilmot made it as difficult as possible for her. The estate was actually mortgaged to one Edward Emmett of London for £2000 (much less than its value), and Wilmot at first claimed that the mortgage meant that he did not own the estate and therefore could make no provision from it. He said that he knew nothing of the jointure, that the lands were not properly described, and that he thought it:

> very hard that the plaintiff (Dorothy) who is a Volunteer[50] and a person of so bad a Character should have any Indulgence of this Court.

Later he attempted to force her to pay Crown rent and mortgage costs, but unsuccessfully.

Having by 1746 secured her jointure, Dorothy turned to the case of her son Edward, who was in that year sent to school at Hereford.[51] In 1747, apart from bringing a suit against Edward Emmett for return of documents, she arranged that 'the Rt Honourable Edward Lord Lisburne, by his next Friend, David Lloyd should petition the Court of Chancery 'in order to be let into possession of the Title and Estates.' The case is therefore known as Lisburne v. Vaughan, i.e. Edward was the plaintiff, claiming to be the rightful Viscount Lisburne, and seeking possession of the Crosswood estate from Wilmot. David Lloyd's appearance is surely significant of his warm interest in the whole affair.

The case dragged on for years while the lawyers collected depositions and drew up voluminous briefs for counsel. Wilmot Vaughan had married Elizabeth Watson, an heiress of Berwick-on-Tweed, who brought a considerable estate in Northumberland and Durham to her husband, and their son was another Wilmot, whose first wife (the marriage took place in 1753) was also an heiress, Elizabeth Nightingale, who brought with her the right to a small estate in Enfield, Middlesex. Family tradition among the descendants of Edward Vaughan maintained that it was Nightingale money that enabled Wilmot senior, her father-in-law, to withstand Edward Vaughan's claim to the Trawsgoed estate and the Lisburne title. Wilmot senior must have been in some financial embarrassment, since the Welsh estate only yielded just over one thousand a year in rent, of which Dorothy was entitled to four hundred, and Malet had to be provided for.

The case was eventually set down for the Court of the King's Bench in 1754, but the hearing was a formality, for the parties came to a last-minute settlement.[52] Edward Vaughan, now twenty-one, gave up his claim to the estate and title in return for payment by Wilmot Vaughan of a lump sum of £200 and an annual pension of £200, to be increased to £300 at the death of his mother the Dowager Viscountess. Mrs Benchley, whose account of the life of Dorothy Vaughan was copied by Herbert Millingchamp Vaughan, quotes an unnamed newspaper of the day:-

> the Plaintiff was told by his Attorneys, in the face of the Court, that he had no chance of success, for that his Mother would perjure herself and would have £1000 costs to pay, and together that his Mother, his Uncle and all his friends would be sent to Garland utterly ruined, if he did not come into some agreement, with which he was terrified and the Court and Jury waiting his Determination, he at last under these Apprehensions and in this flurry and confusion, was brought to agree to relinquish all his Rights to the Estates to the Defendants in consideration of an Annuity of £200 during his and his Mothers life, and £300 a year if he survived her . . . the Consequence of this Verdict is that the Plaintiff acknowledged himself to be a Bastard, which he did not then understand was the case.

I do not understand the reference to 'Garland', but the implication is clear.

The case attracted wide attention. In December 1754 William Morris of Holyhead wrote to his brother Richard in London:

> I had read in the papers that young Lisburne had compromised matters with his uncle at Court, and did expect to see the poor devil outwitted. Rhoedd eisiau'r Llew neu ryw un dewr i sefyll wrth ei gefn o, druan wr. Duw a'm cadwodd hyd yn hyn ac am ceidw rwyn gobeithio rhag trais cyfreithwyr.[53]

At some subsequent date Edward Vaughan became owner of Green Grove in the Vale of Aeron; he married, and fathered three sons, Edward, David and John. His nearest neighbour was David Lloyd of Breinog. I cannot discover how Edward Vaughan came to possess Green Grove, and Herbert Vaughan confessed himself unable to trace either the pedigree of David Lloyd or the previous existence of Breinog, though the family can indeed be traced, and Breinog certainly *did* exist. As for Green Grove, a Morgan Llwyd of Green Grove was High Sheriff of Cardiganshire in 1677. It was supposed by H.Lloyd-Johnes that Dorothy and Edward had purchased the place, but from whom and with what resources he does not say.[54] Is it coincidence that Green Grove and Breinog are so close? Did David Lloyd provide the wherewithal? That is sheer speculation, but it seems plausible.

The connection between Edward Vaughan and David Lloyd (his 'best friend' in the lawsuit) becomes still closer when we examine David Lloyd's will, made in 1769.[55] Bridget, his second wife, is left £30 a year. She and Dorothy are each bequeathed ten pounds to buy mourning clothes and mourning rings, each 'with a lock of my grey hair inlayed' as a token of esteem. Dorothy was to dispose of 'my worst Daily Cloathes' among his servants. Since his only legitimate child had predeceased him, he had to decide to whom to leave his property. Although he had blood relatives, the children of his two sisters, it is possible that the fact that these children were all girls may have influenced him in his decision to choose one of Edward's children as his heir, or there may have been another factor. The girls were left small cash legacies, while Breinog was to go to David, second son of Edward Vaughan. If David were to predecease him, the reversion would go to Edward's other sons, first Edward and then John. If none of the three were to survive, nor leave issue, only then would the reversion go to his great-nephew, the eldest son of his niece Elinor Ashbrook, daughter of Mary Jones.[56]

The inheritance was to be conditional on the boy David's assuming the surname Lloyd, on his attending the University of Oxford between the ages of 16 and 21 with an allowance of £80 a year, and his subsequent dwelling at Breinog. Why choose David? It may be simply that the boy was his godson, named for him; legacies conditional on changes of surname were not unusual. Hitherto I have attempted to set out the evidence with as little personal opinion as possible. But comment cannot be avoided at this point. Who was the father of Edward Vaughan? It is certain that it was not the second Viscount. His behaviour on that point is consistent; it would have been totally out of character for him to have made midnight assignations with a woman he had obviously come to hate, and then to deny the child or children of such assignations when he had no son of his own. Vicious he may have been, but the oath on the communion was not an act even he would have undertaken lightly.

If not the Viscount, it must have been either David Lloyd or Edward Glynne. There is no certainty, but I incline to believe that David Lloyd *thought* he was the father, and indeed probably was, whatever may have been Edward Glynne's indiscretions. This best explains his will. He was perhaps responsible for Edward Vaughan's ownership of Green Grove. If Edward was his son, then Edward the younger, David and John were his grandchildren. David would inherit Breinog while his elder brother Edward would inherit Green Grove, and David would maintain the name Lloyd.

The evidence for this claim is only circumstantial, as is inevitable in the nature of the case. David Lloyd was accused of misbehaviour with Dorothy in 1729, not simply by malicious witnesses from among the servants, but by the local vicar. He remained closely associated with Dorothy for the rest of his life; whenever it was that he returned from Henblas to Breinog, she moved with him, as did his second wife

The memorial of Dorothy, Lady Lisburne, in Llanfihangel Ystrad church, Ceredigion.

Bridget. The association of Breinog and Green Grove, the possible endowment of Edward Vaughan with Green Grove, his will of 1769; all suggest that his association with Dorothy was long and close. Bastard or no, Edward was not without friends; in 1756 he was made a J.P., which provoked a snarl of outraged protest from the parliamentary candidate of 1761, Wilmot Vaughan II, son of the victorious third Viscount, in a letter to the Lord Chancellor.[58]

Edward Vaughan outlived his second son David, and the boy does not seem to have survived long enough to benefit by the inheritance due to him from David Lloyd's will.[59] Edward Vaughan the elder's will[60] leaves his real estate to his eldest son Edward, and a hundred pounds 'to my second son John Vaughan'; David had obviously died. John Vaughan then assumed the surname Lloyd and took up the Breinog inheritance; he is named on the family memorial in Ystrad church as John Vaughan Lloyd of Breinog; he did not pass the Lloyd surname on to his children. Edward Vaughan the elder was buried at Ystrad Church in 1796, where he and his family, including John Vaughan Lloyd of Breinog, are commemorated by an elegant marble slab. The family continued to use the coat-of-arms of the Trawsgoed family, who judged it wiser not to complain.

What of the Dowager Viscountess, Dorothy? She achieved some kind of accommodation with Wilmot Vaughan, since she surrendered an unspecified number of her jointure properties in the Trawsgoed estate in exchange for an annuity of £88.11.6.[61] She too is commemorated in Ystrad church, under the Trawsgoed motto: Non revertar inultus (I shall not return unavenged):-

> To the Memory of the Honourable Lady Dorothy Dowager Viscountess Lisburne who departed this Life the 26th of Novr. 1791 in the 87th year of her Age. Her Ladyship was remarkable for her Humanity and ever employ'd in works of Beneficence and Charity.

'Remarkable for her humanity' she must have been! She managed to get herself a husband well above her social rank and fortune; when apparently deserted by him, she seems to have taken her brother-in-law as lover, to have faced her husband with wrathful pride before leaving him, to have cut herself off from her little daughter, to have been careless of her reputation with her cousin Edward, to have borne three children whose paternity was known for certain only to herself, to have defied her father's wishes and rejected his support when she might most have depended on him, and to have been ready to go to law on several occasions to secure what she felt or knew were her rights. As far as I can understand her character, Dorothy was a true fighter and survivor, an eighteenth-century Becky Sharp who fought and struggled through much of her life in her own interests and endured to a great age. The only published notice of her life is her household accounts for part of the year 1744; she lent 'Mr Lloyd' (i.e. David Lloyd) several sums of money, and gave him £26.5.0 to go to Shrewsbury. There are frequent references to 'my littel boy', i.e. Edward.[62]

As for Wilmot the third Viscount, he had ensured his brother's title and estate for himself, but it was not the easiest of inheritances, and although he seems to have made stout efforts to reduce the burden of debt and to manage the estate more effectively than had the second Viscount, he could not entirely shake off the burden of debt. As we have seen, by his marriage to Elizabeth Watson of Berwick-on-Tweed he acquired a substantial estate in that area, without which he could surely not have survived. His son, the second Wilmot and fourth Viscount Lisburne, married well as we have seen, and when his wife Elizabeth (née Nightingale) died not long after the resolution of the lawsuit, he eventually gained her estates in Devon and married a second time, again advantageously. He became an M.P., gained government office and was rewarded with an Irish earldom, which greatly disappointed him. His acid pen was frequently wielded to express his anger at various affronts, several of which we shall encounter in the next chapter. We have already seen that he was outraged by what he felt was a deliberate slight in the suggested promotion of Edward Vaughan of Green Grove to be a J.P., in 1765. Wilmot Vaughan wrote to the Duke of Newcastle to vent his wrath:

> In this List (i.e. of proposed Justices) is introduced the Person who so long pretended to the Titles & Estate of my Family, whose Illegitimacy has been confirm'd by a solemn Verdict & who now subsists by my Father's liberality. The Contriver & Abettor of this infamous Scheme Mr David Lloyd is another who stands in it a Fellow of the most profligate Life & the most corrupt Principles . . . the Indignity offered to me by framing this List, I shall take upon me to resent in a proper manner but as it also concerns the County I represent, it is my Duty to refer it to your Grace & to protest very seriously against it. I must entreat your Grace to interpose with the Chancellor & to prevent any

regard being payed to this List for I never shall assent to Mr Lloyd or the List as it now stands becoming part of the Commission.[63]

The reverberations of the scandal lasted long indeed.

I have already offered conclusions about the paternity of Edward Vaughan and the nature of the characters involved in the story, based on a reading of the available evidence. However, it is essential to cite the opinions of a witness who, although separated by several generations from the events of the mid-eighteenth century, had the benefit (and disadvantage?) of family tradition as well as years of close reading of the documents, whose preservation we owe to him.

That witness is Herbert Millingchamp Vaughan (1870-1948), to whom reference had been made more than once in passing. He was a direct descendant of Edward Vaughan of Green Grove; the family later moved to Plas Llangoedmore, on the north bank of the Teifi opposite Cilgerran castle. He never published anything about the case, but his surviving manuscripts advert to it in great detail. He supplied Alcwyn Evans, the genealogist, with an account of the story which can be read in Evans's manuscript genealogies.[64] It would be otiose to repeat his narrative here, but it amounts to a defence of the legitimacy of Edward Vaughan on legal grounds, and refers to moves by Edward Vaughan's descendants to re-open the case and lay claim to the Lisburne title and the Trawsgoed estate. He based his opinion of Edward's legitimacy on the fact that Dorothy was not legally separated from her husband, that technically he could have had access to her, and on the supposed close physical resemblance between the second Viscount and Edward Vaughan. He does, however, refer to the good relationship which subsequently developed between the two families, and obviously believed that the situation had long been a *fait accompli*. Supporting evidence appears in a *Cambrian News* account of the funeral of the fourth Earl of Lisburne in 1873; Captain Vaughan of Breinog sat in the second mourning coach with Edmund Vaughan, the Earl's nephew.

To Mrs Benchley's already-quoted account of the life of Dorothy, Herbert Vaughan added his opinions on the dramatis personae in the case with rather less reserve. He believed that David Lloyd was a rough, uncouth character, unlikely to have been Dorothy's lover; he suggested that Edward Glynne is the more likely man, though he was not willing to accept the certainty of this. He certainly believed, apparently on the basis of family tradition, that Edward Vaughan was to say the least a naive and weak character, possessing, in Herbert Vaughan's own words, 'a rather feeble intellect.'

It may be objected that to narrate this episode in detail, giving a whole chapter to one generation's story, overbalances the whole story of the Vaughans and their estate. There is, of course, little drama in unbesieged virtue, so much in conflicts of vice. It is, indeed, a squalid story of deceit, intrigue and effrontery. It may however be argued that it is the very vividness of the details which makes the story worth telling. Suddenly we encounter in uncomfortable proximity not only the major and minor aristocracy of mid-Wales in all their fallibility, but their servants also, stepping out of the shadows to tell us their names and occupations, their opinions and their coarse jokes. This generation of servants had not been banished to the servants' wing, but often according to sex shared a bedroom, even a bed, with master or mistress. Then too the drama of the story is telling; the confrontation of husband and wife, the taking of a solemn oath after Communion, the sudden yielding of the plaintiff in court. It is satisfying, finally, that the three surviving characters in the drama, Dorothy, her son Edward and their opponent Wilmot, all eventually fared well. The first lived to a ripe old age, the second began a successful new lineage of modest squires who did much military service, while the third, with the aid of his son, did their best to restore the drastic damage done to estate and family by the second Viscount Lisburne, the wretched John. Finally, it is worth remembering that during the 1730s, while the second Viscount Lisburne roistered with his mistresses, events occurred in Wales which were to have a dramatic effect on its history. This is the decade in which Howell Harris, Daniel Rowlands and William Williams brought a new fervour to religious and moral life, and in which the circulating schools of Griffith Jones, Llanddowror, brought literacy to an unlettered people, thanks to the support he received from Sir John Philipps and Bridget Bevan, who among the Welsh ruling élite stand at the other end of the moral spectrum from John Vaughan.

NOTES

[1]The substance of this chapter originally appeared as an article, 'The Trawsgoed Inheritance', in *Ceredigion*, XII, no.1 (1993), 9-40.

[2]Lawrence Stone, *The Road to Divorce: England 1530-1987*, (Oxford, 1990), henceforth cited as Stone, *Divorce*.

[3]CD I, 611.

[4]NLW Llidiardau Papers, box 5. I owe thanks to Dr Jill Barber for these references.

[5]According to the Dictionary of Welsh Biography, John's successor Wilmot Vaughan, was the son of the first Viscount's second marriage to one Elizabeth, who died in 1716, and was therefore half-brother to the second Viscount. However, Alcwyn Evans's genealogy of the family (NLW MS 12359D), NLW Castell Gorfod MS 7 (the Golden Grove genealogies) and the Lisburne *Pedigree*, are all agreed that Wilmot was also the son of Malet and therefore full brother to John.

[6]NLW Plas Llangoedmore MS 54.

[7]CD II, 290.

[8]See below. I have not been able to discover any reference to the case in the PRO, but extensive legal papers from the case survive in the Plas Llangoedmore collection in the National Library of Wales, bequeathed by Herbert Millingchamp Vaughan, a descendant of Dorothy, Lady Vaughan. Additionally, his own collection, the H.M.Vaughan MSS, includes two exercise books, MS 88, 'A Life of Dorothy Viscountess Lisburne', a copy made by Vaughan in 1942 from original by E.S.Benchley in 1884, great-great-granddaughter of Lady Lisburne. The following account relies on these two sources; comparatively little remains in the Crosswood Deeds (though see CD I, 883; II, 231).

[9]J.M.Howells, *Thesis* p.61, claims that Dorothy had already been married once, 'to a person named Walter'. He gives no source, and must have been using *The Complete Peerage* (ed. Doubleday and de Walden, VIII (London, 1932), p.34) where it is said her husband was a Mr Waller of co. Cardigan; this may have been the foundation for a similar claim in R.Sedgwick (ed), *The House of Commons 1715-1754*, (London, 1970), p.493. However, all the contemporary sources I have seen indicate that she had not previously been married. Howells also claims (p.62) that the marriage was advantageous for the second Viscount, which is obviously untrue. *The Complete Peerage* also claims that she died at Golden Grove, a mistake for Green Grove.

[10]Henblas is now a farm a little to the west of Llanwnog church. In 1845 (Tithe Map), following the extinction of the male Glynne line, Henblas was the property of the Reverend Devereux Glynne Mytton.

[11]See HMC, *The Duke of Portland's MSS*, VIII, p.322, 'Petitions and Memorials to the Queen, 1704-1708'.

[12]H.M.Vaughan (see below) thought that there was a Bridget Hill who was David Lloyd's second wife, but he could not have married his deceased wife's sister at this time.

[13]Since publishing my article, 'The Trawsgoed Inheritance', I have been advised that Breinog ('place of crows') rather than Braenog should be the preferred spelling for the name which usually appears, misleadingly, as Brynog.

[14]NLW Plas Llangoedmore 22, pp.237 et seq.

[15]It is the use of the plural here which prompts me to believe that there were three Hill sisters: Dorothy, Cordelia (Lloyd) and another.

[16]NLW Plas Llangoedmore MS 2. For marriages which were irregular or clandestine, but not illegal, see Stone, *Divorce*, ch. IV, passim. They were made illegal in 1753.

[17]NLW Plas Llangoedmore MS 5, p.2.

[18]NLW Plas Llangoedmore MS 87.

[19]Stone, *Divorce*, p.224-6.

[20]NLW Plas Llangoedmore MS 22, pp.104-5.

[21]NLW CD III, 23b.

[22]NLW Plas Llangoedmore MS 22, pp.110-1.

[23]NLW Plas Llangoedmore MS 5, p.3.

[24]Stone, Divorce, pp. 237-40.

[25]Ibid., pp.41-43.

[26]NLW Plas Llangoedmore MS 22, pp.122-48.

[27]NLW Plas Llangoedmore MS 15, p.21.

[28]NLW Plas Llangoedmore MS 21, from depositions made at the Red Lyon inn, Welshpool, 28 September 1743.

[29]NLW Plas Llangoedmore MS 13, 24-5; MS 22, 138-9.

[30]NLW Plas Llangoedmore MS 22, p.162.

[31]Ibid., p.174.

[32]Ibid., pp.313-4.

[33]Ibid., pp. 322-3.

[34]Ibid., pp.141-2, 146.

[35]NLW Plas Llangoedmore MS 13, p.29.

[36]NLW Plas Llangoedmore MS 17 is an attested copy of the parish register, which notes that the registration was not actually made until December 1733.

[37]NLW Plas Llangoedmore MS 13, p.12.

[38]Stone, *Divorce*, p. 180. R.Sedgwick (ed.), in *The House of Commons 1715-1745*, (London, 1970), 493, claims that the second viscount had one son and one daughter, the only modern authority to do so.

[39]NLW H.M.Vaughan MS 88, ff.30-1.

[40]Confirmed by Letitia Vaughan, NLW Plas Llangoedmore MS 13, 26.

[41]Ibid., p.25

[42]HMC, *Diary of the First Earl of Egmont*, Vol II, 46.

[43]NLW Plas Llangoedmore MS 13, p.10.

[44]CD III, 4a. The Viscount's two wills are quoted as if they were one document by J.M.Howell, *Thesis*, p.68, and he states that Anne Savage was allowed to stay at Trawsgoed under the terms of the wills, but this was not the case.

[45]CD I, 612.

[46]Scrutore = Escritoire, a writing-desk.

[47]Malet married one Bennet Langley, of Montgomeryshire, and may have lived happily ever after despite her disrupted childhood.

[48]CD I, 805.

[49]CD III, 3a.

[50]NLW Plas Llangoedmore MS 11. The *Shorter O.E.D.* gives a legal definition of volunteer as 'One to whom a voluntary conveyance is made; one who benefits by a deed made without valuable consideration, 1744.'

[51]NLW Plas Llangoedmore MS 5, p.3.

[52]For the Court of King's Bench in family cases, see Stone, *Divorce*, passim, but

especially 233-5, commenting on the swiftness with which cases were settled once before the court.

[53]J.H. Davies (ed.), *The Letters of Lewis, Richard, William and John Morris*, (Aberystwyth, 1907), Vol.I, 323-24. The Welsh reads: It needed the Llew (i.e. Lewis Morris) or someone brave to support him, poor fellow. God has saved me so far - and I hope he may keep me safe - from pillage by lawyers.

[54]'The Lesser Country Houses of Cardiganshire,' *Ceredigion*, II, 2, (1953), 87.

[55]NLW Morgan Richardson MS 1891.

[56]Notes written on David Lloyd's will show that his sisters' families contested the will in Chancery in 1777, but without success.

[57]*West Wales Historical Records*, III (1913) 72-116.

[58]H.M.Vaughan discovered this letter, British Library Addl MS 35,604, f.300, and copied it in NLW H.M.Vaughan MS 88.

[59]When Lady Dorothy made her will in 1777 (NLW Morgan Richardson 1895) David seems already to have died. She left all to her son and grandson Edward.

[60]NLW Morgan Richardson MS 1894.

[61]NLW Llangoedmore MS 116.

[62]H.M.Vaughan, 'Household Accounts of a Welsh Peeress in the XVIIIth Century', *West Wales Historical Records*, V (1915), 293-96.

[63]David Williams, 'Cardiganshire Politics in the Mid-eighteenth Century', *Ceredigion* III, 4 (1959) 310.

[64]NLW MS 12,359-60.

IV. RESTORING REPUTATION

It was in straitened circumstances that Wilmot Vaughan emerged from his struggle with his sister-in-law Dorothy Vaughan and her son Edward Vaughan. The Lisburne title and the Trawsgoed estate were now finally Wilmot's, but the estate was encumbered by the debts built up by his brother and by the subsequent mortgage, by the settlement payable to Dorothy Vaughan, and by the annuity to her son Edward.[1] To add to Wilmot's problems, his late brother had been prosecuted by the Treasury in 1737 because he was in arrears with the Crown rents owed on the Strata Florida lands, but a stay of execution was contrived. Although the aristocracy were able to follow their own whims without too much regard for social sanctions, the episode may have damaged to Wilmot's prestige and political standing in the county, and it is not surprising that he did not follow his brother, his father, grandfather and great-grandfather as a Member of Parliament. However, this chapter will show that the Vaughans made a successful return to political life, while the following chapter will show that finally, like scores of other aristocratic families, they were caught between the Scylla of social change and the Charybdis of economic failure. It may be complained that this chapter is overweighted in favour of a single individual, Wilmot Vaughan the younger (fourth viscount and first Earl of Lisburne), elder son of Wilmot the third Viscount. This is inevitable given, not only his importance as an agent of recovery for the family fortunes, but because he is better documented than any other member of the family, and those documents, especially his personal letters, are of both political and personal interest. Again, a simplified genealogy will help understand family relationships:

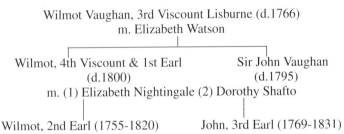

Wilmot Vaughan, 3rd Viscount Lisburne (d.1766)
m. Elizabeth Watson

Wilmot, 4th Viscount & 1st Earl (d.1800)
m. (1) Elizabeth Nightingale (2) Dorothy Shafto

Sir John Vaughan (d.1795)

Wilmot, 2nd Earl (1755-1820)

John, 3rd Earl (1769-1831)

In 1727 Wilmot can have had little hope of inheriting the Trawsgoed estate and the Lisburne title. His brother John had remarried and a daughter had been born, so the birth of an heir could only be a matter of time, or so it must have seemed. In pursuit of his own interest, Wilmot brought off a highly successful marriage, to Elizabeth, daughter of Thomas Watson of Berwick-on-Tweed, a gentleman owning several substantial farms in Northumberland and Durham, as well as fisheries and lime-quarries at Berwick; the estate totalled over a thousand acres, miniscule when compared with the vast acres of Trawsgoed, but earning as much if not more in rent.[2]

Thomas Watson had a son, also Thomas, but the latter never married, so Elizabeth was her brother's heiress, and when the younger Watson died, the estate passed to the Vaughans through her. Had John Vaughan the second viscount produced a legitimate heir, Wilmot would have become a North Country gentleman in right of his wife; as it was, he became responsible for two widely separated estates. He ensured the Vaughan line by fathering two sons, Wilmot and John (the latter by his second marriage), as well as a daughter, Elizabeth.

Wilmot I, as we may call him to distinguish him from his son, inherited a difficult situation from his dissolute brother. However, he was appointed Lord Lieutenant of the county in succession to his brother, thus retaining a good deal of prestige and influence through this key post. Economically Wilmot I did a good deal to restore his Welsh estate to normality; politically he was influential within the county, but it was his son, Wilmot II, who seriously sought to restore the family's political fortunes. It may help to understand something of the background.

Eighteenth-century parliaments were very different from those of today. The House of Lords was of course the preserve of the landed and titled aristocracy of England plus a self-elected representation from among the Scottish and Irish peers. The House of Commons was also controlled by the landed aristocracy and gentry; many M.P.s were sons of peers, or had Irish titles, and the majority of seats were in the control of the great magnates, titled or not, so lesser gentry might only gain a seat by winning the support of one of these men. Other seats were not in the gift of a single family, but were nevertheless the domain of a number of families who would always prefer, if possible, to agree on a single candidate rather than engage in the ruinous expense of a contested election.

During the sixteenth and seventeenth centuries there had been long periods when no parliament sat, and the sovereign ruled directly. However, after 1679 such periods virtually ceased to happen, and parliament met frequently. Most men did not seek election on ideological grounds, and only a minority were desirous of office. Membership of the House of Commons was for most members recognition of their status and power in their own areas, and they would use the influence they had at Westminster to achieve office (especially sinecures) for themselves, their relatives and friends, while keeping out of office their rivals and enemies. Above all, they sought to ensure that their home areas were, in their favourite word, *quiet*.

The early period of Welsh parliamentary representation is barely distinguishable from that of England. Welsh parliamentary candidates played the same game as their English counterparts; they regarded a seat both as the reward of their local importance and a proof thereof. There were critics of the monarchy and friends of the monarchy, but a man might criticise or support the government according to the issue of the day and his own opinion. An individual M.P. who was so minded could make his mark by strength of character and force of rhetoric; this might bring him influence with his fellows, and he might even gain ministerial office, but there was no Cabinet on the familiar later pattern. Many M.P.s never spoke on the floor of the House.

How does Cardiganshire fit this national picture? Although the Vaughans were the largest landowners and the only peers in the county, it was the Pryses of Gogerddan who were generally recognised as the foremost family; during much of the seventeenth century the Phillipses of Cardigan Priory were also important. John Pryse had sat for the county seat in 1553 when Morris ap Richard was still engaged in the enlargement of his small Trawsgoed estate. Pryse's descendants had achieved a knighthood and a baronetcy before John Vaughan gained his knighthood. However, the Pryse family's progress was frequently blighted by lack of a son and heir, or by a minority, and these hiatuses made the family's political life uneven, so that sometimes there was no Pryse available to stand, or the head of the family might be unwilling to stand, in which case an in-law, a distant relative or a crony might be nominated; on rare occasions even a rival family's nomination might be tolerated. For example, in 1747 John Pugh Pryse was under age; Thomas Powell of Nanteos sought the borough seat and John Lloyd of Peterwell the county seat. There was a

conference of Pryse family trustees, who wrote to Thomas Lloyd of
Abertrinant, Powell's representative:

> that if Mr Powell for our future Justification will under his Hand fully
> promise you to promote & preserve the Gogerthan Interest, till Master
> Pryse comes of Age, & then be ready to resign the Burroughs to him,
> that he has our Consent to represent it, & we hope will meet with no
> Opposition from the rest of the Trustees. And as to Mr Lloyd of
> Peterwell he is a Stranger to us but if upon consulting Gogerthan
> Friends you are sensible that 'tis for the Interest and Quiet of the
> County that he should be countenanc'd by Gogerthan, you may waite
> on him, & assure him of our Votes and Interest.[3]

Englishmen with no local estate could represent the Cardiganshire
boroughs at the whim of the controlling family; thus Sir Charles
Cotterell of Lincolnshire, a friend of the Phillips family of Cardigan
Priory, was the borough Member during the years 1663-1679.

Before the advent of John Vaughan in 1628 no Welshman
representing either Cardiganshire seat had made any profound impact
on the House of Commons, and Vaughan's successors were political
dwarfs in comparison with him. We shall see that Wilmot II held
government office, but more usually the county's Members seem to
have been content to gain and keep their places of honour without
further ambition. This does not mean that the Cardiganshire magnates
were dumb. We have already seen how the first Viscount Lisburne
wrote to Queen Anne's minister, Robert Harley, to complain about the
elevation of several non-jurors (men whose loyalty to the Crown was
suspect) to the bench of magistrates; the list was immediately altered.

It may have been this incident, or as Peter Thomas suggests, the
change from Whig to Tory power with the accession of Queen Anne,
which caused Lewis Pryse of Gogerddan to write to William Powell of
Nanteos in 1702:[4]

> I am now in general hopes of putting my Lord Lisbons nose out of joint
> in his arbitrary government in the country and I am now in hopes if not
> assurances that the same stewards which he removed out of the
> judicature shall be restored.

Following the upheavals of the Civil War and the Interregnum,
parliamentary life had resumed with much of its previous form
apparently intact. Political struggles still revolved round the
governmental budget and taxation, with the House of Commons

determined to control the king's governmental expenditure. Charles II steered a cautious line between his desire to favour Catholics and his need to cope with Dissenters; he was determined to maintain his throne and never to resume his travels. His openly Catholic brother James brought disaster after his succession in 1685, and was overthrown in 1688. These great events must certainly have been the talk of local politicians as well as those in London; the Pryses of Gogerddan sympathised with the exiled Stuarts, while the Vaughans of Trawsgoed were unwaveringly loyal to the new settlement. The local details are largely lost to us, but they are symbolised by the state portrait of William III which the king presented to the newly ennobled John Vaughan, first Viscount Lisburne of the second creation, in 1695.

Political life in eighteenth-century Cardiganshire, as in the rest of Britain, was at the national level a matter of power and patronage, and at the local level a matter of family loyalty, fierce inter-family rivalry, and shifting inter-family alliances. Corruption was endemic, while adherence to the Whig or Tory label was a matter of interest rather than principle. In Cardiganshire the Pryses of Gogerddan led the Tory interest, often with the support of the Powells of Nanteos; the Vaughans of Trawsgoed, along with Thomas Johnes of Llanfair and Dolaucothi and the Lloyds of Peterwell were the most influential Whigs; these traditions did not prevent the families from quarrelling fiercely amongst themselves. By the nineteenth century the Vaughans had switched their allegiance to the Tories and the Pryses to the Liberals. Since elections were expensive, and there were two seats, the boroughs and the county, compromise was possible, as in 1761 when John Pugh Pryse of Gogerddan for the county and Sir Herbert Lloyd of Peterwell for the boroughs were elected unopposed.

*   *   *

The complexities of the first century of Vaughan involvement in national politics are best given here in list form (nominations were for the county seat unless shown otherwise):

1628 John Vaughan for Cardigan Boroughs
1640-45 John Vaughan for Cardigan Boroughs
1661-67 John Vaughan
1669-1685 Edward Vaughan
1689 John Vaughan defeated by John Lewis the sitting Member

1690 John Vaughan defeated by Sir Carbery Pryse who d.1694
1694-98 John Vaughan (1st viscount Lisburne 1695)
1727-34 John Vaughan 2nd viscount defeated Thomas Powell

John Vaughan the second viscount did not seek re-election; it is hard
to decide to what extent political manoeuvres and personal problems
were responsible, but he had shown himself loyal to Walpole's
ministry when he voted, even supporting the unpopular excise bill of
1733 which proposed taxes on tobacco and alcohol, and which had to
be withdrawn.

Although four generations of the family had been M.P.s, Wilmot I,
third viscount Lisburne, did not seek election to Parliament. We can
speculate, though without direct evidence, that this may have been
because the embarrassed state of his affairs during and after his
brother's difficult and debt-filled career. However, he was certainly
involved in the bitter county feuds and electoral conflicts of the 1740s.
He wrote to the Duke of Newcastle in 1742 to express his concern
about the offices of Custos Rotulorum and Lord Lieutenant, which had
been held by his late brother:

> The firm attachment my Ancestor's and Predecessor's showed to the
> present Illustrious Family on the Throne, in opposition to all ill
> wisher's, was rewarded by Markes of the Royall favour, haveing ever
> since that Era been promoted to the greatest Honours and Priviliges in
> this Country, but now on the Death of my Brother the severall offices of
> Custos Rotulorum, and Lord lieutenant, of this County becomeing
> vacant, I am under some Aprehensions that these places of Honour are
> endeavourd to be Grasped at, by some Gentlemen; whose Characters as
> yet, I am certain have given em very small pretensions to Claim such
> favour's. Not to incroach farther on your Lordships time, I shall only
> beg leave to intreat your Lordships Countenance in my favour, that I
> may wear the same Marks of the Royall esteem my Ancestors have
> done . . .[5]

His efforts were not wholly successful; he retained the Lord
Lieutenancy, but Thomas Johnes of Llanfair Clydogau became Custos
Rotulorum; these two posts were more usually combined in one
person. Wilmot Vaughan was also a J.P.; the earliest surviving volume
of Cardiganshire quarter sessions records tell us that he attended in
January, 1743, and he was present on the bench at Tregaron when John
Lloyd of Llanddewibrefi threatened to run Herbert Lloyd of Peterwell

through with a pitchfork.[6] He seems to have attended quarter sessions about once a year, and although his name, as a peer, has priority in the lists of those attending, he did not always get his way. In the meeting of January 1743, at Aberystwyth Guildhall, he and John Lloyd of Ffosybleiddiaid presented the petition of the parishioners of Gwnnws for the removal of Margaret Evan, a poor infant and object of charity, to the parish of Caron, and had actually had her removed, but at the April sessions the order was quashed, and the men of Gwnnws had to pay compensation and costs to the men of Caron. In 1744 he was asked to inspect the defects of Llanafan bridge and arrange its repair; in 1745 he performed the same task for Llanbadarn bridge. In 1747 another of his orders for the removal of a charity child, this time from Llanafan to Llanbadarn Fawr, was quashed, and the matter referred to 'the two next neighbouring justices'. This can hardly have pleased him.

On a higher level of political involvement, Wilmot I supported John Lloyd of Peterwell for the county seat in the election of 1747, but relations between Trawsgoed and Peterwell cooled after the election of 1755, though at the same time Wilmot II gained the friendship and support of the Rev. William Powell, Tory squire of Nanteos, a house usually loyal to Gogerddan. In that year, in the absence of a Tory candidate from or supported by the Pryse family of Gogerddan, Wilmot II was elected unopposed in the Whig interest as M.P. for the Cardiganshire seat. This did not please Herbert Lloyd of Peterwell, whose brother John Lloyd had held the seat in 1747 and 1754, dying suddenly in 1755. Herbert Lloyd had had no choice but to submit, however, since Wilmot Vaughan had for some time solicited the support of the Duke of Newcastle, controller of the realm's political patronage, and had savagely attacked the character of Herbert Lloyd in his correspondence.

Wilmot I's health may not have been strong. In 1758 John Owen wrote enthusiastically to Edward Hughes, convinced that Wilmot was on his death-bed:

> Daccw yr hen Lord Lisburne [yn] marw'n deg a dau feddyg yn disgwyl wrtho.[7]

However, he survived the crisis and lived for another nine years.

Although not a Member of Parliament, Wilmot senior had his political interests. He wanted to assume all the rights of his Irish

Wilmot Vaughan (d. 1800), fourth viscount and first earl of Lisburne;
Sir Joshua Reynolds.

peerage but his father, John the first Viscount, had neglected to register his patent, without which he could not sit in the Irish House of Lords. So Wilmot senior began a correspondence in 1760 which apparently resulted in his taking his seat in Dublin in 1765, shortly before his death in 1766.[8]

His son Wilmot II, who was educated at Eton, is a crucial figure in the family history for two reasons. It was he who achieved the rank of earl as a reward for his political services, and it was he who moved the family from Wales for a generation. In 1764 at St George's church, Hanover Square, London, he had married his first wife, Elizabeth Gascoigne Nightingale. This was a most fortunate marriage for him, since his wife was heiress presumptive to her childless brother, Washington Nightingale of the Mamhead estate in Devon. Although the unfortunate Elizabeth died a few weeks after the birth of her son Wilmot III in 1765, the baby boy was now heir to Mamhead, and when Washington Nightingale died, the substantial Mamhead estate became the property of the Vaughans and the favoured home of Wilmot II, the fourth Viscount and first Earl.[9] The Nightingale inheritance also included the Enfield Rectory estate, Middlesex, and two generations of Vaughans were buried either at Enfield or at Mamhead. By 1765, therefore, the Vaughans controlled extensive lands in Wales, Devon, and Northumberland and Durham. It is unclear at what stage Wilmot II actually moved his household to Mamhead, but in 1769 he commissioned Robert Adam to alter the interior of the mansion, and in 1772 he brought in Capability Brown to create a new and fashionable garden.[10]

It may seem perverse to begin a description of a man with his obituary, but the portrait of Wilmot the new (fourth) Viscount in the *Gentleman's Magazine* in 1800 is interesting, if elegantly vague in the manner of the age:

> It is no flattery to his memory to say that his understanding was superior to most, equal to the best. His classical attainments were extensive, possessing all the elegance without the pedantry of the professed scholar, benevolent, charitable, and sincere, he discharged the several relations of life with tenderness, affection, and faithfulness. Beloved by his neighbourhood, and united to his family by the closest endearments, his death is most severely lamented.[11]

It is hard to know whether he was beloved by his neighbourhood; in any case that is more likely to refer to Devon, where he spent most of the last thirty years of his life, than to Cardiganshire. His classical attainments would certainly have been of a respectably high standard, but other than that he went on from Eton to Oxford, we know little. Did he undertake the Grand Tour, as did so many of his English and Welsh contemporaries?[12] It is very likely, but the dearth of family correspondence and accounts in the Crosswood archive leaves us in ignorance. Brief light falls on the level of Wilmot's culture in two letters written to him in 1785 by the Rev. W.J.Temple of Gluvias in Cornwall. Temple seems to have acted as a family adviser, and may possibly have been tutor to one or more of the children. One letter lists several French books that Wilmot sought for his library, and asked him for a list of the Italian books he might require, which could be ordered via the captain of an Italian ship. In the second surviving letter Temple says:

> I have given the list of Italian books your Lordship wishes to have, to a merchant here who has concerns in Italy . . . the Venetian was sailed before I had the honour of your Lordship's letter. I hope Muratori & Petrarch etc are come safe & beg you will honour them with a place in your Lordship's curious and valuable Library.[13]

Fortunately a number of Wilmot's personal letters survive, written to his friends William Powell of Nanteos (from 1755) and James Lloyd of Mabws (from 1767), enabling us to know him better than any other member of the family.[14]

The earliest of Wilmot's surviving letters was written in February 1755, to the Rev. William Powell of Nanteos (1705-1780). Trawsgoed and Nanteos do not previously seem to have been close politically; as we have seen, Nanteos had followed Gogerddan's Tory leanings, while Trawsgoed was Whig, insofar as those titles have any stable significance. However, Trawsgoed needed friends; the two Wilmots, father and son, saw the Lloyds of Peterwell and the Johneses of Llanfair and Abermad as enemies, and cast around for support against them. Wilmot's first letter is couched in the most formal terms, and seeks Powell's support for nomination to the county seat in the forthcoming election. Powell, as a clergyman, could not stand for Parliament; he was originally a second son, but his elder brother Thomas (1699-1752) had died childless.

The stiff tone of Wilmot's letter suggests that they had never previously corresponded, though it is difficult to believe that to be so.

Powell noted his approval on the back of the letter, and within a few months the correspondence becomes warmer. Wilmot, now elected M.P., reported on his meeting with Powell's ten-year-old son Thomas, a pupil at Westminster School, gave a lively account of a Commons debate, and found a naval post for a friend of Powell's. Letters survive until 1783, and the last of them echoes the first; it is a request for electoral support from Thomas Powell. Wilmot's elegant style is not best suited to warm us to him; he flatters both Lloyd and Powell with assurances that each is his best and most valued friend. However, the letters to Powell tell us a little about his life. On one occasion, Powell had obviously complained that he did not know what address would find Wilmot; the latter replied, from Savile Row:

> Sometimes I am here, then in Devonshire & next upon the banks of the Tweed.[15]

On another occasion he explains his plans for 1759:

> I propose going to Bath in a few Days in order to drink the Waters regularly for six Weeks. I am flattered that they will relieve my Complaint in my Stomach, tho I have tried them very often with little Success.[16]

However, we must return to Wilmot II's political career, and the activities of his father.

In 1755, much to the fury of Lewis Morris,[17] the twenty-eight-year-old Wilmot II had been returned for the county seat in a by-election following the death of John Lloyd of Peterwell; he sat until the General Election of 1761, and was briefly Secretary to the Chancellor of the Exchequer. As we have already seen, he could wield a waspish pen, and he continued to correspond with the Duke of Newcastle when outraged by local intrigues, hoping to gain that great magnate's support. He won the day in the matter of Herbert Lloyd's list of JPs in 1756, but he and his father had other problems, great and small, to deal with.

A plot began in the county in 1759 to displace Wilmot from his county parliamentary seat; the leading conspirators were Johnes of Llanfair and Lloyd of Peterwell. The plan was to ensure the election of John Pugh Pryse of Gogerddan for the county and Herbert Lloyd himself for the borough, and it set Wilmot's easily-kindled anger aflame. He wrote to Newcastle:

> As I am in that situation which can alone resist an attempt of this kind I
> have stated it without reserve to your Grace that I may know how far I
> may depend on your Favour & on the support of Government. That will
> in a great Measure determine my Conduct since I never would have
> engaged in Parliamentary Matters if I had not been desirous like those
> of my Family to place at the Head of this County a strenuous & active
> Friend to his Majesty & to his Government.

and again:

> Mr Johnes the Custos of the County & Steward of the Crown Manours
> from motives of envy & jealousy is the great Promoter of this
> opposition. He is armed with all the Weapons that Government can put
> into his Hands & they are employed in the most arbitrary Manner to
> support the Cause of a Tory upon this Occasion. I have formerly
> mentioned to your Grace that these offices were snatched by this
> Gentleman from my Family upon the Death of my Uncle & upon his
> leaving his Fortune in a very embarassed state . . . It is in short
> absolutely necessary (if my Success is to be consulted) to take these
> offices from Mr Johnes & to shew the County by that act that
> Government disapproves of his Conduct.[18]

Thomas Johnes at Dolaucothi got wind of Vaughan's
correspondence with the Duke, and hastened to put his side of the
argument:

> Mr Vaughan & his family have received many singular & great favours
> from the Government, & yet their Attachment has not always been
> most remarkable, which your Grace may well remember in the affair of
> Eskyr Mwyn; and had I not in obedience to your Grace's interposition
> given over all opposition to Mr. Vaughan in his last Election, He had
> not now had a Seat in Parliament . . .[19]

During this period of plotting, Wilmot attempted to gain the office of
Sheriff (an annual appointment) for his friend and supporter Thomas
Hughes of Hendrefelen, near Ystrad Meurig. He was greatly
embittered by the failure of his efforts, and said so to the Duke of
Newcastle:

> This very extraordinary Step taken I suppose upon proper
> Consideration has determined me to decline giving my Friends any
> further Trouble it having been my original Resolution never to stand a
> contested Election in Opposition to Government . . . I shall give your
> Grace no further Trouble but only to signify, that after the Treatment I

have received, my Father Lord Lisburne who is at present Lieutenant of the County of Cardigan does not think he can with Honour continue to hold that office. He therefore with all Duty & Zeal to his Majesty begs Leave to resign it into his Hands, hoping that whoever is appointed to succeed, will serve him with the same Loyalty & uniform Attachment as he has done.[20]

Wilmot II held to his resolution, did not stand for the county seat in 1761 (since he would certainly have lost, expensively), and was reduced to begging the Duke of Newcastle for a nomination elsewhere for that year in humiliating words:

When I waited upon your Grace with Lord Barrington, you were pleased in the Conversation I had with you, to tell me that I should come into Parliament & that you would take an opportunity of considering me, which Assurance you desired his Lordship to remind you of. In Consequence of your Intention so favourably expressed I trust your Grace will do me the Honour to recommend me to a Seat either upon the Vacancys caus'd by the double Returns or upon such opportunitys as to those in your Grace's situation must frequently occur . . . I am not conscious of having done any thing to deserve either the neglect of the Crown or that of your Grace, tho' I now find myself & Family is divested of every Mark of Distinction it has born in its own Province from the Revolution to this Time all which Disappointments I could easily have prevented if I had courted new Friends & new Connections.[21]

In 1762, without a place in Parliament, Wilmot sought Newcastle's backing for the Tiverton seat, conveniently placed for his Mamhead estate, which he preferred to Trawsgoed. This attempt failed, but he eventually succeeded in gaining the Duke's support for his nomination in Berwick-on-Tweed, where the influence of the Northern estate was crucial. This success did not come until 1765. Wilmot's letter congratulating Newcastle on his achieving high office in that year, and begging for his patronage, shows that he could fawn as well as rail:

Give me Leave to Congratulate yr. Grace, amongst the Rest of yr. Graces Friends, on yr. appointmt into that High office & Hope yr. Grace may many years Live to serve His Majesty & your Country with yr. Distinguished Great & Good Character, which you in the Former Reigns so Hapily Established, & will Ever be thought of by Posterity with Respect & Honour.[22]

In 1766 both Thomas Watson of Berwick and his brother-in-law Wilmot I the third Viscount Lisburne died, so that the latter's son, Wilmot II, M.P. for Berwick-on-Tweed, succeeded to both the Trawsgoed and the Northumberland estates. Wilmot had been elected M.P. for Berwick-on-Tweed in 1765, obviously as his uncle's nominee; he was still kept out of the Cardiganshire county seat since the young heir to Gogerddan, John Pugh Pryse, was now of age and took the seat. In 1768 however John Pugh Pryse inexplicably moved to the borough seat, so Wilmot, now Viscount Lisburne, gave up the Berwick seat for the Cardiganshire county seat, and was re-elected without formal opposition from 1768 until 1796, when Thomas Johnes of Hafod Uchdryd took over the seat.

Wilmot's letters to James Lloyd (1721-1800) give us further insight into Wilmot's rather chilly character. James Lloyd, born in 1721 at Carmarthen, was a descendant of the Lloyds of Ffosybleiddiaid, a former pupil of Harrow and a barrister. He married Anna Maria Lloyd, heiress of Mabws and Ystrad Teilo (Llanrhystud), and built Mabws house.[23] One of Wilmot's letters to James Lloyd gives some background to the election of 1768, particularly his sketch of Sir Herbert Lloyd's approaches to him:

> I observe the Account you give me of Sr Herbert's Proceedings which answer the Ideas I have always entertained of the Man & the Game it is necessary for him to renew . . . But tho' he has omitted no Instance of Civility or Attention to me of late, yet he has never explained any of his views to me, doubting I suppose what reception they would meet with. Professions indeed of having no Connection with Mr Pryse & of desiring to act with me in every Thing; to all of which I replied by a civil Bow, knowing the Nature of the Man.

For himself he claimed, not without a certain smooth hypocrisy:

> I am less eager than ever to appear upon that Stage [i.e. politics], but at the same Time I think it my Duty to serve my Country [i.e. county] to the best of my abilitys, or at least to prevent it sinking into improper & worthless hands.[24]

The relationship between Wilmot and John Pugh Pryse of Gogerddan is intriguing, and some light is thrown on it by the survival of more of Wilmot's letters to William Powell of Nanteos from 1768 on. In 1761, as we have seen, Wilmot had been forced from the county seat, to be replaced by the Gogerddan heir, who was twelve years the younger. It is clear that although Wilmot was Cardiganshire's only peer, the commoner John Pugh Pryse was really the leading man in the county. Wilmot was careful not to quarrel with Pryse, who seems to have borne a somewhat erratic character; we have seen that he gave up his county seat in Wilmot's favour in 1768, at the same time exercising his patronage to ensure that his relative Pryse Campbell of Stackpole took the borough seat. Campbell died within a few months, and Wilmot wrote to Powell at Nanteos in December 1769:

> [Mr Pryse's] Idea & mine perfectly concurred, in leaving to yourself principally Mr Lloyd of Mabus & the Gentlemen at Cardigan the nomination of the Candidate [i.e. for the borough seat]. Your son, Mr Thos Powell, if he should be inclined to stand, was our first object and next, Mr Pryse thought of offering the Seat to either of Mr Campbell's Sons . . . In matters relative to the Borough I never attempt to interfere further, than by my honest & impartial Advice, when required. If Mr Thos Powell should offer, which I most cordially wish, who can be so agreable to me, as the Son of my best Friend?[25]

However, the nomination went to Ralph Congreve, presumably on the insistence of Pryse, and when an election was again in the offing in 1773/4, Wilmot suffered a severe snub at Pryse's hands. He had written to Pryse, who had departed suddenly from London for Italy, to consult with the gentlemen of the county before naming a candidate for the borough seat. However, Pryse eventually returned to London in December 1773 and wrote a curt letter (copied out by Wilmot for Powell's benefit), naming a remote cousin, Sir Robert Smyth, as his favoured candidate. Wilmot was obviously astounded by the choice, and by the lack of consultation, describing it as 'this sudden Event, for which I am in every respect little prepared', and referring to the 'Trouble & Embarrassment' caused by the lack of consultation.[26] Yet the way Wilmot swallowed his distress and supported Pryse at the latter's insistence reveals how powerful was the Gogerddan interest.

However, despite Pryse's influence and Wilmot's support, the borough election was to be contested. Thomas Johnes of Dolaucothi and Hafod Uchtryd wrote to Wilmot early in 1774 proposing that his son, also Thomas, the famous member of the family, should stand for the borough. Wilmot wrote to James Lloyd of Mabws, expressing his astonishment not only at Johnes's temerity in putting his son forward, but in proposing that Wilmot should bear half the costs of the election! Wilmot was additionally concerned that in fact Thomas Johnes junior might contest the county seat against him.[27]

In the event, Smyth outpolled Johnes by 1488 to 980, but Johnes's appeal against the result was allowed, and he took the seat; Wilmot's reaction is not recorded. Pryse's death in 1774 must have been a relief to the Trawsgoed interest, but we have no letters to Mabws from that year. A few letters do survive in the Pigeonsford (Llangrannog) correspondence; these show Wilmot exercising his smooth diplomacy; in the election campaign of 1784 he paid for a chaise to carry squire George Price to Cardigan and back.[28]

Despite his constant apprehension that he might have to fight elections, Wilmot II seems to have enjoyed the world of politics. Although the background details are not apparent, he became a friend as well as a follower of leading politicians, and the combination of useful friendships and his own ambition ensured his appointment to government office, first under Grafton, then under Lord North. He was a Lord Commissioner of Trade (with a salary of £1000 a year) from his election in 1768 until early in 1770, when he became a salaried Lord of the Admiralty. After he had been ten years in that office he complained to James Lloyd that Lord North had done little for him in the way of patronage; nevertheless when the Prime Minister in the same year offered him the court post of Comptroller of the royal household, with a Privy Councillorship, he refused them, preferring to remain at the Admiralty, until Lord North's ministry fell in 1782.

In 1776, Wilmot was elevated to an Irish earldom, being but one of what Horace Walpole called 'a mob of nobility'.[29] This reward for his loyalty to the government was in fact a deep disappointment; he had been lobbying his political friends and acquaintances for an English peerage, which would have given him a seat in the House of Lords, and in 1783 Lord North actually recommended him for the Lords. He was obviously on good terms with the prime minister; in 1782 he had been favoured with a letter from North stating his attitude toward the current political situation and his own political intentions, and North was still in correspondence with him later in the decade.[30] At that time however, George III, was unwilling to make additional English peerages at the request of a government (the Fox-North coalition) of which he disapproved, mainly because he was at cross-purposes with Lord North who himself held only a courtesy title but wanted to move to the Lords in his own right. While the king refused a peerage to his prime minister, he could hardly ennoble anyone else. A later correspondence campaign by Wilmot to gain the elusive English peerage brought him no success.

When Lord North's ministry fell in 1782, Wilmot wrote to James Lloyd in Horatian terms:

> The sudden Change in every Department of Government, tho' long foreseen by me, which has just happened, having left your Friend a private Man, I trust he [i.e. Wilmot himself] will at least derive this Advantage from it, that he will in future be more Master of his Time, & more able to attend to his personal Concerns. I look with some Satisfaction to that Ease & Quiet, which have been so long interrupted & in the general Confusion of the State, to which none have more contributed than the new Rulers, the Loss in Profit or Consequence is little to be regretted. If I preserve the Esteem of a few Friends, amongst the most valuable of Whom is Yourself, I shall consider this Event with perfect Indifference, wishing only it may be productive of every real Good to this distressed Country.[31]

Wilmot's expressions of reluctance to assume a seat in the Commons and of relief at the loss of office should be taken with a large pinch of political salt. When the Fox-North coalition collapsed at the end of 1783, and Pitt's replacement government was struggling in early 1784, Wilmot's antennae twitched vigorously. Would his county seat be safe? He wrote to William Powell at Nanteos seeking his support once again.[32]

He must also have written to James Lloyd expressing his concern, for Lloyd's reply survives:

> You may make yourself quite Easy if there should be a dissolution for I am fully satisfyd that you will meet with no opposition. Not the least Rumour at present prevails and the whole county is as quiet as you can wish. (24.1.1784)[33]

For a while Wilmot was convinced that the young Thomas Johnes of Hafod was his enemy, plotting with Edward Loveden of Gogerddan and Thomas Powell of Nanteos to replace him in the county seat. As if that were not bad enough, he felt the government itself was after him:

> A Dissolution of Parlt is still expected & every Measure taken on the Part of Government to disturb the Seats of those who have asserted the due Weight & Importance of the House of Commons in the Scale of the

Legislature. As such I have not escaped Notice & from the best
Authority I learn that setting aside his solemn Promise in Writing &
every verbal Assurance Mr Johnes will be prevailed on to raise an
Opposition in the County & do every thing in his power to prevent my
Reelection. (17.3.1784)

Although contested elections were rare, Wilmot needed to be
extremely active to head off possible rivals for the nomination, and he
had to work as hard as anyone to save his seat. Despite his long
friendship with William Powell, the latter's son Thomas, whom
Wilmot had befriended when still a pupil at school in London, seems
to have been actively canvassing for support to oust Wilmot from the
county seat. This was certainly devious in a man whom Wilmot had
previously encouraged (in vain) to stand for the borough seat. From
London Wilmot sought James Lloyd's advice:

> Will it be advisable for me to come into & make a general Canvass of
> the County, or to appear with my Friends at the Gt Sessions to counter
> what may be intended there. (17.3.1784)

Thomas Johnes swore friendship and support that very day, and next
morning Wilmot wrote in high spirits; a rare event, but his political
blood was heated:

> I have written to the High & Under Sheriff intimating that I purpose to
> attend at the Sessions & desiring they will summon my Friends & as
> they have assured me they will attend to every Request I may make, I
> doubt not they will do every thing to favour me. (18.3.1784)

James Lloyd replied with vigour, laying out energetic canvassing
tactics for the ensuing week. On Monday Wilmot was to visit Cil-pyll,
Brynallt and Mynachty, sleep at Tŷglyn, visit Abermeurig,
Llanvaughan, Waunifor, Alltyrodyn, Gernos and Bronwydd, sleep at
Cilgwyn, visit Llysnewydd, Penywenallt, Blaen-pant and Pigeonsford,
sleep at Cardigan, and then visit three more houses on Thursday:

> Send to Llandovery and order your chair to meet you on Teusday [*sic*]
> night at Tuglyn you will save yourself great fatigue for you have an
> excellent chaise . . . Do not think of employing your time in writing
> letters at present you must do all in Person within the County
> (27.3.1784)[34]

A week later, following a chilly eight-hour ride from Llandovery, Wilmot was at Trawsgoed, and he fired off salvoes of short letters to James Lloyd as he moved round the county canvassing the freeholders in a state of high excitement as he assembled his supporters:

> I am not easy whilst there remains the least Doubt. If the Canvass was briskly carried on, I think Mr Powell would quit the field . . .
> We called on Davies of Cwmnant but did not see him. We imagine he kept out of the Way, Mr John Lewis having just past him in the Road
> . . .
> Time daily grows more precious . . .
> If all the Wheels of the Machine were in Motion I should be satisfied, but at present it seems our progress is not what it might be . . .

There speaks a true politician.

James Lloyd offered every support and encouragement, assuring Wilmot that of 240 freeholders in the south of the county, not twenty would vote against him. His friends would sweep the parishes of Llangranog, Llantysiliogogo, Llanarth and Dihewyd on his behalf; his son and nephew had canvassed all the way from Ffair-rhos to Mabws, finding only two hostile voters. John Bowen of Cardigan likewise offered advice and support.[35]

Wilmot was indeed successful; Powell quit the field, so Wilmot kept the seat without a poll. However, the correspondence shows how a campaign had to be mounted even when there was no subsequent contest. Only scattered correspondence survives after 1794; one later letter does survive referring to the long illness of his wife and his own fragile health. Despite that, Wilmot held on to his parliamentary seat until 1796. A single stray letter to Lloyd from the election year 1788 shows Wilmot seeking his friend's support yet again in his campaign to retain his seat against the canvassing of the Gogerddan and Nanteos interest.[36] The letter is written (from Bath) in a most tremulous hand, well indicating his poor state of health, but it clearly shows his determination to cling to his seat.

In 1796 he gave up the seat, but although very weak and housebound at Mamhead, he took a close interest in the election of that year. The Gogerddan interest lay in the hands of Mr Loveden of Buscot, Oxfordshire who had married the Gogerddan heiress; Thomas Johnes was keen to move from his Radnorshire county seat to Cardiganshire, while Thomas Powell of Nanteos had not given up hope of election, though he was subservient to Loveden. Wilmot, for his part, was determined that his second son John Vaughan should be elected. Several letters from William Young, the London solicitor whom Wilmot employed as his principal agent in his Welsh affairs at this time, show how intricate were the relationships and manoevres which eventually ensured the election of Thomas Johnes for the county and John Vaughan for the borough seat.[37] The election meeting at Cardigan was described to Wilmot by Edward Lort:

> Mr Johnes bringing forward all his friends and [was] nominated by a great Majority, but I did not expect Mr Cambell [sic] and Capt Owen Lloyd of Abertrinant to be so warm against Mr Vaughan. The former open[ed] the meeting and a warm altercation took place between him and Mr Lloyd of Deal in Consequence of Mr Lovedens and Mr Powells Letters to Mr Lloyd requesting him to stand for the County, so you see my Lord how paultry Mr Loveden has acted.[38]

William Vaughan's investigations had revealed to Wilmot that Loveden had written that he wanted:

> to give our Interest to any Gentleman that may Oppose Mr Vaughan as I trust there is sufficient spirit left in the County of Cardigan at Large to pervent [*sic*] such Hereditary Claim, and I perfectly Agree with Mr Lloyd of Mabus that it is high time to Curtail it.[39]

If this indictment of James Lloyd was a blow to Wilmot, it did not entirely dissolve the friendship, and Wilmot can hardly have complained at the outcome, since John Vaughan took the borough seat. By Samuel Rush Meyrick's account John Vaughan was a most agreeable man personally, but feckless; he certainly had no political talent whatsoever, and his extravagance would bring the family deeper into debt.

Wilmot was the most politically active of all the Vaughans after Sir John, spending thirty-seven years in the House of Commons without ever contesting a poll; fourteen of those years he spent in office. As well as discussing politics, Wilmot's letters to James Lloyd offer comment about both local and national politics, as well as his personal affairs. Although he lived at Mamhead and worked in London, he tried to visit Trawsgoed every summer; in the letter of 1767 already cited he says, with even more than usual sententiousness:

I am as much resolved as human accidents will allow to visit Crosswood the first Week in April, & hope the Plan I propose . . . as well for improving the Farm as putting the House into some decent order, will show clearly that my Intention is not to neglect what so well deserves my Care & Notice.

He could be even more earnest:

The Political Sky appears as much clouded as the natural one, & I am afraid little Sunshine is to be expected. The Rulers of these Times have been trained rather in the School of Pleasure than of Business & I think answer no more the Idea of Statesmen, than Punch & his Friends give us of a wise & well-regulated government. (24.11.1768)

There are occasional glimpses of the Earl as the Welshman in London:

Capt Lloyd of Danyrallt & some of our Countrymen dined with me . . . (3.5.1777)

Your brother from Plymouth is in Town . . . We meet often & today dine with all our Friends at a new Welsh Club established in Bond Street . . . I am going tomorrow for the Holydays to Lord Thomond's in Essex. (25.3.1765)

During the 1770s James Lloyd often pressed Wilmot on local matters, especially the stationing of dragoons in Newcastle Emlyn because of widespread smuggling, to the outrage of the Excise authorities. One of Wilmot's replies is especially revealing:

As to the Board of Excise, I have seen the Report to the Treasury upon my Application. It therein states, that neither Commonalty nor Gentry of the Higher Class pay any regard to the Excise Laws within the County of Cardigan, that the Contempt & Infringement of them is constant & notorious, & that a military Force is absolutely necessary . . . in the Neighbourhood of Newcastle (Emlyn) there can be no Writ or Process served without a military Aid. (3.5.1777)

Lloyd also pressed his friend for governmental influence on behalf of his young soldier son John Lloyd, and for other friends. Wilmot professed to be doing everything in his power, but complained of the long waiting lists for office. Young John Lloyd was sceptical, and wrote to his father:

> Thanks to you my Dearest Sir for sending me Lord Lisburne's Letter
> which I return you with one Observation which you must not be angry
> with me for, That all his Letters are the same And even if he dictates to
> another how easy it is to smell him out. (26.11.78)

Young Lloyd's scepticism seems to have been unjustified in the event,
because he gained civilian employment with the Navy at Plymouth,
which would have been in Wilmot's gift, and wrote frequently to
Mamhead on matters of passing concern.

Wilmot was a sceptic in international affairs as in home matters; the
great issue of the day was the American War of Independence, into
which the North ministry had entered so reluctantly. On March 7,
1778, he commented:

> The public Prospect is very gloomy. We have taken every Step & made
> every Concession even to a degree of Humiliation to induce the
> Americans to make Peace, but I entertain no sanguine Hopes of
> success, as I have ever believed these Troubles have arisen more from
> Motives of Ambition, than of real grievance.

The saddest letters are those concerned with Wilmot's eldest son,
born in 1755 of his first marriage to Elizabeth Gascoigne Nightingale.
Wilmot refers to his son by the courtesy title of Lord Vaughan, and we
may do the same, since his Christian name Wilmot is confusingly that
of his father and grandfather. He seems to have had a normal
childhood, and was educated at Eton between 1765 and 1772, then at
Magdalen College, Oxford. However, he developed severe personality
problems. In a remarkable outburst on July 27, 1779, Wilmot the father
laid his heart open to James Lloyd:

> With respect to Lord Vaughan, I have no Hopes, he can be brought by
> any Means to a proper Sense of what becomes him in any shape. I have
> made him every offer & given him every Assurance, that Affection,
> Indulgence and even Forgiveness can suggest. But all in vain. He will
> not disclose what his Situation or difficultys are to me or any indifferent
> [= unbiassed] Person, he keeps no appointment he makes with me or
> anyone . . . but flys all over the Kingdom in a Post Chaise & four
> without a Servant, Linnen or common Necessarys. He never stirs out
> without loaded Pistols in his Pocket, has very good Lodgings in Town
> & yet lives at Pero's Baigno. He will do nothing nor attend to any
> Business even where he is most immediately interested. He at the same
> time appears perfectly calm & composed . . . He is totally unfit to have
> the management of himself, yet I can do nothing to restrain him, tho'

all his Actions prove clearly a disordered understanding. At the very Time he can appear to transient Observation in his Exterior at least for certain Intervals, not unlike other Men. The Effect this has had upon my Peace & Comfort, & the whole Plan of my Life for these three years past, I cannot describe to you. It has robbed me of every Satisfaction, & I see no End or Remedy for the Evil. Common Irregularity & Extravagance are too prevalent, but these are of a Species I never traced in any other Man. There is no guessing what he aims at & he has neither a Friend or Acquaintance left, who will associate with him. His Sollicitor, Mr Lloyd, a Man of Character whom he employed with Mr Dunning to examine all the Titles I had to my several Estates, when he found he could not answer his purpose, he has left, just as he has done others, & in one Word I am utterly at a Loss, what to do with him, or even how to divest myself of him . . . Every Duty of the Parent & of the Friend, every Attention & Care, every Indulgence has been shown on my Part, after such Indignitys offered, such Insults received, every Rule of Order & Decency violated.

Wilmot had remained a widower for almost eight years after Elizabeth's death in 1755, but in 1763 at St Andrew's church, Holborn, he took Dorothy Shafto, eldest daughter of John Shafto M.P., as his second wife. She soon bore her husband two daughters, Dorothy (1765) and Mallet (1766), and then a second son, John (1769), who eventually, after the death of his unfortunate half-brother, became the third Earl of Lisburne. Fortunately one of her letters to her husband survives, suggesting a happy marriage. Wilmot had been away from his wife and his Mamhead home in 1780, electioneering in Cardiganshire. Dorothy wrote:

My Dearest Love, I received your very kind letters . . . all of which I return you thanks most sincerely for. They are my only comfort for I must say it has been a long absence. I hope however by this time I have an opportunity of giving you joy of getting your election & that you are almost on your return Home. I do assure you, nothing but the satisfaction of believing you happily Elected for your County could at all reconcile me to the disappointment of not seeing you so much longer than I expected . . .

After telling him the election gossip from Devon, she concluded:

I know I need not beg you to avoid the Passage [i.e. across the Severn] if the weather is not favourable, as you always think tenderly of me and mine, I am happy to find by Grey you are tolerably well . . . Adieu my dearest Love we are all well and join in duty & Love & I am ever yrs most faithfully . . .[40]

The Lisburne-Northumberland papers, though filling only one box, show clearly how the head of a great estate was involved in a mass of correspondence of a kind which has virtually disappeared from the Trawsgoed archive. Letters poured in from penniless curates and their patrons seeking promotion to Welsh parishes, from naval officers and from their widows, from creditors, and above all from the lawyers and agents employed by Wilmot. Occasional intriguing flashes of light are cast on his life; in 1796 one Charles Este wrote from a Soho address:

> I am much obliged to Your Lordship by your Offer of the two Negroes to Colonel Picton and myself [but] under the Circumstances as they stood, the Boys were left in the West Indies.[41]

A number of letters survive from 1786 on the death of Wilmot's brother-in-law, Thomas Lloyd of Abertrinant, paying tribute to the dead man's open and honest character, and expressing concern about the widow's emotional and financial condition.

Wilmot Vaughan, fourth viscount and first Earl of Lisburne, died in 1800 and was buried at Mamhead. During his career he had done a great deal for his estate, as we have already briefly seen in the first chapter, and will see again. He exchanged lands, bought lands, improved lands, and made other investments. Despite his disappointment over the English peerage, and the tart nature of much of his political correspondence, he may well have deserved the obituary from the *Gentlemen's Magazine* previously quoted. We may attempt to judge his position in society from a Welsh viewpoint by comparing him with his younger contemporary, Sir Watkin Williams Wynn, the fourth baronet (1749-1789), of Wynnstay. Both had been sent to eminent schools; Wilmot Vaughan to Eton, Watkin Williams Wynn to Westminster (it so happened that the Commons intake of 1761, which included Wilmot, had no fewer than 111 'Old Westminsters'). Both men had been to Oxford. We do not know whether Wilmot was sent on the Grand Tour; he may have been forced to avoid it as an economy measure, although economy measures were rarely favoured at this social level. Sir Watkin's bills were formidable; in 1768 he went to Paris (where he took fencing, dancing & language lessons), Switzerland, and Italy, including Rome, where he and his companions had a group portrait painted. The cost of this trip, though less than a year abroad, was £8,643.

Sir Watkin was a figure of note in his time, and we have gossipy descriptions of him. His famous 1770 coming of age, celebrated in London and Wynnstay, included feasting at the latter on 30 bullocks, 50 calves, 80 sheep, 50 hogs, 18 lambs, huge quantities of fish, hams, tongues, pies, poultry, 18,000 eggs, 73 hundredweight of bread and 120 dozen of wine, with a Great Room built for the event. He was a collector and connoisseur of art, a friend of Reynolds & Robert Adam, a patron of blind John Parry and other well-known musicians. David Garrick visited Wynnstay in 1777.[42] Intriguing though he may thus seem to us in retrospect, Sir Watkin was mortgaging the future of his estate by his conspicuous consumption; his posthumous debts were said to be £160,000, and his successor had a miserable time in consequence. Wilmot Vaughan, from his much smaller economic base, was a comparatively successful politician and left his estate in less catastrophic condition.

It is worth dwelling briefly on Wilmot's achievements in the light of the comments of F.M.L.Thompson.[43] Although Thompson does not deal specifically with Wales, many of his remarks are apposite. He suggests that the end of the eighteenth century and the beginning of the nineteenth was the high-water mark of the English aristocracy. It is not easy to define groups within the aristocracy; the titled English nobility (barons and above) were a small group, even following the the younger Pitt's creations. Some of them owned less land and had smaller incomes than the wealthiest commoners. The general estimation seems to have been that a man with £10,000 a year was either a lord in fact, or could act like one. It is impossible to establish Wilmot's income during the late eighteenth century, though at a guess he may not have been far below that £10,000 group. As Earl of Lisburne, an Irish creation, Wilmot was not of the core of the aristocracy, but he was well-placed. He and his father had saved and restored the family fortunes in terms of land (the increased estate), money (the clearance of much debt) and political influence (tenancy of the county seat and minor government office).

Several factors, however, combined to ensure that the family and estate did not reach still higher status, and that within thirty years of the first Earl's death, the estate would start to shrink. The first factor was the failure to achieve an English peerage; Thompson lists other

Irish peers who were more fortunate.[44] The second was the failure of subsequent generations to achieve marriages as successful as those of Wilmot and his father, which had brought in the Northumberland and Devon estates. The third was the problems caused by Wilmot's own sons, the insane Wilmot III, the heir, and his younger half-brother Colonel John Vaughan, the gambler.

*   *   *

Wilmot the first Earl's sister Elizabeth and younger brother John had had their lives arranged for them. Elizabeth married Thomas Lloyd, squire of nearby Abertrinant in Llanfihangel-y-Creuddyn, worth £600 a year. The marriage of a viscount's daughter to an obscure squire may seem a social setback, but there were more peers' daughters in the marriage market than there were available heirs to peerages, so many had to be ready to marry down a level. Wilmot's younger half-brother John joined the army in the classic manner of younger brothers, and was extremely successful, so much so that he deserves extended treatment here. At the request of a cousin, Wilmot wrote out the following description of his brother John's military career:[45]

> In December 1727 Wilmot 3rd Viscount married Elizabeth daughter of Thomas Watson of Berwick-upon-Tweed, Squire, and dying at Crosswood Jan 19, 1766, left issue two sons and one daughter, Elizabeth married to Thomas Lloyd of Abertrinant in the Co of Cardigan Esquire, and died Jan 1784. John the second son was in 1746 appointed a cornet in the 10th regt of Dragoons, and proceeding through the several ranks, served the last wars in Germany, North America and the West Indies, particularly at the taking of Martinico (= Martinique), where he commanded one of the battalions of Grenadiers that distinguished themselves at the reduction of that island. On the 11th May 1755 he was appointed Colonel of the 46th regiment, which being ordered to North America, he served as Brigadier and Major General on that staff. On the 29th January 1777 he was appointed Major-General on the British establishment and led the Grenadiers to the attack of the rebels at Brooklyn, in Long Island. At the landing on New York Island he first advanced at the head of the same corps and in ascending the heights was wounded in the thigh. He commanded the attack at Fort Montgomery on the North River where his horse was killed as he was dismounting to lead the troops to storm that fort, in which he succeeded and is noticed by Sir Henry Clinton's orders dated

the 9th October 1777, in these words "Fort Clinton is henceforth to be distinguished by the name of Fort Vaughan in memory of the intrepidity and noble perseverance which Major-General Vaughan shewed in the assault of it." After the campaign of 1779 he returned to England and was in December appointed Commander in Chief of His Majesty's forces in the Leeward Islands.

That account omits some facts: John Vaughan served in America 1760-1767 and 1776-79, and spent the years 1779-82 in the disturbed West Indies, and was even considered for the post of commander-in-chief in America. He was briefly governor of Fort William in the

Lieut-General Sir John Vaughan(1747-95). Unattributed.

Highlands of Scotland, 1779-80, and was appointed sinecure Governor of Berwick Castle 1780-95. Apparently he had intended to leave the Army in 1775, having become an M.P. in 1774, and there a surviving address expresses the regret of the Grenadiers at his intended departure, but the American War of Independence changed his mind for him.[46] Wilmot had loyally acted the part of the elder brother from the first; in 1767 he had tried to secure for John a position on the staff of the Lord Lieutenant of Ireland.[47]

Other references to John Vaughan may be traced in contemporary correspondence. He had actually been nominated for the command in America in 1779 when General Cornwallis changed his mind and decided after all to accept the responsibility he had previously sought to avoid. Lord George Sackville-Germain, who as Secretary of State for the American colonies 1775-1782 bore the main brunt of directing the British efforts in the American War of Independence, wrote to William Knowle in 1779:

> Vaughan's commission may be recalled but I cannot advise doing so slighting an act to an officer who has behaved so well, and who has the merit of remaining steady whilst others were so ready to resign.[48]

Not everyone thought so highly of him; James Hare wrote to Lord Carlisle in 1782:

> Vaughan is talked of for the command at New York, though I cannot believe they will appoint so very improper a man as he is generally thought.[49]

A Major Wemyss wrote of him:

> Without abilities, he was ill-tempered and capricious, ever censuring the conduct of others, particularly his senior officers.[50]

However, these opinions do not apparently represent the general judgement; Francis, Lord Rawdon, had written from the field to the Earl of Huntingdon in 1776:

> I find myself very strongly inclined to cultivate the acquaintance you recommend to me with General Vaughan. He has an open manly manner which prejudices me much in his favour.

Like some other prominent public servants, General Vaughan felt neglected by Lord North, the Prime Minister. In 1781 Horace Walpole wrote to a friend:

Neither Lord North nor his master [i.e. George III] thank or take notice of those that have done their best. This is strictly true. General Vaughan, their own creature, has not had his service mentioned to him, and I could name a dozen more equally disgusted.[51]

By referring to Vaughan as 'their own creature', Walpole simply means that he was loyal to the King and Prime Minister, and had been promoted by them. As it happens, Walpole (or his informant) was quite wrong. In 1778 General Howe, who had already congratulated Vaughan on his military success, on his spirited conduct and gallantry, had written from Philadelphia to Lord George Germain:

> The approbation which the King has been graciously pleased to express of the judicious and spirited conduct of Sir Henry Clinton and Major-General Vaughan I shall immediately transmit to those officers.[52]

Vaughan had certainly done a good deal to inspire confidence in those who knew him. When he left the North American theatre for the West Indies in 1779, he received addresses from the loyal refugees of North America, lamenting his departure and thanking him for his kindness.[53] He was eventually made a Knight of the Bath in 1792. While serving in the West Indies he had contact with other men from his home county. Captain (later Admiral) John Thomas of Llanfechan (son-in-law of Wilmot Vaughan's friend James Lloyd of Mabws) captained the *Ulysses* in the Caribbean in 1780-81, and Captain (later General) Vaughan Lloyd of Ffosybleiddiaid (1736-1817) served under John Vaughan's command early in the 1790s.[54]

Wilmot refers to his younger brother several times in his letters to James Lloyd. Most notably, he commented in April 1777:

> Every dispatch informs me of the various risques my brother has run, except his own Letters, which are always silent upon that subject.

Wilmot, as a Lord of the Admiralty, was closely involved in the management of the war, and his name appears frequently as a signatory to official correspondence. The Trawsgoed archive contains several addresses of gratitude to General Vaughan from communities in America, and a 1777 letter of congratulations from General Howe on his gallantry already referred to.[55]

As commander-in-chief of West Indian land forces, under the overall command of Admiral Rodney, Vaughan led the troops who

captured St Eustatius in February 1781, and who were granted a share
of the booty, which he valued at three million pounds.[56] Vaughan's
official and private correspondence shows great interest in the matter
of booty, which was the usual way for officers and men to enrich
themselves in war. During 1781 he complained of ill-health, and after
accepting the surrender of Martinique in November, he insisted on
returning to Britain in December; his brother Wilmot had helped
secure his return.[57] However, Vaughan's real motive in returning seems
to have been the need to defend himself (and Admiral Rodney) against
a motion in the House of Commons inspired by citizens of St
Eustatius, whose property he had taken and divided with his troops as
booty. He conducted his defence with vigour and success.

Despite his military career, much of it overseas, Sir John Vaughan
played an important part in the management of the Trawsgoed
possessions. In 1773 he had paid £10,000 for a considerable estate in
the parishes of Llangoedmor, Llanfihangel Ystrad and Trefilan, in
mid- and south Cardiganshire. He held a number of farms from the
Trawsgoed estate, and lent quite large sums to his brother in his efforts
to clear, or at least to stave off, the permanent burden of Trawsgoed
debt. Presumably he financed these operations with his West Indies
booty; an army officer's pay was notoriously insufficient to support
the necessary style of life (though there were perks for officers), and
he did not derive his capital from the family estate.

As we have seen, Sir John was involved in politics as M.P. for
Berwick-on-Tweed (thanks to the family connection) from 1774 till
1795; his long periods of absence on overseas service were not
allowed to interfere with his tenure of the seat. He was also a member
of the Irish parliament, representing St Johnstown, from 1776 till
1783. Like his brother Wilmot, Sir John supported the North ministry
and opposed Pitt. A lifelong bachelor, he died at Martinique in 1795,
and his body was brought home to be buried at Mamhead.

NOTES

[1]The second viscount had borrowed money from John Johnes, Dolaucothi, who could not recover the debt from either Wilmot père or fils. See NLW Schedule of Dolaucothi Correspondence, XII, 74.

[2]For brief details of the Northern estate, see Appendix I.

[3]Quoted in David Jenkins, 'The Pryse Family of Gogerddan, II', *NLWJ*, VIII, 2 (1953) pp.176-198. This article throws vivid light on the intrigues and corruption of the period.

[4]For fuller coverage see P.D.G.Thomas, 'Eighteenth-century elections in the Cardigan Boroughs constituency', *Ceredigion* V (4), (1967), 402-423; 'County Elections in Eighteenth-century Cardiganshire', ibid. XI (3) (1991), 239-58; David Williams, 'Cardiganshire Politics in the Mid-Eighteenth Century', *ibid.* III (4) (1959), 303-18.

[5]David Williams, op.cit. p.307.

[6]Bethan Phillips, *Peterwell*, (Llandysul, 1983), p.63. This invaluable book gives a lively picture of political and social life in eighteenth-century Cardiganshire.

[7]Hugh Owen (ed), *Additional Letters of the Morrises of Anglesey, II*, (London, 1947) p.942: 'Here is Lord Lisburne, fairly dying, and two doctors waiting on him.'

[8]NLW CD III, 16.

[9]Wilmot Vaughan was born on 9 April 1765; his mother was buried at Enfield on 24 May in the same year.

[10]T. Gray, *The Garden History of Devon: an illustrated guide to sources* (Exeter, 1995). 145-46.

[11]S.R.Meyrick, *History of Cardiganshire*, (Brecon, 1907), p.344.

[12]For an interesting Welsh example, George Lewis Langton, see R.J.Colyer, 'A Breconshire Gentleman in Europe 1737-8', *NLWJ*, XXI (1979-80), pp. 265-97.

[13]NLW CD III, 55.

[14]His letters to Powell are NLW Nanteos L.133-158; to Lloyd they are in a bound volume, NLW MS 14,215C. A few of James Lloyd's letters are preserved in the unscheduled NLW. Lisburne-Northumberland archive, bundles 5 and 7. A number of his letters to Edmund Burke in the Sheffield City Archive will be the subject of a separate study.

[15]NLW Nanteos L.143.

[16]NLW Nanteos L.145.

[17]ML I, 353.

[18]David Williams, *op.cit.*, p.312.

[19]Ibid. p.314.

[20]Ibid. p.315.

[21]Ibid. p.315.

[22]Ibid., p.316.

[23]NLW Alcwyn Evans genealogies (NLW MS 12,359D), p.90.

[24]NLW MS 14,215C, ff.1-2.

[25]NLW Nanteos L.149, subscribed 'From my Bed Thursday morn 5 oclock'.

[26]NLW Nanteos L.156.

[27]NLW CD III, 24. The document is Wilmot's retained copy, the correspondent unnamed, but the references to 'my dearest Friend' indicate that James Lloyd was the addressee.

[28]Evelyn Hope, *Llangranog and the Pigeonsford Family*, (Cardigan, 1931), pp.12-13.

[29]Cited in Glyn Roberts, *Aspects of Welsh History* (Cardiff, 1969), p.170.

[30]A. Valentine, *Lord North*, vol.2, (University of Oklahoma Press, 1967), pp. 341, 421.

[31]Loc.cit., f.93; it should be located in the correspondence of 1782, not 1784.

[32]NLW Nanteos L.158.

[33]NLW Lisburne-Northumberland archive, bundle 5, unscheduled.

[34]Ibid.

[35]Ibid.

[36]NLW CD III, 62.

[37]NLW Lisburne-Northumberland papers, bundle 7, unscheduled.

[38]Ibid.

[39]Ibid.

[40]NLW CD III, 39, dated 8.10.1780.

[41]NLW Lisburne-Northumberland papers, bundle 7.

[42]See T.W.Pritchard, 'Sir Watkin Williams Wynn, Fourth Baronet', *Denbighshire Historical Society Transactions*, 27 (1978), pp.5-48, and 28 (1979), pp.18-67

[43]F.M.L.Thompson, *English Landed Society in the Nineteenth Century*, (London, 1963), passim, using the edition of 1971.

[44]Ibid., pp.10-11.

[45]NLW CD III, 137. Wilmot tells his cousin that he has copied out an extract from 'A Peerage of England, Scotland and Ireland' printed for W.Owen in Fleet Street London 1790.

[46]NLW CD III, 26, dated 29.7.1775.

[47]NLW CD III, 22a.

[48]H.M.C. *Manuscripts in Various Collections*, VI, p.157.

[49]H.M.C. *The Manuscripts of the Earl of Carlisle*, p.562.

[50]Cited in Piers Mackesy, *The War for America 1775-1783*, (London, 1963), 329.

[51]Valentine, Lord North.

[52]K.G.Davies, *Documents of the American Revolution 1770-1783*, vol.XV, (Dublin, 1976), 52.

[53]NLW CD III, 32, 33.

[54]Lloyd Theakston & Davies, *Family Records & Pedigrees of the Lloyds . . .*, Appendix, p.ix, p.98.

[55]NLW CD III, 32, 33, 29.

[56]K.G.Davies, op.cit., 38.

[57]H.M.C. *The Manuscripts of Mrs Stopford-Sackville*, I, p.74.

V. 'YOU ARE ONLY A MAN'

We saw at the beginning of chapter I how the Vaughan family and the Trawsgoed estate seemed to have survived intact into the ninth decade of the nineteenth century. However, this chapter will show how the currents which eventually swept away so many great families and their estates had already begun to undermine the Vaughans and their hold on their estate long before the end of the century. The growth of factory-based industries and the huge increase in commerce meant that ownership of land was no longer the major prop of the wealthiest families, nor was agriculture any longer a potent source of wealth. The development of sources of cheap food in Australia and the American continent, and of improved means of bringing first corn and then meat to Britain, undermined both agrarian and pastoral farming. The Corn Laws were an attempt to hold back the tide, but they could not last; the population was increasing much faster than the capacity of British farmers to meet their needs. These changes, together with the spread of democratic ideas, retarded by the negative reaction to the French Revolution, but aided especially in Wales by the growth of nonconformist Liberalism, were to decimate the estates of the Welsh aristocracy and gentry. Twentieth century wars, agricultural depression and taxation wrought further havoc among them. Some families, apparently exhausted, simply ran out of children and disappeared. Others, lacking the ability to adapt or develop, moved to live in more modest circumstances. Eventually most were left with no more power and influence than their personal talents allowed, save for a residue of habitual respect.[1]

It is only to be expected that these great changes are barely visible in the sources for the Trawsgoed estate and the Vaughan family history. Estate administration continued, family settlements were made and remade, attitudes remained firmly traditional. In religion, for example, the Vaughans supported the established church; Capel Afan in Llanafan is one of few nonconformist chapels built on Lisburne land, and then it was tucked decently away out of view. They were not actively intolerant of nonconformity, as is well shown in the biography of Isaac Jones, a Wesleyan Methodist minister from Llanfihangel-y-Creuddyn. An undated incident, probably during the 1840s, describes how the local Wesleyans used to meet in Rhyd-y-cochiaid in the home of one of the Earl of Lisburne's shepherds, in full view of Trawsgoed mansion. According to the author, Lord Lisburne cared nothing about theology, but those attending the meetings were frightening the pheasants, and they felt well advised to leave Rhyd-y-cochiaid for Cnwch Coch; both Lisburne and Powell refused to allow them land for a chapel, but they found a free patch and built there in 1844.[2] In politics, too, the family maintained its Tory loyalty without question, and they seemed quite deaf to the questions being asked more and more insistently from outside their own circle.

The barest outline of descent will help the reader follow the Vaughan family story in this period; since three of the six married twice and another married three times, matrimonial complications are not acknowledged:

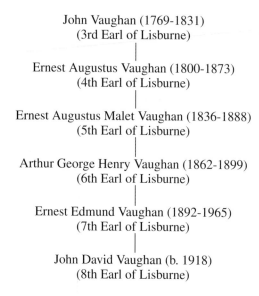

John Vaughan (1769-1831)
(3rd Earl of Lisburne)

|

Ernest Augustus Vaughan (1800-1873)
(4th Earl of Lisburne)

|

Ernest Augustus Malet Vaughan (1836-1888)
(5th Earl of Lisburne)

|

Arthur George Henry Vaughan (1862-1899)
(6th Earl of Lisburne)

|

Ernest Edmund Vaughan (1892-1965)
(7th Earl of Lisburne)

|

John David Vaughan (b. 1918)
(8th Earl of Lisburne)

The previous chapter described how Thomas Johnes of Hafod took over the county seat from the ailing first Earl of Lisburne, while the Earl's second son, John Vaughan, became the member for the Cardigan boroughs. To the aged Wilmot Vaughan, first Earl of Lisburne, his two sons were disappointments. As we have seen, Wilmot the elder son, was afflicted with mental illness and caused his father a great deal of distress. Nevertheless, even in his wretched and certified condition, he inherited the Trawsgoed estate and Lisburne title in 1800, though trustees acted for him. Unfortunately for the estate, his younger half-brother John Vaughan was a gambler, who had begun accumulating debts before his father's death in 1800.[3] Like so many second sons, he joined the Army with a purchased commission, which would have been at his father's expense; he was appointed Lieutenant-Colonel of the Loyal Sheffield Regiment in 1794, and Colonel in 1800.

In August 1798, at Powderham, Devon, John Vaughan married the Honourable Lucy Courtenay, the fifth daughter of William, Viscount Courtenay, and with her he acquired a dowry of £5,000. After the death and burial of his father at Mamhead in January 1800, John was principal trustee of the family estates for the mad Wilmot, whose personal welfare was the responsibility of Wilmot's half-sisters, Lady Dorothy Palk and Lady Mallet Vaughan. John Vaughan retained the Cardigan borough seat unopposed through the elections of 1802, 1806 and 1807. In 1812 he was opposed by Herbert Evans of Highmead, but kept the seat with the support of the squires of Hafod, Nanteos, Bronwydd and Llysnewydd, as well as by dint of securing many scores of new voters at Cardigan, which was no longer under the control of Gogerddan.[4] However, at the 1818 election Vaughan did not stand again. Although a sitting M.P. could not be arrested for debt, John Vaughan's financial problems must have already have become intolerable. On leaving the Commons, he found himself obliged to live at Tours in France for extensive periods until his death in 1831, in order to escape his creditors. When the lunatic Earl died in 1820,[5] John Vaughan inherited the title, along with the estates and many debts both inherited and self-inflicted. He and his advisers were able to act to reduce the long-term debts by selling the Mamhead estate, but the financial embarrassments detailed in the next chapter were a permanent problem, which like many of his aristocratic contemporaries he seems to have ignored as far as possible.

Surviving letters of Elizabeth Parry and E.M.Parry to George W. Parry of Llidiardau shed a gossipy light on John Vaughan's problems:[6]

> Mr Vaughan talks very much of going to England to educate his children. The 2 eldest they say are to go to France to be brought up there. They fix the day often for going, but are at home yet. 'Tis thought that money may be scarce. (18.2.1815)

> Mr Vaughan and Family have left Crosswood this good while, tis
> thought this way that they are not likely to return. The farm has been
> rented and everything belonging to it sold. (15.7.1816)

> The Vaughans of Crosswood are yet in Paris, now that he is out of
> Parliment he cannot appear in England because of his Crediters. What a
> pity a man of his property should involve himself, whereas a little
> economy, a little punctuallity in paying would have averted all his
> difficulties and he might yet have been our member with credit, but
> when one sees what gentlemen his Agent and the Nanteos are, tis partly
> accounted for. (4.9.1819)

George Parry commented curtly:

> As to Mr Vaughan, I understand he is a Gambler, if so, he is less to be
> pitied. (16.12.1819)

The two Parry ladies later tell of the junketings when John Vaughan
finally became third Earl in 1820 and his son attained his majority in
the following year:

> I am told the Vaughans are expected to Crosswood in a month's time.
> Great preparations, ale has been brewed as strong as brandy.
> (21.5.1821)

> Lord Lisburne [i.e. Ernest Augustus, Lord Vaughan] has been at
> Crosswood some little time & then returned to London. Tis said his
> Father sent for him and tonight they are both expected to Crosswood.
> Tis thought there will be a good deal of rejoicing etc. on the birthday
> the later end of this month. One very large ox to be given to the poor &
> one to be roasted whole, a smaller one.

As well as gambling, John the third Earl was also reckless in
another way. While there had been a growing tendency among landed
families to have fewer children than in earlier times, thus reducing the
need for expensive dowries and allowances, John Vaughan and his
wife Lucy (who died in France in 1821 and was buried at Enfield)
produced five sons and a daughter. The daughter, Lucy Harriet, never
married, and the first-born son, John Wilmot, born in 1799, died in
France in February, 1818, leaving the next son, Ernest Augustus, as
his father's heir. The loss of the eldest son at the age of 19 must have
been a shocking blow, but no references to it remain in the archive,
and no family correspondence appears to survive elsewhere. Two other

brothers, George Lawrence (1802-1879) and William Mallet (1807-1867), both married and have many living descendants.[7]

The new heir to the estate, Ernest Augustus Vaughan, did not make a promising start. In 1825 he was involved as plaintiff in an unfortunate action for assault against a neighbour; the episode is described in chapter VII below, and reflects little credit on the young man. Like his father, he was a heavy spender, and in 1827 he was taken to the Marshalsea prison, since he could not repay a debt of £3,000 to one Henry Wheeler. Readers of *Little Dorrit* will recall that all levels of society were represented in the debtors' prison.[8]

When John the third Earl died in May 1831 and was buried at Enfield, Ernest Augustus Vaughan succeeded to the burden of estate debts and the honour of the family title. By this time, as is described in the next chapter, the estate had begun to shrink. The Devon estate had gone and the Northern one was reduced; however, income from the Cardiganshire lead mines helped compensate for the loss. Ernest Augustus had hitherto remained a bachelor, but in 1835 he married his cousin Mary Palk, daughter of Sir Lawrence Palk, one of the trustees of the estate and husband of Lady Dorothy, Ernest Augustus's aunt. There is comparatively little about the fourth Earl in the archive, other than estate deeds, despite his long possession of the title and lands. It seems possible, though not directly proveable, that he was responsible for the splendid interior of the Library.

When John Vaughan left the Commons in 1818, the Vaughan leadership in county politics lapsed for the first time for seventy years. The period of that lapse was a dramatic one in British political history; the Reform Bill was passed in 1832, and was followed by the reform of local government. The title Liberal replaced that of Whig, and there was a more apparent difference between the two great parties than there had previously been. Despite the conservative influence of such Methodist leaders as John Elias, the swelling tide of nonconformity in Wales was to lead men towards supporting the Liberals, though the power of Tory landlords and the lack of a secret ballot forced radical tenant farmers to be discreet. Politically the Vaughans were almost totally inactive at this critical period; debts, enforced Continental residence and estate sales sufficiently account for this lapse.

When Ernest Augustus, the fourth Earl, finally decided in 1854 to enter Parliament, he was the last of the Vaughans who was able to take his seat (for the county) uncontested. The opportunity arose on the

Ernest Augustus Mallet Vaughan (1800-73), 4th earl of Lisburne.
Unattributed.

retirement in 1854 of William Edward Powell of Nanteos, who had
been returned unopposed since 1816. The Earl sat as a backbench
Conservative supporter, and was returned unopposed in 1857, but
retired at the General Election of 1859, when the heir to Nanteos,
William Thomas Rowland Powell, replaced him, staving off the
Liberal challenge of Arthur Saunders Davies. Thus ended a
remarkable period in the Vaughan family's history: it had produced
eight Members of Parliament in an unbroken run of seven generations

since 1628: Sir John Vaughan, Edward Vaughan, John Vaughan father and son, Wilmot the first Earl, his brother General Vaughan, John Vaughan the third Earl and Ernest Augustus the fourth Earl. Only the Pryses of Gogerddan, with twelve family M.P.s, produced more Parliamentary representatives for Cardiganshire and the boroughs than the Vaughans.

After the Liberal versus Liberal county election of 1865 when no Tory stood, the Conservative Vaughan interest made a further effort in 1868, in one of the most famous of all British General Elections. This followed the extension of the franchise, a development which was likely to favour the Liberals, though it affected the borough seats more than the counties. The Conservative candidate for the county seat was Edmund Mallet Vaughan of Lapley (Staffordshire), son of William Mallet Vaughan, grandson of the third Earl, and nephew to Ernest Augustus the fourth Earl. Edmund Vaughan had been born in 1840 at Mabws in Cardiganshire, but apparently spent little time there before the call to follow the family's Westminster tradition. He and his campaign are cruelly but realistically described by Ieuan Gwynedd Jones:

> the best that could be said of him was that he was young, and the worst that his digestion was stronger than his intellect . . . he scarcely campaigned at all. His Address, a perfunctory, ill-composed, platitudinous document..was greeted . . . even by men sympathetic to him, with derision, and he was compelled to publish a slightly more explicit one.[9]

It is perhaps fair to comment that the Cardiganshire Tories did not practise campaigning in the modern sense of issuing statements of policy or making public speeches, though they canvassed vigorously. A gentleman relied on tradition, believing that the electorate would trust him, that he had the right to vote according to his conscience, and he expected loyalty from his tenants and his network of friends and associates. Policies in the modern sense were hardly to be mentioned, though the disestablishment of the Irish Church was such a fraught issue nationally, and so relevant to the Welsh situation, that it figured prominently in the 1868 election. But the Conservatives hoped that their landed interest and influence with the county's lawyers would bring their candidate safely home. The landed interest brought pressure of various kinds to bear on tenants, who were embarrassed by the lack of a secret ballot. Both Vaughan and the Liberal E.M.Richards were virtual outsiders to the county. Richards was hardly a Radical candidate; Professor I.G.Jones has shown how he was able to use the Gogerddan landed interest in his favour. Ironically, the original polarisation of 1700 with Gogerddan as Tory and Trawsgoed as Whig had switched round many generations before 1868; the Pryses were now Liberal (of a very conservative kind) and the Vaughans Conservative in the party sense. At the vote E.M. Richards finally scraped home by 156 votes. The election must have been a strain for the Earl, virtually coinciding as it did with the murder of his gamekeeper Joseph Butler, described in chapter 7 below.

Following Vaughan's defeat, the Tory *Carmarthen Journal* cried 'foul':

> The Conservative party need not envy the triumph of their opponents, won by means which no one can justify. Dissenting ministers were specially imported from Glamorganshire into Cardiganshire to excite the feelings of the tenant farmers, to vilify the landlords, and misrepresent the character of the clergy of the Irish Protestant Church . . .

The voters were 'unnaturally primed with the prevalent bigotry entertained by a foreign clique' (i.e. nonconformist ministers!) and the party would have to learn to fight 'if the yoke of Radicalism is not to enslave the county'.[10]

The attempts made in 1868 by some landlords in some areas of the country to influence their tenants, and the subsequent expulsions of the disloyal, led to the establishment of the Hartington Committee and eventually to the secret ballot. Expulsions were commoner in south Cardiganshire than in the north. A generation later the Royal Commission on Land in Wales and Monmouthshire heard evidence throughout Wales in the early 1890s. The Commission was the result of years of agitation and complaint in the Welsh countryside. Campaigners claimed that rents were too high, compensation for improvements was not paid, the Game Laws were harsh, tenancies were awarded or taken away for political and religious reasons, and agents and landlords alike were often non-Welsh-speaking. These grievances were given every opportunity for expression by the Commissioners, who sat in virtually every agricultural town in Wales.

When the Commissioners collected evidence in Cardiganshire in 1894, many bitter memories of 1868 came to the surface, and three former tenants of the Trawsgoed estate came forward to give evidence. One of the three recalled an incident involving the Vaughans and the 1868 election. He was the Rev. David Davies of Hafod-hir, who complained that he had lost his Lisburne tenancy in 1868 for voting Liberal. The estate's agent, Robert Gardiner, countered this; he admitted that the Earl had gone round the farms *asking* for their votes but saying 'we will not press you to give your vote'. Davies, according to Gardiner, was a special case; he was a known Radical, who had compromised with Lord Lisburne by promising not to campaign against the Vaughan interest. He had, however, reneged on his promise, and was therefore expelled.[11] The other two cases are recounted below.

The fourth Earl held his title for forty-two years, longer than any of his predecessors. Much had changed in the Ystwyth valley between his accession in 1831 and his death in 1873. Most dramatic, surely, was the arrival of the railway in the Ystwyth valley in 1867, running from Carmarthen through Tregaron and Trawsgoed to Aberystwyth. This brought the estate a limited amount of useful cash for land sold, but was far more valuable for its extension of horizons and its transformation of the local economy. Coal and lime were more easily accessible, and merchants in both commodities established themselves at Trawsgoed station. Previously, most goods had been brought to Aberystwyth by sea and then carted up the valley, but now they could come directly by rail to the station. It became possible during the shooting season to send game to merchants in south Wales or the Midlands. That remarkable publication, *A Hunting Diary*, records how during the 1870s the Cardiganshire gentry took advantage of the railway to extend their hunting range.[12] The Gogerddan hounds would be put on the morning train to Machynlleth or Strata Florida, returning in the evening.

It is not always easy to date the many nineteenth-century developments on the estate and in the locality, but to Ernest Augustus Vaughan belongs the credit for providing the Llanafan village school of 1865, the Earl of Lisburne School, and for several years the Earl actually maintained the school. In 1866 a plan was drawn up for rebuilding Llanafan church; that particular plan was not carried out, but the subsequent complete rebuilding of the church had certainly happened before his death in 1873, at a cost to the Earl of £1,600.[13]

Llanafan church, and its Lisburne connection, deserve a little more detailed attention. The site is possibly that of a pre-Norman foundation, and in the mediaeval period it was an outlying chapelry of Llanbadarn Fawr. For centuries it remained a curacy, with the unfortunate priest being paid £6.8.0 a year, while the parish tithes (£136 a year in 1845) went straight to the Chichesters of Arlington, Devon, who contributed nothing to the Christian well-being of the parish or the fabric of the church. John Vaughan the second Viscount (d.1741) is the first member of the family whom we know to have been buried in the family vault. It is fair to assume, though there is virtually no evidence, that the family connection with the church was weak during the decades when Mamhead in Devon was to all purposes the family's home. Two generations of the family were baptized and buried either at Mamhead or at Enfield, Middlesex. But after the fourth Earl built the new church, his descendants and relatives over several generations endowed it generously with family memorials: several excellent stained-glass windows (and others more pedestrian), funeral hatchments, a splendid organ, and a box for the communion plate, as well as memorial tablets. On the right of the nave is the Lisburne chapel on its higher level having its own entrance, with obvious social implications. Did the pre-Victorian building have a squire's fireplace, perhaps, such as still survives in Llanddwywe church in Meirionnydd? In late nineteenth-century memory and for obvious reasons the main doorway to the nave was known as the

The Earl of Lisburne School, Llanafan in 1888.

Welsh Door, and the entrance to the Lisburne chapel as the English Door.[14] Despite this, and despite the family memorials on the walls, the church does not have the overwhelming feeling of a squire's church to which the public is only admitted on sufferance; rather it is, thanks in large measure to the Lisburne gifts, to priestly care and the pride of the congregation, most attractive.

Social relations between the Trawsgoed family and the local community before the twentieth century are difficult to fathom for lack of direct evidence. The cult of deference was of course overwhelming, as is implicit throughout this book. What did the family feel about the growth of Calvinistic Methodism in the Ystwyth valley and throughout the parishes where they held land? The estate leased plots of land for chapels at Blaencwmystwyth, Pontrhydfendigaid and Llanafan, leases which were eventually converted into grounds. Consent was also given to leases by landowners who owed chief rent to Trawsgoed, including Swyddffynnon, Trisant and Rhydyfagwyr. Did the tenants resent paying tithes? Surely they must have done, though hostility cannot have been directed against the Church or the Vaughan family, since the tithes went almost entirely to the Chichester family of Arlington in Devon (see below, chapter 8).

How did the Welsh-speaking tenantry communicate with the Vaughan family? It has already been suggested that Edward Vaughan (d.1684), son of Sir John Vaughan, may have been the last head of the family to speak fluent Welsh. His son and grandsons, the first, second and third viscounts, all born at Trawsgoed, may have acquired a little from wet-nurses or in dealing with their tenants, but the first Earl, as we have seen, spent much of his life in Devon and London, as did the next generation in the early nineteenth century, adding France to their family range. The sale of Mamhead meant that the family headquarters was once more in Wales, but it is likely that they remained thoroughly anglicised, with the one remarkable exception described below. That is not to say that members of the family may not have picked up a smattering of Welsh, since the womenfolk dealt with servants, and the menfolk with tenants and labourers. Such evidence as there is, however, shows that many servants were recruited from England and Scotland; the tenantry, on the other hand, were almost entirely Welsh.

The fine description of the fourth Earl's funeral, in the *Cambrian News* for November 21st 1873, is splendid evidence for the continued

public deference referred to above, though it is too long to quote here;
Ernest Augustus was the first Earl of Lisburne to be buried in the
family vault, though as we have seen his great-great-grandfather the
second Viscount had been buried there in 1741, and other members of
the family were already entombed there. The newspaper account tells
us that:

> The hatchment of the late earl has been placed above the main entrance
> of the hall, where it will remain, according to custom, for one year.

Two such hatchments, large wooden diamond-shaped panels, bearing
different versions of the family arms, now hang in the chancel of
Llanafan church.

An undated newspaper cutting of the same year, preserved in a
family scrapbook, gives the Earl a flattering but interesting obituary.
After acknowledging his headship of the Conservative party in the
county and his kindness to his tenants, the writer pays particular
tribute to his improvements on the estate:

> Nothing could exceed his fondness for beautifying Crosswood, and
> improving the large estates he succeeded to, a large amount being
> constantly expended in carrying out many material improvements, and
> with so much wisdom that it is gratifying to know his life was
> sufficiently prolonged to enable him to reap, to a considerable extent,
> the fruits of his policy. To those unacquainted with the Crosswood
> estates forty years ago, it is almost impossible to convey an idea of how
> much they have been changed, the results of the planting alone being
> marvellous . . . His herd of Hereford cattle was the largest and finest in
> the western division of Wales; while his flock of Shropshire Downs was
> the subject of his lordship's constant attention . . . No estate in Wales
> could offer a more complete illustration of confidence subsisting
> between landlord and tenant.

Four children had been born of the fourth Earl's marriage to Mary
Palk: Ernest Augustus Mallet (1836), Wilmot Shafto (1839), Edward
Courtenay (1841) and Elizabeth Mallet, who outlived all her brothers,
dying in 1921. Wilmot Shafto died young (1853). The Countess, their
mother, died in 1851, and in 1853 the Earl married one Elizabeth
Mitchell. She bore him a daughter, Gertrude, and died in 1883. We
have one small clue to the early upbringing of the children. The 1841
census for Aberystwyth reveals that Ernest Lord Vaughan aged 3 (a
mistake; he had been born in London in June, 1836), the Hon. William

Vaughan (a mistake for Wilmot) and Lady Elizabeth Vaughan, were in residence at an unnumbered house on Marine Terrace, probably Grosvenor House next door to the Belle Vue Hotel. Their parents were not present, nor were they at home at Trawsgoed. Four female servants were counted, and the head of household was one David Lewis, aged 60, a carpenter. Parental care of their infants was not apparently a priority with the Earl and Countess.

The eldest son, whom we may for the moment call E.A.M. Vaughan (Ernest Augustus Mallet) to distinguish him from his father, was educated at Eton (1848-52) and Christ Church, Oxford. Like his father and grandfather, he spent money on too lavish a scale, involving himself in severe debt, even appearing as a defendant for debt in the Court of Common Pleas over which his great ancestor had once presided as Chief Justice, though unlike his father he does not seem to have been imprisoned. His enjoyment of 'the races, and other places of fast entertainment' had led him to trust his name as security for a bankrupt gambler, Edward Courtenay (presumably a relative of his grandmother Lucy née Courtenay) a trust which cost him £2,000.[15] Most interestingly, he learnt Welsh, a skill forgotten by his recent ancestors, and when in 1888 his turn came to be laid in the family vault in Llanafan church, his will laid down that the service should be conducted entirely in Welsh.

E.A.M. Vaughan became the fifth Earl of Lisburne on his father's death in 1873, an occasion marked by the need for the first time to pay death duties (Gladstone's Succession Duty Act had been passed in 1853). The bill was for £2,006. The new Earl, who had been educated privately, had already married once, in 1858, but his wife, Laura Burnaby, had died in childbirth in 1865. Following his accession to the title, he pensioned off one Elizabeth Morris, a London mistress whom he had kept for a time, and he married again in 1878, his new wife being Alice Probyn, of Huntley Manor in Gloucestershire. After borrowing large sums from the Lands Improvement Company in 1874 and in subsequent years, the fifth Earl was able to make improvements to his inheritance. Originally the loans were for farm improvement, and some of the money was so used, but he gained the permission of the company to use much of the money to improve Trawsgoed mansion, a process which reached its climax after his death (in 1888) with the building of the new and ugly west wing of the mansion in 1891.

Unfortunately for the fifth Earl's posthumous reputation, an incident of 1875 is recorded in detail among the statements given in evidence to the Royal Commission on Land of 1891-5. David Jenkins, formerly of Cwm-meurig Uchaf between Ystrad Meurig and Ffair Rhos, told the Commissioners the story of his farm over the previous hundred years. His great-grandfather, grandfather and father had improved the farm with much work and expenditure, but in 1875:

> my father and a neighbour were looking at a swede crop, which was being destroyed by hares and rabbits. His neighbour advised my father to set a few traps to catch them, which he did. When he went to look at the traps the following morning, he was met by two gamekeepers who at once reported the matter to his lordship . . . he received notice to quit . . . the sin was an unpardonable one, being an offence against one of the most sacred laws of the estate. Thus my grandfather was turned out of his own house, where he had intended spending his declining years, and my father out of the farm where he had spent the best years of his life, working hard for its improvement, and upon which he had spent hundreds of pounds, to fare as best he might with his family of seven children, the eldest only 13 years of age, without a penny piece of compensation.[16]

The agent Robert Gardiner's response was a model of diplomatic tightrope-walking:

> It was considered a bad case at the time. It is long ago. Although he was a good tenant, Lord Lisburne decided to part with him, because he was right in the middle of his preserve lands . . . .I was sorry for the man at the time, but it was a case in which the landlord had to make a little example.[17]

It is good to record that descendants of David Jenkins are successful farmers to this day in the north of the county, and salutary to conclude that it was the estate which suffered by the expulsion of a good tenant.

The fifth Earl felt no desire to continue the family's long and active political tradition. While his father had represented the county in the Conservative interest, and aided his nephew's vain effort to recapture the seat in 1868, the son was criticised by Matthew Vaughan Davies, who wrote to Lord Salisbury:

> Lord Lisburne . . . will do nothing. He does not even subscribe to the Registration Fund . . .[18]

The fifth Earl's death in 1888 is splendidly recorded in the local newspapers of the day. He had died on March 31st at St Leonard's on Sea, Hastings, and the body was brought back to Trawsgoed by special train. On the afternoon of the funeral, the tenants, farm servants, neighbours and those who had arrived from Aberystwyth in brakes, carriages and by rail were marshalled in order. The Countess drove to Llanafan church in advance of the funeral procession, which was led by four doctors, six priests, the family solicitor and a deputation of the oldest tenants. Following the bier came the heir, Arthur Henry Vaughan, with other close relations, local magistrates, a choir, three hundred of the tenantry and a large number of the general public, especially from Aberystwyth, and 33 carriages. All the local gentry, old and new, were there: Powell of Nanteos, Waddingham of Hafod, Loxdale of Castle Hill, Pryse of Gogerddan, Bonsall of Fronfraith, Parry of Llidiardau, Vaughan Davies of Tan-y-bwlch. The attendance was about a thousand in all, and the procession to Llanafan must have been impressive, but the congestion outside the little church would have been considerable.

The *Cambrian News* obituary of the fifth Earl is worth citing as an example of the diplomatic skills a journalist had to exercise at that time:

His Lordship did not take a very active part in the affairs of the county, either in the administration of its finances at Quarter Sessions or in its political representation. He sustained the traditions of the house in being a Conservative and a member of the Established Church, but in respect of politics he was not unreasonable, and in respect of religion he allowed everyone about him to exercise the most perfect liberty of conscience. That he was a good landlord was testified by the enthusiasm of his tenants on the occasion of his return home after his marriage with Lady Lisburne, and again when the whole neighbourhood assembled to take part in rejoicings in 1884 to celebrate the coming of age of Lord Vaughan (i.e. the Earl's eldest son). He lived almost continuously at Crosswood and took a deep interest in his estate and the welfare of his tenants. He gave employment to a large number of men, by whom he will be greatly missed as well as by the poor for miles around. He assisted them in an unostentatious manner; and in this work he was helped by Lady Lisburne. Indeed, there was not a sick and poor person living within a very large circle around Crosswood who is not personally known by her Ladyship.

The Earl's widow Alice (who according to family tradition had done much to develop the Trawsgoed gardens) did not remain the family dowager for long; she escaped the embarrassment of being dowager Countess with, as we shall shortly see, her younger sister as the new Countess, by marrying the Earl of Amherst in September 1889, and after his death she married a Polish prince, Jean Sapeika Kodenski in 1914.

The sixth Earl, Arthur Henry George, was nothing if not energetic. Within seven months of his father's death he had married his father's sister-in-law, Evelyn Probyn of Huntley Manor, whom after a brief honeymoon he brought home to scenes of enthusiasm which were extensively described in the press; the passage is worth quoting for a glimpse of a social occasion now unimaginable. The couple arrived at Aberystwyth by train and transferred to the Manchester and Milford (Carmarthen) line, accompanied by a brass band and many friends and supporters.

> The engine steamed off for Trawscoed, amid the firing of fog signals and the hearty huzzas of the congregation of people . . . Others travelled by road, large parties going in two well-appointed brakes from the Lion Hotel . . . every farm house and cottage some miles distant from Crosswood were decorated with bunting.

Trawsgoed station had been specially decorated for the occasion, with a triumphal arch and flags. The couple were warmly welcomed, and a procession formed, led by the brass band playing 'See the Conquering hero comes'. Trawsgoed bridge was a mass of greenery, as was the entrance to the drive, where a speech of welcome was delivered by the Rev. W.J.Williams, vicar of Llanafan. The couple's barouche was then pulled to the mansion by a number of the tenants and workmen. At the house they were photographed, and a local poet, Joseph Morgan of Pontrhydygroes, delivered a brief Welsh welcome in banal verse.

The headmaster of Ystrad Meurig, the Rev. John Jones, gave addresses of welcome to the Earl and Countess, and presented her ladyship with a diamond bracelet, subscribed for by the tenants and others. Even more impressive than the bracelet's price (£267) was the size of the committee which had been empanelled to choose it and collect the subscriptions; it had no fewer than 78 members, including the captains of the lead mines still working on Trawsgoed land. Lady Lisburne responded briefly, and her husband at greater length, announcing by way of climax a rebate of 15% on the half-yearly rents

Trawsgoed station on the arrival of the sixth earl and his bride.

payable at Christmas. There were refreshments for all at Birchgrove, and in the evening Chinese lanterns were hung along the drive, while fireworks were let off and a huge bonfire burned on top of one of the hills facing the mansion.

The new Earl threw himself into local activities. He proposed the resurrection of the County Agricultural Society, and was extremely energetic in promoting the improvement of horse and cattle stock. He provided, and attended with his wife, Sunday School treats and treats for the Earl of Lisburne school. Interestingly, the accounts of these events close with the Sunday Schools singing 'Land of My Fathers' while the day school treat closed with 'God Save the Queen'. The Earl announced rent reductions again in the spring of 1889.

In December 1888 the Earl declared his candidature for the new Cardiganshire County Council, for the Strata Florida ward. Parliament's establishment of the County Councils to take over the responsibilities of the Quarter Sessions and other bodies for local government, represented an enormous change in political life. The Quarter Sessions, which had borne the brunt of local government, had been an unelected body, and was in effect the exclusive province of the local gentry. A number of democratically elected bodies had come into existence as the result of reforms and organisation of schools, water supplies and poor relief. The whole ad hoc structure was to be streamlined in the form of elected county councils (though they did not immediately gain responsibility for education). The aristocracy and gentry saw that they must submit themselves to the hazard of the ballot-box if they were to retain the influence they had previously exercised as JPs, and in Cardiganshire a number of the gentry stood for election. The Earl of Lisburne was fortunate in being unopposed when the voting took place in January 1889, and some of the gentry won seats in the Conservative interest. J.C.Harford of Falcondale defeated a Liberal in Lampeter, Col. Evans, the Lord Lieutenant, defeated a Unitarian minister in Llanwennog, Dr J.T.Morgan of Nantceiro defeated the headmaster of Ardwyn School and in Llanilar G.T.Parry of Llidiardau defeated a Llangwyryfon shopkeeper. There was a Conservative conflict in Llanfarian, with Morris Davies of Ffosrhydgaled defeating Matthew Vaughan Davies of Tan-y-bwlch (the future Lord Ystwyth).[19]

However, Waddingham of Hafod was defeated in Devils Bridge, Major-General Alexander Jenkins was beaten in Blaenporth, Sir Marteine Lloyd of Bronwydd lost in Troedyraur and Henry Bonsall of Cwmclarach in Bow Street, all to Liberals, and overall the Liberals had a comfortable majority on the new council. Lord Lisburne was one of the few Conservatives to be elected aldermen, but although he could certainly have expected re-election without question, he did not seek to carry on after the first term, perhaps because he had been defeated in a contest for the chairmanship of the council by an Aberystwyth coal-merchant. He was in demand locally as a chairman, and when the Society for the Utilization of the Welsh Language, the brainchild of Dan Isaac Davies, held its half-yearly meeting in Aberystwyth in May, 1889, the Earl was in the chair for the public session in the evening, held in the College Hall, and he was the first of a dozen speakers, and showed that he was not unaware of the changing tide of public opinion in Wales:

> I do not see why every Welsh boy and girl should not have an opportunity of acquiring a correct knowledge of their native language. The use of Welsh as a medium for the teaching of English [this was the aim of the Society] will, I am sure, commend itself to all (Cheers). If utility is not sacrificed to sentiment and this two-sided danger is avoided, I am confident that the utilization of the Welsh language can be made conducive to good results, particularly in Welsh speaking districts. (Cheers).

Much of the Earl's energy was spent in estate projects. In the Trawsgoed archive of maps and plans there are a number of designs which were submitted for his approval. Unfortunately some of these are both undated and undateable, but they belong either to the early 1890s or the early 1920s; both the sixth and seventh Earls loved a project. Their plans and achievements are discussed in chapter 6 below. The biggest project of all, of course, was the large extension of the mansion in 1891.

The sixth Earl sought to be popular. He was at least partly responsible for the rebuilding of Ystrad Meurig and Gwnnws churches. The Countess regularly distributed blankets to the poor in the upland parishes, some of them the gift of her sister, now Countess of Amherst.[20] A colourful account survives of a servants' ball at Trawsgoed, and though the year is missing from the newspaper source in the Lisburne family album, it smacks of the sixth Earl's era. A hundred people attended, including tradespeople and professional men as well as friends of the employees. Dancing began in the Library at 9 p.m., led by the Earl and Countess, followed by midnight supper. The meal was served 'in the large dining hall, around which are hung

Trawsgoed domestic and demesne staff, 1888.

portraits of different members of the Vaughan family. Dancing continued until 6 a.m. to the strains of Mr Wheatley's Quadrille Band.'

Such junketings may have succeeded in suggesting to contemporaries that all was well with the Vaughan family's long tenure of the Trawsgoed estate, but the rentals and the lists of mining royalties show that income was dwindling just as political influence had done. Deeper forces were at work. Like his father, the sixth Earl did not fare well at the hands of one of the witnesses before the Royal Commission on Land. David Morgan was tenant of Gilwern, a small farm in Llanfihangel-y-Creuddyn Isaf. Gilwern was part of the Cwmnewidion estate, acquired by the Vaughans a century earlier and now in the hands of Captain Vaughan, uncle of the sixth Earl. Gilwern was a small farm, and David Morgan had sought the soon-to-be-vacated tenancy of Rhos-rhudd, a 300-acre hill farm above Gilwern. Captain Vaughan's agent gave him permission, and with his blessing Morgan moved his corn to the new site and paid for the Rhos-rhudd sheep, in anticipation of the move. Then Lord Lisburne's keeper caught Morgan's 13-year-old son with two other lads just inside Lord Lisburne's plantation next to Gilwern. They were killing a rabbit.

The result was that the Earl persuaded Captain Vaughan to cancel David Morgan's new tenancy of Rhos-rhudd, although he was not expelled from Gilwern. Morgan was upset, not least because of the costs of the move, and when he met Lord Lisburne near Gatiau Gwynion, he attempted, despite his poor English, to reason with him, but was met with a volley of oaths and curses. Morgan's reaction is symbolic of the change that swept Welsh (and English) society towards the end of the nineteenth century:

> I told him it was a shame for his lordship to use such language, and I begged him again to let me speak. He then cursed and swore again. I then said 'Don't you think, my lord, that I am a dog. I am a man, and you are only a man.'[21]

When Robert Gardiner, Lord Lisburne's agent, gave his evidence, he deftly sidestepped a question on this case, as he was technically right to do, since he was not Captain Vaughan's agent and therefore had nothing to do with the matter. That the Land Commission received so few complaints about the Trawsgoed estate was probably due to the skill and experience of Robert Gardiner, who handled the most awkward of the Commissioners' questions with aplomb.

The Nineties seem to have been, at least in retrospect, a strange period in the life of the Welsh gentry. Politically they had become virtual ciphers, so near had Liberalism come near to extinguishing Conservatism as a popular cause in Wales. New democracy was, at least in popular perception, triumphing over ancient privilege. Abandoning the House of Commons as a lost cause, some gentry had tried to enter the new County Councils only to find, if they gained seats at all, that a Nonconformist shopkeeper or farmer might be elected chairman, and that as Conservatives, they were always in a minority. Some had already lost their estates. Others, like the Lisburnes, had been forced to begin selling, and though they still commanded large incomes, they had large outgoings as well. In 1873 the Trawsgoed estate was reckoned to be 42,720 acres, almost all of it in Cardiganshire where it was much the largest estate. During the Nineties the Trawsgoed rental was still over £9,000, and indeed remained at that level until the start of the First World War, though seriously affected by debt and sales.

The world of the traditional aristocracy in both Wales and England was in steep decline before the end of the nineteenth century. Dr Richard Moore-Colyer has charted the fate of the Cardiganshire gentry.[22] Wealth in land was not increasing in capital value or in real income, while the coal mines and manufacturing industry boomed phenomenally. It was the age, no longer of great agricultural landowners, but of Sir John Guest of Dowlais (d.1852), of David Davies Llandinam (d.1890), and of D.A.Thomas (d.1918), though of course Guest transformed himself into a Dorset landowner, so strong was the appeal of tradition to the nouveaux riches. True, the aristocratic Marquess of Bute was enormously wealthy and a landowner, but his huge wealth was due in part to his good fortune in owning much of Cardiff at the right time, including land where he could build the docks to export coal from his mines. In general, political power had shifted away from the aristocracy and gentry; industrial magnates, lawyers and union leaders were to be the early beneficiaries of this change. Death duties loomed over the great country estates at a time of low rents and poor farm incomes. In many areas, though perhaps not at Trawsgoed, servants became more and more difficult to obtain, since men and women were less willing to work in demeaning circumstances for meagre wages. All is summed up in those fateful words of David Morgan of Gilwern: 'I am a man, and you are only a man.' The century-old message of Tom Paine had reached the depths of the Welsh countryside; the age of deference was rapidly passing.

This collapse of the gentry and aristocracy seems to have been far more marked and complete in Wales than in England. The upper class in Wales, although apparently in control of so much of the land, lacked the great depth of wealth of the English magnates, and had less capital to fall back on when harder times came. There were no Welsh dukes, although there were dukes who owned land in Wales. The huge Liberal surge in Welsh politics, the shift of wealth from land to industry, death duties; these and other factors ran parallel with an increasing lack of self-confidence among the Welsh upper class. English peers could still lead in politics; Lord Salisbury was Prime Minister in 1900, and there were always peers in the Cabinet. But the world of Welsh politics was dominated by T.E.Ellis, Lloyd George and Mabon, with Keir Hardie to come. The elegaic mood of the Welsh squirearchy was admirably captured in *The South Wales Squires* (1926) by Herbert M. Vaughan, himself a direct descendant of Edward Vaughan the son of Dorothy Vaughan.[23] Many seem to have been reconciled to their own extinction as a class, determined to pass away gently, gun on shoulder and dog at heel, rather than rage against the dying of their world. Paradoxically enough, oral evidence seems to suggest that only when they were in apparently terminal decline did the aristocracy become popular. Many spent less time away from home, and involved themselves more in local and charitable activities.

Of course the Trawsgoed family's decline was comfortably padded. When in 1899 the sixth Earl died of cancer, aged only 47, an inventory of all the goods in the mansion and Lodge farm had to be drawn up in accordance with the requirements of death duties.[24] The inventory is truly astonishing; it fills some ninety long pages of a ledger, even though, for example, the 'twenty large oil-paintings' displayed in the hall only fill one line. A fine stained-glass window in Llanafan church was commissioned by his widow in the Earl's memory. It is much superior to the general run of nineteenth-century stained glass; one half shows St Hubert, patron saint of the Earl's favourite sport of hunting; the other shows King Arthur, with a lower panel depicting the three Queens gently laying the wounded king in their Avallon-bound ship. This was in tribute to the Earl's Christian name, as well as to his interest in his Welsh roots. The glass shows real skill and delight in flowers, trees, birds and animals, and the tiny hooded figure of a friar is the Whitefriars studio trademark.

The *Cambrian News* of 8 September, 1899, published both an editorial and an obituary on the death of the sixth Earl. The editorial is in the typical style of John Gibson, the paper's remarkable editor, although he restrained his often acid pen:

> The late Earl took no prominent part in public life. He discharged his duties as a magistrate and was the President of the County Conservative Association, but he was not eager for public positions, and the bulk of his time was spent in attending to his estate. He was an extensive game preserver and took great delight in field sports.

Much of the rest of the passage is in praise of Mr Gardiner, the agent.

The sixth Earl's early death was a drastic blow to the family, leaving a minor as inheritor for only the second time in its history. Ernest Edmund Vaughan, born in London in 1892, was still a small boy when he lost his father. He was sent to Eton, spending holidays at Trawsgoed, and it is at this time that an unexpected source provides a little insight into social life at the mansion. The source is that remarkable yet profoundly boring book, *the Life, Travels, and Reminiscences of Jonathan Ceredig Davies*. Davies, a widely-travelled man of many interests, printed seventy copies of his 436-page autobiography, a page at a time, on a tiny platen press at Llanddewibrefi in 1926. While living at Llanilar in the early years of the century, he was a frequent visitor at Trawsgoed, and was befriended in particular by the young Earl's thrice-married grandmother Evelyn, Countess of Amherst. Davies, an unashamed tuft-hunter, was delighted to hobnob with the county aristocracy. For example, in 1906:

> I again had the honour to be at Crosswood. We were about ten altogether at table, namely, the Countess of Lisburne, the Lady Enid Vaughan, Earl of Lisburne, Lady Elizabeth Inglis-Jones, Mr and Mrs Inglis-Jones of Derry Ormond, a son and daughter of Mr and Mrs Inglis-Jones, a sister of Mrs Inglis-Jones, and myself. When luncheon was over, I entertained the whole company by telling them a story about Fairies. (p.218)

The young Earl joined the Scots Guards in 1912, was briefly named an officer in Owen Rhoscomyl's Welsh Horse Yeomanry, and transferred to the Welsh Guards when that regiment was created in 1915. Trustees had managed the estate during his minority, and for part of the War the mansion housed convalescent British infantrymen. The young Earl survived the war, though wounded, and returned home to preside benevolently over the much-diminished Trawsgoed possessions. He did make one excursion into politics. In the turbulent electoral period of 1921-24, when the Cardiganshire seat was a cockpit in the struggle between the followers of Lloyd George and of Asquith, the Tories had not intervened in the by-election of 1921 nor the General Election of 1922, but gave their support to the Liberal, Ernest Evans, who was victorious in 1921 but defeated in 1922. In the 1923 General Election, the Tories put forward the Earl of Lisburne. He polled over six thousand votes, and was narrowly third behind the victorious Rhys Hopkin Morris and Ernest Evans. The Vaughans had produced MPs in the seventeenth, eighteenth and nineteenth centuries, but would not do so in the twentieth century.

The Earl married one of the great beauties of her day, Maria de Bittencourt (Regina), daughter of the Chilean Ambassador to Britain, who is still remembered with great affection in the neighbourhood for her kindness and striking good looks. When the Second World War began, the Earl returned to uniform, working at the Guards' Depot, and his son John also joined the Welsh Guards and was commissioned. During the war the Earl loaned the mansion for the storage of works of art evacuated from London during the Blitz. After the war, tacitly acknowledging in 1947 that the days of the great Welsh estate were done, the Earl sold the mansion and park to the government for £50,000, and most of the remaining farms to their tenants. It might be reasonably claimed that this was the end of the Trawsgoed estate, since the mansion had gone, but it was not the end of the *Lisburne* estate; the Earl retained a number of farms in the neighbourhood of Pontrhydfendigaid and Tregaron, and thousands of acres of shooting land, reaching from Cors Caron up to Teifi Pools, much of which remains in family ownership.

The sale of the mansion ensuring its maintenance for the future, though internally it was much altered for bureaucratic occupation. The sale was made with a reversionary interest in law, which is to say that although the Government's tenure was to all intents freehold, nevertheless the family had the first refusal should the Government decide to sell the mansion and demesne, and this right was eventually

Regina, Countess of Lisburne, by Sir Gerald Kelly.

exercised in 1996. The family also had the right to be consulted before major changes could be made. The sale of 1947 was a move both fortunate and wise; had the seventh Earl clung to the mansion for the rest of his life it might eventually have had to be abandoned like Hafod Uchdryd, or run down like Nanteos, since the burden of proper maintenance would surely have proved unbearable. The war years had seen the death of the Countess in 1943, and the Earl joined with her parents to place a stained glass window to her memory in Llanafan Church. He eventually married again in 1961, only four years before his death.

Not surprisingly in view of his early inheritance, the seventh Earl held the title and estate longer than any of his predecessors. He made over the residue of the estate to his son in 1963, and died in 1965. He loved farming, and between the wars he experimented with this building and that idea; the black-and-white dairy building near the main drive was one of his creations, as was the fine avenue of lime trees. He sent his only son, John David, the present Earl (b.1918), to

Eton and Oxford, and had his three daughters educated at home and at
Heathfield School, Ascot. As will be seen in the next chapter, income
from the estate shrank drastically after 1918; nevertheless, local
people warmly remember otherwise unrecorded acts of kindness and
generosity: a pension here, help with education there, hospital
assistance, gifts of money and food. At the same time the family took
frequent holidays with friends and relatives in England and Scotland,
in Egypt and on the Continent. Seen with hindsight, from outside the
charmed circle, it appears as a kind of dreamlife, extremely
comfortable, but entirely lacking in that arrogant and confident
ambition which had driven previous generations to alternate success
and excess.

The present Earl and his sisters, the Ladies Gloria, Honor and
Auriel, are the last generation of the Vaughans to have spent a major
part of their lives with Trawsgoed mansion as their home. In the 1960s
and 1970s the Earl bought back several of the estate's old farms,
including Cruglas, Swyddffynnon, and until recently divided his time
between London and Cardiganshire. Though his business interests
were London-centred, he continued his family tradition of serving in
Welsh public life, being President of the Wales Council of Social
Services, and Deputy Lieutenant of Dyfed. He sold Cruglas in 1995
and has retired with the Countess to live near Ludlow.

The present heir, Viscount Vaughan (David), was born in 1945,
only two years before the final sale of the mansion; his two brothers
were born later. David Vaughan lives in Glasgow; his brothers Michael
and John in London. It is John Vaughan who has been principally
responsible for the remarkable reversal of fortune by which the
mansion is once again in private ownership, in the form of a limited
company of which he is a director, and developments are awaited with
interest.

NOTES

[1] See for example G.E.Mingay, *Land and Society in England 1750-1980*, Longman (1994), passim.
[2] John Hughes, *Bywyd y Parch. Isaac Jones* (Liverpool, 1898), pp.39-42.
[3] Not 1813, as erroneously stated in DWB.
[4] R.G.Thorne, *The History of Parliament: the House of Commons 1790-1820* (1986), p.488.

[5]He was buried under the Communion table at St Andrew's Church, Enfield, on 9 May 1820.

[6]Dr Jill Barber kindly supplied me with all these quotations from the Llidiardau papers in NLW, the first two and last two from Box 14, the second two from Box 8.

[7]I am most grateful to Miss Diana Vaughan, a descendant of William Mallet Vaughan and therefore of Ernest the fourth Earl of Lisburne, for her kindness in giving me a copy of her detailed genealogy of the family.

[8]NLW CD I, 720: 'Henry Wheeler Complains (at the King's Bench) of the Honorable Ernest Augustus Vaughan commonly called Lord Vaughan being in the Custody of the Marshall of the Marshalsea.'

[9]I.G.Jones, 'Cardiganshire Politics in the Mid-Nineteenth Century', *Ceredigion* V, 1 (1964), pp.32 & 35. The article sets out the background to the 1865 and 1868 elections, and is an invaluable guide to their understanding.

[10]*Carmarthen Journal*, editorial, 4.12.1868.

[11]Royal Commission on Land in Wales and Monmouthshire, *Evidence*, Vol.III, p.720.

[12]Newton Wynne Apperley, *A Hunting Diary*, (London, 1926).

[13]NLW CD I, 1752.

[14]NLW David Thomas Papers, Llanafan bundle.

[15]NLW CD I, 1941.

[16]*Loc.cit.*, pp.676-7.

[17]*Loc.cit.*, p.720.

[18]Cited in Kenneth O. Morgan, 'Cardiganshire Politics: the Liberal Ascendancy, 1885-1923', *Ceredigion* V, 4, p.320. This valuable article contains another interesting if enigmatic opinion on the characters of the fifth Earl and his heir, this time from Viscount Emlyn, also writing to the Prime Minister: 'He is young, and, I am told, a nice fellow, but his father had one dreadful failing [*sc.* womanising] and I am not sure the son is entirely free from it.' Loc.cit. p.320.

[19]Results in the Cambrian News, 25.1.1889.

[20]See e.g. Cambrian News 10.2.1899, p.3; 17.2.1899, p.3.

[21]*Loc.cit.*, pp.684-5. In Morgan's words as printed, 'dog' is followed by a question-mark, which seems to me redundant, and indeed meaningless.

[22]R.J. Colyer, 'The Gentry and the County in Nineteenth-Century Cardiganshire', *Welsh History Review*, X (1981), pp. , and 'Nanteos: a landed estate in decline 1800-1930', *Ceredigion* ix, 1 (1980), pp 58-77. See also John Davies, 'The End of Great Estates and the Rise of Freehold Farming in Wales', *Welsh History Review* VII (1974).

[23]H.M.Vaughan, *The South Wales Squires*, (1926, reprinted Carmarthen, 1988).

[24]"The death of the Earl of Lisburne took place at his seat, Crosswood, near Aberystwyth, at three o'clock on Monday morning, Sept.4. His lordship took to his bed about three weeks ago, suffering from a tumour growing on the back. He was attended by several doctors, who performed an operation on Thursday, August 31 . . . The earl . . . was of a most genial and pleasant disposition." *BYE-GONES relating to Wales and the Border Counties*, Vol.6, 1899-1900, p.205.

VI. HOUSE AND GARDEN

Trawsgoed mansion stands in the Ystwyth valley, nine miles south-east of Aberystwyth. The site is obviously a favoured one, despite being open to the winds from most directions. In Cardiganshire broad stretches of low, level and reasonably fertile ground are rare, especially ground not subject to flooding, though small streams water the Trawsgoed site effectively. The river Ystwyth emerges from a spectacular canyon at Grogwynion, and two miles further down it turns west at Llanafan bridge and broadens out into a wide expanse of comparatively good farmland most of the way to the sea. The mansion itself stands on an alluvial terrace of glacial material: pebbles, clay, rubble and loam. The house is concealed from the road to Pontrhydfendigaid by a long strip of woodland, which has been sadly

Trawsgoed mansion in 1684 (Thomas Dineley).

ravaged by the gales of 1989 and the invasion of the rhododendron weed. Rather unexpectedly, the building faces north-east towards the foothills of the Cambrian range, defying the winter winds which blow across the open parkland between the surviving oaks.

The pattern of approach-roads to the mansion was originally very different to what it is today. From Aberystwyth there were two routes. One came over Banc Magwr from Llanfihangel-y-Creuddyn, following the present zig-zag road past Llannerch-yr-oen farm and perhaps close to the line of the Roman road. It skirted round the north-east sides of the demesne, then divided. One branch went to the mansion, the other met the roads from Tregaron and Llanilar close to the site of the present Tŷ Gwyn. The other road from Aberystwyth came via Llanilar; it forded the river close to the later bridge and for a short distance followed the line of the present main road through Coedcae, but then bore left to meet the road from Tregaron. This came via Llanafan and originally crossed the fields of Wenallt and passed Llanafan mill on Nant-yr-haidd. Particularly striking must have been the avenue of trees which ran north-east from the house to the road (now a track) from Llanfihangel-y-Creuddyn. All these features are clear from the 1756 demesne map which also preserves the second early view of the house. All except the avenue of trees are also clear in the minutely detailed map of the demesne made by Henry Mercier in 1771,[1] and from Thomas Lewis's maps of the neighbouring farms made in 1781.[2] Evident in the two early maps is the small palisaded deer park, of which no oral memory remains in the locality, but which is named in several documents, and consisted of 144 acres.[3]

Like any old house, Trawsgoed has undergone many transformations, not only in its actual fabric, but in its immediate surrounds and its relationship to the valley in which it stands. We know nothing of it before the first picture, drawn by Thomas Dinely in his account of the Duke of Beaufort's tour of Wales in 1684.[4] The Duke was President of the Council of Wales and the Marches, and would have expected to be accommodated in the best local houses. Unfortunately the pictures of 1684 and 1756 are not easy to reconcile. Although it is possible to argue that the house has been re-orientated; i.e. that the front was originally to the south-west, whereas it is now on the north-east side, careful study of the plans of 1756 and 1771 show clearly that there was no roadway or drive to the south-west side of the house. It seems certain therefore that the house always faced north-east.

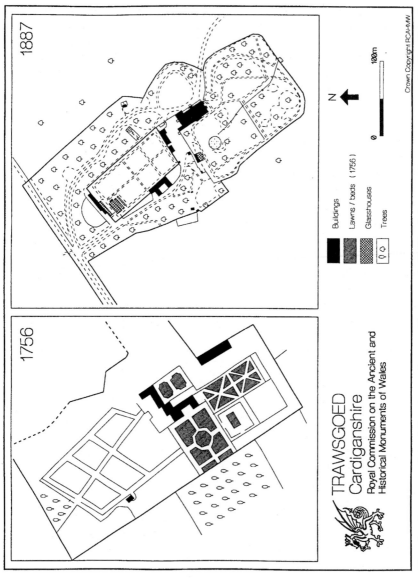

The development of the historic gardens at Trawsgoed digitised from early map sources by the Royal Commission on the Ancient and Historical Monuments of Wales. Crown copyright.

If it can be assumed that the ground plan of the house as shown in the maps of 1756 and 1771 is accurate (and they certainly resemble one another very closely), then the view of 1756 must be from the north-east side, the present front. This is clear from the nature of the westerly wing of the house, which in both the plans reaches forward and then sideways, corresponding to the 1756 picture. As for the 1683 picture, I now believe it to have been taken from the opposite side of the house, from the south-west, but I suspect that it cannot be considered entirely accurate, but that it may have been redrawn from memory. The 1756 picture shows a wall with arches piercing it on the right-hand side; a similar arch is just visible on the *left* in the 1684 picture.

That it was taken from the south-west may become even clearer by comparing it with the photograph taken about 1888. On the left of this picture is a lower wing with a complicatory extension to the rear; in general plan, these match very well in the 1683 sketch. Moreover, we know that this apparent addition to the house was demolished in 1891 to make way for the present large wing. The work involved taking out ancient oak beams with Latin inscriptions, supposed to have come from Strata Florida. It should be remembered that local abbeys are popular in folk tradition as a probable source of furnishings for churches or mansions, and it was the Stedmans, not the Vaughans, who owned the site of Strata Florida, but since the two families

Trawsgoed mansion in 1756.

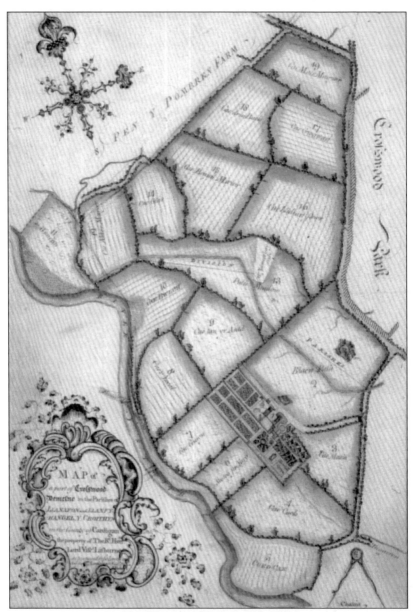

The Trawsgoed demesne in 1771.

intermarried closely in the early seventeenth century, such an origin is theoretically possible. It cannot be verified, however, since the beams have long disappeared. Fortunately the inscriptions were copied by Mr H.H. Herring, the headmaster of the Earl of Lisburne School, Llanafan, and published. Most of them are quotations from the Psalms; one is a verse from Isaiah and another from Luke's Gospel, both quoted in the Latin Mass, so that the Strata Florida origin of the beams is certainly plausible.[5]

I venture to suggest, in the light of that discovery, that what was demolished in 1891 may have been the oldest surviving part of the house, dating back perhaps to the mid-sixteenth century, to which the main body of the house shown in the 1683 sketch was added in the seventeenth century. Whether the extended L-shaped wing shown in the 1756 and 1771 plans existed as early as 1684 is therefore unclear, since it would have been hidden from the southerly viewpoint. One problem in distinguishing the 1683 and 1756 pictures is that there is a remarkable similar gateway shown in each. Either they were a matching pair, one front and one rear, or the 1683 view included the gates from a confused memory of the site.

It might be wise not to take the 1684 picture at its detailed face value. The view is perhaps better understood as an impression of a fine Jacobean or Carolean house with an interesting garden, fashionable in plan and elegant in execution. I tentatively propose that this house was largely the creation of Sir John Vaughan at some time before his death in 1674, but it possibly embodied earlier fabric. If the Roundheads had wrought havoc at Trawsgoed as Sir John claimed, then the Dineley house in part and perhaps the whole garden may date from 1660-1674. The picture of 1756 includes that house, probably with early eighteenth-century embellishments and extensions.

Further evidence for change in the house and its surrounds is to be found in J.Probert's survey and Henry Mercier's map of the demesne, commissioned in 1771 by Wilmot the fourth Viscount.[6] This delightful map, in Indian ink and watercolour, goes into minute detail; even the design of the farm gates is clear. The demesne map is accompanied by Probert's description of the house, and a detailed series of suggestions on reorganising the use and management of the demesne land and the neighbouring farms. The house is described as:

> a large, old irregular Stone Building, covered with slate, and Consists
> of 2 Handsome Parlours, a large Hall, which may be converted into a

dining parlour and passages, a good Kitchen with Scullery, Larders etc, to which adjoins a Housekeepers parlour and Closset on the Ground Floor, over which are 6 good Lodgeing Rooms, 2 dressing rooms and Clossets, and over them - Garrets.

At one End whereof adjoins at present 2 other small parlours with 2 rooms over them much decay'd and ruinous and therefore should be taken down . . . There is also adjoining the Kitchen between it and the proposed Farm Yard an old Brick Building with Slate Cover, formerly a Brewhouse which should be repair'd and fitted up for a Brewhouse and Bakehouse, and the room over it being upon a Level with the Kitchen, converted into a Servants' Hall, there being no such Room at present.

Before the Kitchen and Brewhouse is a paved court which may be divided into a forage Yard etc and at the North end of the present Stables is a large Bay of Brick Building which may also be converted into a good Stable, and in case his Lordship shou'd not think proper to Build a Wing answerable to that on the West side the Court, another Stable and Coach house might be Built at a small expence, about the place where the farthest old Building now stands between the garden and Cae Main near the end of the proposed Road which wou'd be nearly hid from the House by the Grove of Oaks and others may be planted for that purpose so that a Temporary Habitation with Offices might be made at an easy Expence for his Lordship to Reside in for a Month or two in a Year, while settling the Estate in Cardiganshire, or during the time of Building another House, if such should be his Lordships intention.[7]

Unfortunately it is impossible to know exactly how many of Probert's suggestions were realised. Wilmot Vaughan the fourth Viscount and first Earl regarded Mamhead as his principal home, and he spent time in London and on the estate in Northumberland, but he never forgot that the Welsh estate was the family's *fons et origo*. The classical re-modelling or rebuilding of the house in the late eighteenth century was almost certainly his work, though there are at present only two documentary clues. Following his father's death, Wilmot preferred to live at Mamhead, Devon, when not in London, but he visited Trawsgoed every summer when not detained by government duty. In 1767 he wrote to his friend James Lloyd of Mabws:

I am as much resolved as human accidents will allow to visit Crosswood the first Week in April, & hope the Plan I propose . . . as well for improving the Farm as putting the House into some decent order will show clearly that my Intention is not to neglect what so well deserves my Care & Notice.[8]

A decade later, in May 1777, he wrote to Lloyd:

> I have wrote to Mr Ed Hughes [of Aberllolwyn, the agent] to know if I can get two or three Beds at Crosswood, which I thought I might have, as so many Rooms are finished.[9]

Hughes's reply survives:

> I think your Lordship may with safety reside at Crosswood for a short Time, I can't say it is fit for the reception of My Lady Lisburne, the Room over the Gilt Parlour and that over the Hall have been well Air'd.[10]

A week later he wrote:

> the Colonade is not yet covered but slates and materials are ready for that purpose . . .

and it is evident that work on the house had almost finished. It therefore seems clear that Wilmot did indeed remodel or rebuild the house. The ground-plan of the main building does not seem to have altered as a result, but the fate of the west wing is unclear. It had disappeared before 1880, probably long before.

If we ignore the 1891 wing and consider the mansion as it appears in photographs taken in the 1880s, it gives a first impression of being all of a piece, a single creation, apart from the addition of the pillared portico. However, the structure of the house contains older timber, and the extensive cellars are perhaps of an earlier date. Part of a seventeenth-century stone stairway survives in a first-floor room, and the present main staircase is early eighteenth-century work. That there was an older house is obvious from the family's history, but it was on the same site; there was no shift of site as happened at Hafod Uchdryd. Thus the house must have been rebuilt piecemeal and not created totally anew, and it is not surprising that earlier features such as the cellars and timber survive, at least in part.[11]

Moreover, it is clear from the manuscript Ordnance Survey map of 1820 that what may be called Wilmot's house of the 1770s retained the two small south-projecting wings shown in the earlier ground-plans, while lacking the present library, but by the time of the Tithe Map of 1845, the library was in place, having been added presumably after the sale in the 1820s of the Mamhead estate, which paid off enough debts for development to seem possible once more. This magnificent room, one of the finest rooms in mid-Wales, has kept its

The Trawsgoed Library in 1888.

extraordinary nineteenth-century pillars and plaster ceiling with splendid medallions, though until recently agricultural journals lined the shelves, in place of the 3,900 leather-bound books referred to in the 1899 inventory. The superb carpet once on the library floor was cut up and sold in pieces to memento-seekers at the last sale in 1947. The extraordinary ceiling-painting is reputed to have been done by travelling Italian artists recruited by one of the nineteenth-century Earls; the Earl is said to have interfered so much with the artist's work that he flung down his brush, told the Earl he should do his own painting, and returned to Italy in a huff. Unfortunately his name is lost. The Library fireplace and the huge mirror over it are in good condition, and so are the splendid doors. Through the tall french windows there is a splendid view of magnificent evergreen trees and the Victorian-Edwardian garden.

The only other rooms which retain some aesthetic interest are what has recently been the Conference Room (once the Billiard Room), which has a good plaster ceiling, fine windows and an attractive plaster medallion over the door, and the entrance hall, marred though it necessarily has been by a security booth. In 1994 the hall still had a couple of stuffed stags' heads, a row of wooden chairs bearing the family badge of a raised fist, and several fireplace ornaments. However, the family portraits and other fine pictures that once filled the walls, and that can be seen in early photographs, have long gone, though most of them remain elsewhere in family ownership (see Appendix).

The exterior of the mansion is more pleasing from the southerly side, with the library swelling out from the main building-line, and the roof-line ornamented with a balustrade the length of the building. The north or front face is rather forbidding; the main entrance is covered by a heavy pillared portico of early Victorian date, perhaps 1840. The Ionic capitals of the limestone pillars have been unnecessarily damaged, and the pillars themselves show signs of repair, but the family crest of the Earls of Lisburne still looms above the entrance. The grim motto, *Non Revertar Inultus* (I shall not return unavenged) is still there; the origins of this motto and of the coat of arms are unknown, even to the College of Heralds, suggesting considerable antiquity.[12]

It is fortunate that a number of photographs show the mansion as it was before 1891. In that year the sixth Earl put into effect the recommendations of a surveyor who assured the Earl that:

> Crosswood Mansion is old, badly arranged and the accommodation is very inadequate . . . the sanitary arrangements are bad and very limited, and the home altogether quite unfit to be the permanent residence of the Earl of Lisburne and his family.[13]

Larger offices and servants' quarters were recommended, and the building properly serviced. Thomas Aldwinckle of London was called in, and it was he who designed the large ugly west wing which overwhelms the proportions of the original house, and in which a Turkish bath was installed. In addition, alterations were made to the old house, a lodge was built, the water supply greatly improved and the outbuildings reconstructed and extended; the expense was met partly from the sales of land during the 1880s and partly from borrowing. The surveyor was certainly right to advise modernisation; the sanitary arrangements and kitchen were probably very poor, and the family employed many servants. An extension of even larger proportions was made to Gogerddan mansion, with the same end in view. However, the age of servants was drawing to a close; a much smaller extension would have been far wiser in view of the inevitable costs of maintenance on an estate income that was not increasing. However, we may nevertheless be grateful for the 1891 wing; had it not been built, it may be doubted whether the Government would have seen fit to buy the mansion for conversion to offices, and had that not happened, it might by now have simply been abandoned. Aldwinckle proposed fitting stained glass between some of the portico pillars, but fortunately this ghastly plan was never executed.[14]

It is unfortunate that so little evidence survives for the domestic life of the house; such evidence as there is has already been cited in previous chapters. The lack of information is partly due to the dearth of personal correspondence in the archive, and partly to the fact that from the mid-eighteenth century two generations of the family lived in England and France, and the house spent long periods being rented out. It is doubtful whether aristocratic life in Cardiganshire differed much from that described by Mark Girouard in English country houses; to a large extent Trawsgoed must have been an English island in a Welsh sea.[15] Domestic and estate staff were often English or Scottish; the family was anglophone and anglican.

The mansion owes its present good condition to Government expenditure. Following the purchase in 1947, the building was adapted for use as offices of the Ministry of Agriculture and Fisheries, and until 1995 was the Welsh headquarters of the Agricultural Advisory Service and also part of the Institute for Grassland and Environmental Research (IGER), which still retains the home (Lodge) farm. A laboratory block built in the 1970s lurks discreetly behind trees, as well it may. Unfortunately the fine old Lodge farm house, almost certainly built of local bricks, was demolished in recent times.

From the mansion steps the view northwards is still essentially park-pasture, created towards the end of the eighteenth century. Capability Brown had worked with the first Earl of Lisburne at Mamhead, and his indirect influence seems evident in Trawsgoed park.[16] The photograph of the park taken in 1888 shows a scene of typical open parkland, and some of the individual trees are still recognisable today. However, the maps of 1756 and 1771 show a rather different scene. A formal avenue of trees strode towards the north (originally the rear) of the house, and beyond it was the small deer park.

The evidence for the first Earl's alterations to the park is clear enough. In a memorandum of 1788 for tasks to be done at Trawsgoed, he says:

> Hedges on the Demesne to be all made up, Banks repair'd, Water Courses opened in Palu & elsewhere, the Hedges on each side the Avenue fronting the House to be levelled & taken away so that the whole may look like one great Lawn [my italics] from the Avenue of Oaks, to Palu.[17]

Other drastic changes were made, perhaps as late as 1850. Immediately to the east of the original demesne was the farm of Maesdwyffrwd, once itself the centre of a tiny estate. It was mapped in 1781, and looked like any other of the estate's lowland farms.

The vanished farm of Maesdwyffrwd, 1781.

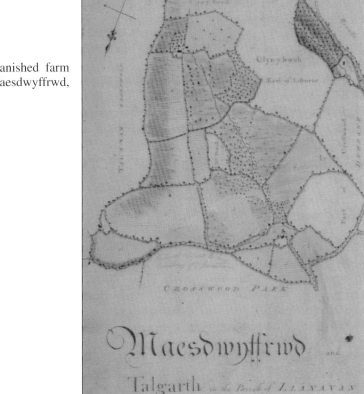

Eventually it was converted (even the buildings disappeared) to tree-scattered grassland and plantations. Beyond these are further plantations on the slopes of Tal-fan. Separating the front garden from the pasture today is a curved wall with fine gates and a ha-ha; the gates resemble those to be seen in the earliest picture of the mansion; like the curved wall, however, they were the work of the seventh Earl in the early twentieth century, based either on the gates shown in the 1683 Dinely picture, of which a copy once hung in the house, or the 1756 picture. Photographs of 1888 shows the ha-ha, but no wall or gates.

Between the rear of the mansion and the road, but still screened by trees from public gaze, is the present garden, a splendid nineteenth and early twentieth century creation whose great trees are now mature, and are even starting to show signs of over-maturity. The site has been gardened for centuries, and sensitive archaeological investigation might teach us a great deal about its history. At present the best guide are the plans of 1756 and 1771, and for the purpose of this discussion it will be assumed that the house has always faced north-east (despite the misgivings expressed earlier), and this survey will progress from the front clockwise round the building.

In the 1756 plan, to the front of the house are the twin lawns which are also clearly seen in the 1756 picture. It is difficult to determine to what extent the 1771 plan, intended to illustrate alterations to the demesne which are proposed in the accompanying document, is an actual representation of what was on the ground at the time. A major discrepancy between 1756 and 1771 is the absence in the former of the grove of trees indicated in the latter to the south-east side of the front lawns. In 1771, according to Probert's survey, the trees were tall enough to screen a stable block. They must have been planted in the late 1750s.

Next to the site of the oak-grove, the 1756 plan shows two areas divided into triangles; in 1771 this is rather obscure, but they may have been ornamental shrubberies. Next to this area are the bowling green and what seems to be a rectangular pond; these are clearly unchanged from 1756 to 1771. The feature directly to the rear of the house is, in both 1683 and 1756, a quartered lawn. By 1756 there was a circular central feature; by 1771 this was an octagonal pond, which today is round. Finally there is to the north-west what appears to be a large walled or hedged garden, as might well be expected, though the plans for 1756 and 1771 differ considerably in layout.

Unfortunately the house, demesne and garden plan has been cut out of the survey of 1781, though the schedule survives, and the Tithe Map of 1848 contains little detail; however, the walled garden and curvilinear paths are indicated. More detailed is the evidence of photograph albums, and a few details that can be culled from documentary sources. Photographs from 1884 till about 1890 are mostly of the rear lawn and pond. They show many flowerbeds dug in the lawn, a large greenhouse on the north-west side, and numerous deciduous trees beyond the pond, whose surround was stepped into the water. On the bank to the south-east of the lawn stood a summer-house, and beyond it a large grassed area, half of which was a tennis court, and beyond that again a number of recently-planted trees and shrubs. The view of this area shows, as one would expect, that the oak-grove south-east of the house was well-grown.

Trawsgoed garden: a heraldic beast.

The most important detail in the garden's recent history must be the date of its major extension south-westwards. The 1756 and 1771 plans both show two small fields, Scotch Fir Yard and Cae Gwyn, between the garden and the road, and they were still in place in 1845. A sketch in pencil and crayon dated 17 July 1889 seems to be the design for this later extension of the garden.[18] The two fields were taken in and planted with what today are mighty conifers and fine araucarias. This collection of trees is a notable one, and in mid-Wales it is only excelled by Powis Castle.

As well as the wellingtonias and araucarias, and the fine English oak and beech, the garden holds good specimens of more exotic trees: Bhutan Pine from Afghanistan, Incense Cedar, Nootka Cypress and Smooth Arizona Cypress from North America, Sawara Cypress from Japan, Myrobalan Plum and Pissard's Plum from Asia, Willow-Leafed Pear from Asia Minor, Hinkoi Cypress from Japan, and many more. Hyde and Harrison noted a number of specimen trees in the Trawsgoed garden, including a Western Red Cedar which was 95' tall in 1969 and a Silver Birch of 69'.[19] Fine trees were also planted at chosen spots on the estate in the Ystwyth valley. For example, prominently placed at Tan-yr-allt, Abermagwr, there was a mighty Silver Fir, felled alas by the great gale of 1976, and there are several fine trees of various species near Dolau-afan, Llanafan Bridge and at Birchgrove (the estate dower house) by Trawsgoed bridge.

The sixth Earl (d.1899) was a key figure in the development of the garden. One photograph shows that the south-east bank was terraced, and had two flights of steps up the terraced bank to the summer-house which seem to be brand-new; all these details are indicated in the sketch-plan of 1889. The terracing between the main lawn and the south-west extension was certainly his work, including the fine garden statuary which ornaments the work. For this we have not only surviving plans, but also the evidence of the Earl's obituary:

> The gardens on the south side were also relaid and terraced and ornamented with fountains and summer houses and hot houses. . . . His collection of orchids was varied and valuable . . .[20]

Following the Earl's death in 1899 it is likely that little was done to alter the gardens until the seventh Earl's return from the First World War and his marriage. The new Countess undertook a number of projects. Her small but dramatic water-garden, exploiting the little stream which feeds the pond, survives. The present Earl recalls the importance of the pond to his maternal (Chilean) grandmother, who despite her loathing of the countryside, paid annual visits to Trawsgoed in the 1920s. Her only rural pleasure was fishing in the pond, which had to be well-stocked before her arrival; the family's children were employed to bait her hooks, from which servants duly detached the fish she caught. Her daughter the Countess also created a large rose-garden on the south-east terraces, whose memory survives in a photograph of c.1930, but which have been totally swept away. The seventh Earl was a man of projects, several of which he carried into effect. One was the black-and-white dairy house which survives near the main drive; according to the present Earl, the cattle did not thrive there. Another was the present wall bounding the garden to the north-east front of the house. A projected golf-course never came to fruition, nor did an east lodge at Gatiau Gwynion.[21]

*   *   *

Although access to the gardens during their period in Government ownership from 1947 till the time of writing was not advertised to the public, neither was it denied; applications to visit were rarely refused, and the tennis court (not the one shown in the c.1890 photograph mentioned above) was available for local use. Visiting the gardens has always been a delight. To the south-east the splendid grove of large oaks is very different from the poorly nourished, much-coppiced and now neglected sessile oak scrub which still survives in ecologically valuable patches on the Ystwyth valley's slopes. In spring, bluebells cover the ground here, filling the air with perfume. In May fine rhododendrons and azaleas blaze among the trees, of which some were commemorative plantings, by the Prince of Wales in 1923 for example. By the main lawn a stream tinkles down through the Countess's water-garden, running past a large wading bird (apparently a giant metal heron) and a small stone pelican. Large golden orfe lurk in the formal round pond at the lawn's centre.

The main lawn is wide open to the sun, yet sheltered from the winds, but the large tree plantation has a different atmosphere. The trees rise, dark, enormous and resinous on either side of a grass walkway which ends in a splendid curved garden seat almost overwhelmed by a tree. A path to the left takes the visitor round the periphery of the garden, at first under the branches, but then in more open shrubland, past the tennis-court and eventually to the oak-grove. Visiting Trawsgoed gardens was always a delight, and it is intended that this pleasure will be renewed under the reinstated family ownership. This will not be cheap to arrange; at the time of writing the garden needs a good deal of professional attention.

*   *   *

The layout of early roads in the vicinity of the mansion was briefly described in the second paragraph of this chapter. It was oddly roundabout and inconvenient, and was bound to be rationalised at some point. That point came with the establishment in 1770 of a turnpike trust to administer and improve the county's roads; Wilmot Vaughan, like all the other local landowners, was a trustee,[22] and received interest payments on his loan of £550; it was his banker who managed the trust's investments.[23] The trust allotted sums of money to contractors (often local gentry) to improve or create roads. Between 1773 and 1786 the present B4340 from Aberystwyth (Southgate) to Llanafan bridge via New Cross and Abermagwr was gradually brought into being. This brought drastic alterations to the local road pattern. The old roads were nearly all downgraded or abandoned. As well as the new main road, a new access road to Llanafan was made (still known as *Ffordd Newydd*), and an entirely new access to the mansion itself, the present main drive, was provided. The main road must have prompted the planting of the tree belt which gives privacy to the house and demesne. At some later date the splendid but now sadly neglected white gates (*Gatiau Gwynion*) were sited where the south-east drive meets the main road.

By the time of the first Earl's death in 1800 Trawsgoed mansion and its surroundings had been completely transformed from their appearance at his accession, and would have been recognisable to us today, despite the absence of later features such as the library, the west wing of the mansion and the enlarged garden. The Tithe Map of 1848, sadly lacking though it is in detail, shows how much had changed since 1756 and 1771. The house had been virtually rebuilt. Numerous trees had been planted. The park-pasture had been brought into being at the expense of the shadowy deer-park enclosure. An exchange of lands with Thomas Johnes of Hafod, dealt with in the next chapter, resolved the anomaly of the little strip of meadow in the middle of the park-pasture which had belonged to Hafod. The great meadow at the heart of the new park is still known by its 1756 name of Palu, but the view was completely altered.

Trawsgoed mansion cannot compare with the finest Welsh mansions such as Erddig or Tredegar, nor are its gardens comparable with Bodnant. Nevertheless, in a mid-Wales context, and even more so in Cardiganshire, Trawsgoed is an interesting house with a fine garden, and its survival, with prospects for future development, is a cause for gratitude.

In Trawsgoed garden, 1990.

NOTES

[1]NLW CD III, 23C. Mrs Ros Laidlaw's help in revising this chapter is gratefully acknowledged.
[2]Available in the N.L.W. Department of Maps and Prints.
[3]NLW CD I.1257.
[4]Thomas Dinely, *The Account of the Official Progress of His Grace Henry the First Duke of Beaufort Through Wales in 1684*, ed. R.W.Banks (London, 1888).
[5]*Transactions of the Cardiganshire Antiquarian Society*, I, 4, p.64.
[6]NLW CD III, 23B (demesne) and CD III, 23C (farms). These maps are in the NLW MSS collection, not the Maps and Prints Department.
[7]NLW CD III,23B.
[8]NLW MS 14,215C, f.1.
[9]NLW MS 14,215C, f.26. Edward Hughes, of Hendrefelen, Ystrad Meurig, and Aberllolwyn, Llanfarian. He was Wilmot's friend, and may have watched over the estate in its owner's absence.
[10]N.L.W. Lisburne-Northumberland papers, bundle 5, unscheduled.
[11]I am grateful to the staff of the Royal Commission on Ancient and Historical Monuments, Wales, for allowing me access to the Trawsgoed mansion file.
[12]For this information and much else I rely on the family pedigree commissioned in 1921 by the seventh Earl of Lisburne from the College of Heralds, and compiled by York Herald of Arms. The unique copy on vellum is in the possession of the present Earl, and I am grateful for being given access to it. The arms are described as: Sa. a chevron, between 3 fleurs de lis, arg.; crest an armed arm, embowed, ppr., holding a fleur de lis, arg.; supporters dexter, a dragon, regardant, wings endorsed, vert, gorged with a collar, sa., edged, arg., and charged with 3 fleurs de lis, of the last, thereto a chain, or; sistister a univorn, regardant, arg., armed, maned, tufted and unguled, or, collared and chained as the dexter.
[13]NLW CD II, 1557, 1558.
[14]NLW Crosswood Plans 309.
[15]Mark Girouard, *Life in the English Country House*, (Yale, 1976).
[16]Dorothy Stroud, *Capability Brown* (Faber, new edn. 1975). Mrs Ros Laidlaw kindly drew my attention to the likelihood of Brown's influence.
[17]NLW CD III 61
[18]NLW Crosswood Plans 316.
[19]H.A.Hyde (revised S.G.Harrison), *Welsh Timber Trees* (Cardiff, 1977).
[20]*Cambrian News*, 8.9.1899.
[21]NLW Crosswood Plans 310 (1919).
[22]NLW Cardiganshire County Roads Board Records, A1 1770-1792 (unpaginated).
[23]NLW Cardiganshire County Roads Board Minutes, vol.1.

VII. MANAGING THE ESTATE

The problems of landowners in relation to their tenants have been well summarised by J.V.Beckett.[1] How could a reasonable income be derived from tenant farmers? What length of lease should be offered? Should leases be auctioned to the highest bidder? How could tenants be persuaded to invest in land they did not own? How could they be prevented from overcropping at the end of a long lease, thus leaving the property run-down (an agrarian form of asset-stripping)? Some but not all of these questions can be discussed in the light of the Trawsgoed archival evidence.

From 1547 till the middle of the seventeenth century we know virtually nothing about the early administration of the estate. Professional agents are not named in the Trawsgoed documents before the eighteenth century; David Lloyd of Breinog is the first of whose name we can be sure, and he left his post in 1729 following the fiasco of the second Viscount's marriage. Yet the size of the estate even before the acquisition of the Strata Florida granges in 1630-2 must have forced the head of the family to rely on a good deal of assistance, both from relatives and from employees. Unfortunately no papers survive from that period. One of the earliest rent-documents is a collectors' book of 1668, entitled:

> Rent Book containing the severall receipts of the severall summes received by mee since may 1666 before this time I never receaved any moneyes from ye Rent gatherers.[2]

The title is not quite accurate, since there are partial rentals for some of the Strata Florida granges from 1661, 1663 and 1664.[3] What is important is that the book was kept, rather clumsily, by John Vaughan's son Edward, who managed the estate for his father, and he lists the men who collected for him, countersigning a number of the pages with some revealing comments:

> This rent was payd my mother as appears by the old booke . . . Hee payed my Sister Lucy amongst other moneyes . . . Hee discounts for arers uppon Nantyfynaches in my mothers hands.

Obviously the whole family, including the womenfolk, were involved in accepting rents, though paid collectors certainly worked for them.

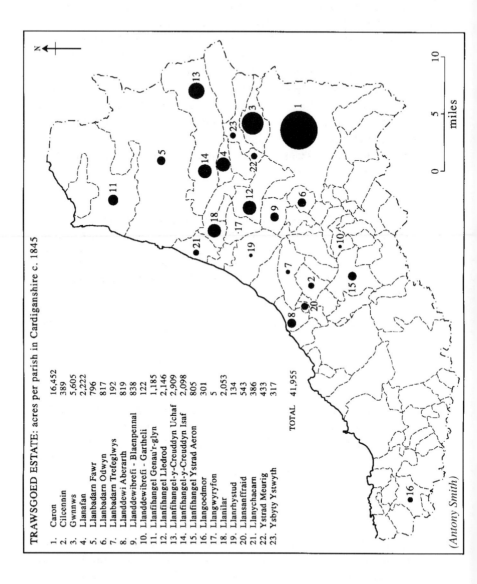

TRAWSGOED ESTATE: acres per parish in Cardiganshire c. 1845

1.	Caron	16,452
2.	Cilcennin	389
3.	Gwnnws	5,605
4.	Llanafan	2,222
5.	Llanbadarn Fawr	796
6.	Llanbadarn Odwyn	817
7.	Llanbadarn Trefeglwys	192
8.	Llanddewi Aberarth	819
9.	Llanddewibrefi - Blaenpennal	838
10.	Llanddewibrefi - Gartheli	122
11.	Llanfihangel Genau'r-glyn	1,185
12.	Llanfihangel Lledrod	2,146
13.	Llanfihangel-y-Creuddyn Uchaf	2,909
14.	Llanfihangel-y-Creuddyn Isaf	2,098
15.	Llanfihangel Ystrad Aeron	805
16.	Llangoedmor	301
17.	Llangwyryfon	5
18.	Llanilar	2,053
19.	Llanrhystud	134
20.	Llansanffraid	543
21.	Llanychacarn	386
22.	Ystrad Meurig	433
23.	Ysbyty Ystwyth	317
	TOTAL	41,955

(Antony Smith)

Only two Trawsgoed leases survive from before the middle of the seventeenth century. One is an enormous vellum document of 1633 in which John Vaughan rents to Jenkin Price two parts of Castle Flemish for £1.1.6 a year, which cannot have paid the cost of drawing up the document![4] Its real value was set out in detail the whole history of Strata Florida's original ownership of the land, and it must be presumed that John Vaughan—a lawyer of course—generated a mass of such documents for all the monastic lands he acquired and rented out for the first time, of which this is the sole survivor, and indeed is unique in the archive.

The first surviving body of leases is a series of copies made in a notebook; some are signed and others are not. The leases are for the spring of 1652/3, and take the form:

> Memorandum that Thomas edward hath taken his lands the 29th day of January in the yeare of our lord 1652 and his terme begininge at May next followinge in the yere 1653 payinge yearely during the terme of four yeares the sume of five pounds six shillings . . . and all duties heerin exprest viz 12 Chickin 4 geese 4 Shroue hens and a hogg and 4 work men for harvest work.

I postpone comment on these surviving medieval rents in kind in order to examine the early leases more closely.

These leases are for varied numbers of years: four, five and six years are the commonest periods. As well as rents in cash and kind, most tenants were bound to pay 'all duties, discharge rates and taxations', and to provide services to the landlord which varied widely. Some farms bore an extensive range of obligations to plough, reap, harrow and carry corn for the landlord. David ap Evan Thomas had 'to fodder two Barren beasts in the wynter' on Nant-gwyn and Esgair-maen in 1656. These brief leases never refer to land management and only occasionally to timber, as when Rowland Griffith leased his (unnamed) tenement from John Vaughan in 1657; he was entitled to 'herbage' (i.e. tree-foliage for fodder) but not timber.

Not all leases followed conventional patterns. In 1654 Hugh ap Richard leased the demesne land of Maenarthur from John Vaughan on most interesting terms. He leased not only the land but stock as well: eighteen milch cows, four oxen and a bull. He paid one pound per animal per annum:

> those kine are to be prised by two or more indifferent (i.e. unbiassed)
> persons att or aboute the first of May next according to the Markett rate
> and att the end of the tearme Hugh ap Richard is to deliuer soe many
> kine or the price agreed upon att the choice of his landlord.

This leasing of animals may explain the frequency of references in
seventeenth-century farmers' wills and inventories to animals in the
care of other farmers.

Maenarthur is high in the Cardiganshire hills between New Row
and Pont-rhyd-y-groes; no farmer would grow arable crops there
today, but for centuries virtually every hill farm grew at least some of
its own crops. As well as leasing the cattle, Hugh ap Richard had to
herd on the land sixty ewes in the summer, paying a stone of cheese
for every half score, and claiming every fourth lamb and fleece. He
had to winter a hundred ewes if his landlord required it of him. The
crops he harvested were to be divided equally between landlord and
tenant, with the tenant keeping the straw. Two Shrovetide hens and six
chickens were the only other requirements. Although the lease was for
eight years, Hugh ap Richard could deliver it up at the end of three
years if he chose; however, he renewed it in 1660 for a period of ten
years.

The notebook contains some eighteen farm leases, drawn up in a
variety of hands, and the lease of Dolfor Mill, next to Dolfor farm,
Llanilar, drawn up in February 1661/2:

> David Morgan Powell hath taken Dolevawre mill for the Tearme of
> one yeare payeing Twelue Teales of Corne and one hog six chickins
> yearly which tearme is to Commence at May next likewise John David
> and Thomas Jenkin both of the parish of Llanilar doe stand bound to
> John Vaughan of Trouscoed in the County of Cardigan Esq for
> performance of the said yearely Rent and are accountable for what
> Corn is received . . .

Apart from the intrinsic interest of these early leases, it is tempting
but frustrating to speculate on their author. The variety of hands seems
to rule out a single agent, and they are not in the hands of Edward
Vaughan or his father. Both men, as lawyers, could have drawn up far
more complex leases had they deemed it necessary. Yet the leases are
competently worded, suggesting a professional ambience. They are of
course in English only; they would have been explained orally to the
Welsh-speaking tenants, who had to trust the agent and landlord.

The thousands of acres in the Trawsgoed estate required considerable supervision. One early list of leases, perhaps from 1670, includes the kind of comments a surveyor might make. Of the grange of Doverchen (Tirymynach, Penrhyn-coch) we learn that John Stedman paid £60 a year for the whole grange, but:

> Ieuan Thomas Gitto holdeth the best Tenement in the Graunge all the houses decayed & down The dwelling house only Standeth unrovd [= unroofed] two ffoot thick of muck the Doors open & Cattle having recourse into the Same at their pleasure he hath paid no Rent for these three or four years past.[5]

Leases of the later seventeenth century are fairly brisk and straightforward; they are most often for three lives at predetermined rents. This was advantageous to tenants, since although inflation could be very slow at times, the tendency was always upwards, meaning that tenancies became increasingly profitable. The agreements usually contain only a minimum of information about land management. However, the numerous leases copied into a book of 1670 shows some development, and from 1670 onwards there tends to be more detail, with tenants more likely to have to give a bond (usually for £20) for observation of the conditions.[6] Tenants were usually bound to grind their corn at the appropriate mill (worked by another tenant of the estate), with a heriot, usually of oxen or other cattle, payable after his death. Tenants had to pay all rates and taxes, and sometimes were specifically bound to keep the buildings in good order, though this seems often to have been taken for granted, sometimes covered by the phrase 'with the usual covenants'. They might be forbidden to sublet without the landlord's permission, although this was not easily enforced. In 1665 Lewis David of Gwnnws took Pantyreirin, one quarter of the ancient demesne of Hafod-fraith, with a guarantee from his father to repair the mansion and out-houses. In the same document occurs an early mortgage notice for a property in Blaenaeron grange:

> David Laurence payes eighteen shilling yearely for this rent of ffiefteene pounds by waye of Morgage upon esgyr Saeson he payed me the interest to Michaelmas 1670 att which time he was to redeeme his lands, but I promised to Mediate with my father, that he should have time till Michaelmas 1673 to redeeme his lands he payeinge the interest annually.

In 1663 Thomas ap Evan ap Rees of Blaenaeron took the lease of Esgairberfedd-isaf, on the unusual condition that he should erect a barn and:

> one sufficient Dwellinge house with three Couples . . . for the erectinge of which . . . John Evan of Llwyn y Boydy in the parish of Lledrod, Smith, and David Mathias of Castell flemish in the said Parish of Caron, yeoman, have likewise Covenanted and undertaken.[7]

Sub-letting was occasionally acknowledged; Edward Vaughan's 1661 lease of Glennydd to Rees David Parry is bound in with Tyddynycoedcae, Llwyn-y-garn and Glennydd Mill, and the subtenants were named. Rees's brother Harry had already taken the neighbouring lands of Cwmbrenan, Llwynrhingyll and Tyddyn-y-maengwyn, but no subtenants were named.

Tenants might attempt to deceive their landlord; Edward Vaughan notes a payment of £1.6.0 by Griffith John 'for a litle tenement neuer enterd on the book but conceald by Watkin Thomas.' More unexpected is the demand made on David Lewis, lessee of Berthdomlyd and Tynyrhelyg, that of his rent of six pounds, two should be paid directly to one Agnes Thomas towards her dowry. Was this provision for someone's mistress?

A lease made in 1681 for twenty-one years between Edward Vaughan of Trawsgoed and Lewis David, of the farm of Tan-yr-allt in Abermagwr, names as rent six and a half teals of 'good and markettable Rye or Pilcorne', the second best beast for a heriot, six chickens at Whitsun, two geese at Michaelmas, one fat hog at Christmas, one fat hen at Shrovetide, two men to reap, two horses to carry corn, two horses to carry turf and two horses to harrow yearly.[8] There was an obligation:

> to make or raise one Perch of New Ditch sett with quick (i.e. hawthorn) uppon the sayd Demised premisses Every year . . . And Alsoe to Keepe the houses Ditches and Fences in Sufficient repair . . . And not to Cutt any wood

In 1731 Clwt-y-cadno (now *Cwrt*-y-cadno) in Llanilar was leased to Jane Evans on condition that she maintained a dunghill for manuring, though we cannot know whether such conditions, especially about cutting wood, were enforced.[9] Both these are early examples of attempts to ensure maintenance and improvement of farms by their tenants. A later twenty-one year lease of 1740 is more verbose, and lacks any reference to land management other than the ban on cutting wood, and a clause allowing Lord Lisburne 'full and free liberty To digg Trench and Search for Ore Coal or any other mines', with compensation for any damage.[10]

The eighteenth-century Trawsgoed leases retain the colourful, if apparently clumsy, rents of the mediaeval period, which had more or less disappeared across England and parts of Wales. Bryneithinog, in Caron parish, was leased in 1734 to Thomas David for £3.10.0, a hen and twenty eggs at Shrovetide and a heriot of the second best beast. 'The public house' at Llanfihangel-y-Creuddyn (now a private dwelling known as Lisburne House) was leased to William Hugh, yeoman, for £1.8.0, a Shrove hen with twenty eggs and six Whitsun chickens. Gwair-y-llyn (now Gwar-llyn) in Llanafan was rented to William Morgan, carpenter, for £1.15.0, a Shrovetide hen and twenty eggs, six Whitsun chickens, a Michaelmas goose, one day's harrowing with two horses, one man to reap the usual days, and a heriot of the second best beast.[11] These rents in goods and services survived on several Cardiganshire estates until the late 19th century, when for example Rogers of Abermeurig still claimed loads of peat and Shrove hens, though he admitted that he did not use the law to enforce his entitlement, and that it was often neglected by the tenants.[11] Many of these rents may have been commuted to money payments. An undated document in the hand of Wilmot Vaughan, the fourth Viscount and first Earl of Lisburne, entitled "Memorandums of Business to be done in Wales", begins:

> To receive my rents and Money for the Corn due & other Dutys according to the Rate they have sold at this Year at Market. To have a Rental of the Estate as it now stands, also of the Corn Rent, Heriotts & Dutys. Duty Lime & the Hogs to be paid for at Market Price.[13]

This suggests clearly that the rents in kind were being commuted for cash. On the other hand we know that in 1818 the local Trawsgoed agent, George Robson, ordered bills from Samuel Williams, the Aberystwyth printer:[14]

> 200 Notices to bring in Fowls, Eggs, &c.
> 200 do to bring in the Fee Farm.. or Chief Rents,&c.
>   (viz 100 in English & 100 in Welsh).[15]

Not only did Trawsgoed retain many mediaeval rentals, it also inherited such survivals of Welsh princely government as *gwestfa*, originally the king's food-render from his freemen, and *comortha*, a Welsh tax payable every three years. The right to collect comortha was highly disputed, but gwestfa was certainly collected in 1673, if not thereafter.[16] In turn, the estate still owed the so-called chief or Crown rents on the Strata Florida lands, the main advantage of these rents to the estate being that they were fixed in perpetuity, and were therefore devalued by inflation. However, the estate was often in arrears with payment.

Tenants' rents, too, were quite often in arrears, although at the end of the eighteenth century William Young, the London agent, commented favourably on the willingness of the Welsh tenants to pay their rents. For example, in 1796 he wrote:

> I find every Thing going on well here [Trawsgoed] . . . the Tenants pay their Rents better than I ever experienced.

Young seems to have been skilled at sympathising with the tenants while persuading them to pay. Rents were regularly raised on the estate; for example a group of farms paying £202 a year in 1762 had been raised to £340 only four years later. Between 1773 and 1820, which included the period of the Napoleonic wars, the rent for the Court farm (Penrhyncoch) rose from £39 to £115; for Llety Synod (Llanfihangel-y-Creuddyn) from £15 to £40.

Tenants expected their landlords to be willing to renew tenancies in favour of their widows and sons. Actually proving from the documents that the Vaughans met this expectation is not easy in the case of sons. The rentals do not survive with sufficient regularity, and on most occasions the documents were drawn up from scratch, so that neither parishes nor farms appear in the same order. Farms changed their names, or simply disappear in one document only to re-emerge in the next. During the period 1746-1793 many Trawsgoed estate farms paid rent to Dorothy Vaughan, the dowager Lady Lisburne, and it is not clear who managed the tenancies during these years; could it possibly have been David Lloyd, her friend and lover, formerly the estate manager?

As if that were not enough, the vagaries of Welsh surnames, and the frequency of a few names both Christian and paternal, makes identification of family succession risky. For example, the farm of

Cwmllechwedd was held in 1747 by John Thomas Jenkin. In 1759 Joseph Jones was tenant; by the rules of Welsh nomenclature he could have been the son of the 1747 tenant, but there is no certainty. In 1747 Berthdomlyd was held by Richard Owen; was William Owen, the 1759 tenant, his son? By English rules he could have been, but again there is no certainty. Only in a couple of seventeenth-century rentals are there direct references to filial succession; in 1670 the lease of Hafod-yr-abad passed from Richard Edward to his son, also Richard Edward, but by 1684 it was in the hands of Morgan Rees. In 1670 Lewis Morgan was given his father's tenure of Lledwenau, and it was renewed in 1678.

Despite these reservations, examination of selected rentals suggests that some leases were passed from father to son over several generations. Berthdomlyd, already named above, was in the hands of tenants surnamed Owen from 1747 to 1820. Maesbanhadlog was held by tenants surnamed Griffith from 1773 till 1850. Gwar-y-gorclawdd (later renamed Tanygeulan) exhibits the following series of names:

1759, 1767 & 1780 Edward Owen
1797 Morgan Edward (perhaps son of previous tenant)
1820 & 1835 Thomas Morgan (perhaps son of previous tenant)
1850 Evan Morgan

However, such tenancies seem to have been in a minority. In the case of sixteen farms in Llanafan and Lledrod whose tenancies it is easy to trace from 1759 till 1850, only Gwar-y-gorclawdd seems to have been held by the same family throughout. However, of the other fifteen, at least six passed once from father to son. Widows' names appear from time to time as tenants.

The habit of deference to the powerful has been referred to more than once, but this should not be taken to mean that the tenants were invariably deferential, nor were they always efficient. In 1777 Edward Hughes negotiated the leases of Maenarthur and Tan-yr-allt (both in Llanfihangel-y-Creuddyn) with 'two substantial farmers from the North' who were 'startled at the very ruinous Condition of Maen Arthur', and who haggled successfully for improvements in buildings and reduction of the rent.[17] Sitting tenants could be obstreperous, as William Young commented in 1795:

the Young Man who succeeded Walter Morgan at the Park [i.e. the Lodge or Home farm] turns out as unpleasant a Tenant as old Morgan

> was, having conducted himself improperly towards Mr Vaughan. This
> and other reasons induced me to give him Notice to quit at May next.

Young expelled another tenant 'as an Example to all others'.

It should be clear from the evidence of the first three chapters that
the Trawsgoed estate passed through two major periods before its final
decline. The first period, till about 1700, was one of growth and
wealth, with the estate in credit. But from 1700 onwards there were
nagging problems of debt, never fully resolved, and despite periods of
administrative effort and retrenchment, these problems combined with
national political and social change eventually brought the estate to a
virtual end.

We have already seen in detail how the estate suffered during the
period 1721-41 while the second Viscount drank, wenched and wasted
away his patrimony, creating a burden of debt that none of his
successors could entirely shake off. Oddly enough, however, the
archive gives the misleading impression that his reign began well. The
years 1721-5, immediately after the accession of the second Viscount,
saw the issue of almost a hundred new leases to tenants, suggesting a
tightening of the administration. This was presumably carried out by
David Lloyd of Breinog, since he was the estate's agent during these
years. Indeed, the archive is especially full for the whole period of the
second Viscount's rule as well as that of his brother and successor
Wilmot, the third Viscount, who died in 1764. Particularly interesting
is the 1721 lease of all the estate's mineral rights to a consortium of
West Country businessmen, for a royalty of one seventh of all the ore
raised.[18] Unfortunately we have no idea what income this may have
brought to the estate. It is plain, however, that the apparent sense of
efficiency conveyed by the archive must have been due at least in part
to the second Viscount's financial plight. In other words, the burden of
debt had to be met by greater administrative efficiency.

Despite the large number of leases carefully made during the later
life of John Vaughan the second Viscount, the colourful rent practices
detailed in the documents and the income from lead royalties, the
estate was still in debt and mortgaged in 1741. We have seen that
already by 1721 there were debts of over £5,000, and an increasing
number of additional debts are known by 1741. The year 1728 had
seen the creation of the £2,000 mortgage on the estate, which as we
have already seen was Wilmot Vaughan's excuse for not paying Lady
Dorothy's jointure. In 1733 the rents of a number of farms were made

over to Michael Helme of Westminster, victualler, valued at £211 yearly, until a debt of £900 due to him should be paid. Wilmot Vaughan's financial position when he became the third Viscount Lisburne in 1741 must have been extremely difficult. Although he is seen by J.M.Howells as the man who saved the estate from immediate ruin by his good management, Howells also allows that Wilmot's measures were short-sighted, like those of his contemporaries in similar straits.

Simplistically, it could be argued that these problems arose from the measures which John and Wilmot's father, the first Viscount, had made to protect the estate. By an arrangement of 1720 the estate was henceforth to be held in strict settlement for male heirs only; each owner was really a life tenant, with virtually no power to sell entailed land. It was therefore easier to raise a mortgage than to pay off a debt with cash, since money could not be raised by selling the settled property. Of course it could be argued that without strict settlement, the problems of debt caused by conspicuous consumption would have led to the early selling of land and the dissolution of the entire estate. As it is, the archive is full of mortgage arrangements made by Wilmot the third Viscount, his son the fourth Viscount and first Earl, and subsequent owners until the end of the nineteenth century. Wilmot in particular had to make efforts to resolve a debt of £7,000 to Andrew Jelfe of Surrey in 1755.[19] Further settlements were necessary to raise money for marriage portions and for relatives in 1764/5, 1768, 1776, and 1792.[20] These arrangements never succeeded in totally clearing existing debts, and were usually followed by fresh borrowing to meet cash-flow problems. Despite the arrangements of 1768, there was still an outstanding debt of £5,000, and it was a disappointment for the fourth Viscount to find that his Berwick, Durham and Northumberland estate was also debt-ridden. Parts of this Northern estate had to be sold between 1769 and 1775, which raised no difficulty as these lands were not part of the strict settlement on the home estate, and were therefore disposable.

Occasionally the deeds give us glimpses of the contemporary landscape; in 1734 the Viscount leased to widow Margaret Lloyd of Abertrinant a slang of ground 131 yards by eleven yards running north and south in Pen-dre fields (Llanfihangel-y-Creuddyn), bounded on the north by Pen-dre Hill, and on the south by the high road leading from Llanfihangel to Devil's Bridge.[21] Since Llanfihangel was probably a bond vill of the Welsh lords of Creuddyn, the land round about may well have been organised in strips in mediaeval times. The earliest surviving map in the National Library of Wales to show any Lisburne land is that of 1741 showing the Llanafan farm of Ty'n-rhyd (now Pengrogwynion), belonging to Gogerddan. Scattered around are small fields owned by Lord Lisburne, but most of the land was obviously waste and open, rocky ground. More maps survive of this farm than of any other, since the area was worked for lead during the eighteenth and nineteenth centuries, as the scars, levels and tips still show. Nanteos and Trawsgoed maps of 1763 and 1781 show how much unenclosed land there still was on the Cardiganshire estates.

The Trawsgoed archive conveys an impression of regular activity in coping with other problems. In 1755 it became possible to arrange the remittal of debts to the Crown on arrears of chief rents, due in perpetuity on the Strata Florida lands. In 1760 there were legal difficulties involving lands in Cilcennin in mid-Cardiganshire. Over a century earlier, in 1635, John Vaughan had leased these lands on long terms to his brother Henry; when the leases fell in a century later, other landowners moved in to claim the lands, whose boundaries and divisions were not clearly defined. These claimants must have been descendants of Henry Vaughan by his three daughters and co-heiresses. A case was heard in Chancery in 1761 and a commission established, and a settlement was reached in 1767.[22] An attempt was made to sell some of the Cilcennin lands in 1765, but we do not know with what success; certainly the Cilcennin demesne was still part of the Trawsgoed estate in the 19th century.[23]

However, if financial and legal issues were pressing, Wilmot I, the third Viscount, had resources to comfort him in looking to the future. We have seen that he had married well in 1727, at a time when he could not have anticipated inheriting the Trawsgoed estate from his elder brother John, who could still have been expected to beget an heir. He had thus acquired the eventual reversion of the Northern estate, and his son Wilmot II's marriage in 1754 brought in the Mamhead and Ashcombe estates in Devon, as well as a money dowry: £4,000 of Bank of England joint stock, and a £3,000 investment in a trading company. Mamhead was to become Wilmot's preferred residence, and his children were born there, the first generation of Vaughans to be born outside Wales, and some members of the family were buried at Mamhead. However, the Welsh estate was still regarded as the kernel of the family's possessions, and was of course in strict settlement, so that selling it was impossible.

After David Lloyd of Breinog, the next agent of whom we know anything is Thomas Morgan, an Aberystwyth attorney, and an interesting letter of his, written in 1763 to Wilmot the younger, survives. Both he and his master seem to have been a little vague on the geography of the estate: Wilmot had written asking to know where Llety Marchnad was, to which Morgan was able to give a clear answer, but he was ignorant of the whereabouts of the substantial Llanfihangel farm of Llwyn-brain. The agent was questioned about the acreage of the disputed lands in Cilcennin, to which he replied:

> I fear that if I pretend to take an Account of the Number of Acres there I shall do harm as the Welch Acres are infinitely less than the English. If I say that a ffield is but five Acres the Inhabitants will affirm the same to be Ten. You will certainly loose Ground there by counting the Acres unless you employ a proper Person to survey the whole.[24]

Thomas Morgan's letter shows that tree-planting was also in train:

> The Colonel desires to know your pleasure with respect to the firr trees. And wants to know where you would have them planted he thinks Alltvedw Hill a proper Place, so do I . . . The Colonel also desires you would be pleased to send down Seeds as soon as You conveniently can.

The Colonel was Wilmot's younger brother, John Vaughan, who despite his military commitments took an interest in the family estate, and had part of it in his direct care; he had also purchased in his own name the Llangoedmore estate near Cardigan. Tree-planting was a major activity for late eighteenth-century landowners, in conformity with the taste for beautifying the landscape, and was indeed an obsession with Trawsgoed's near neighbour, Thomas Johnes of Hafod.

Although Wilmot the younger spent most of his time in Mamhead and London, he knew his Welsh estate well despite the errors just referred to, and his *Memoranda* show some concern for its improvement. On the matter of scattered slangs and consolidation, he undertook:

> To inquire where the Slang call'd Camawr in old Morgan Parry's Grounds lies. It appears by the old rental to be let at 19s a year with a fine. By the old Survey it consists of 18 acres . . . whether the rent may not be much advanc'd. It ought to be distinguish'd & survey'd.

There appears to be some slangs belonging to the Philipp's in Havod Perveth Tenement which belongs to Kilkinnin. Wou'd it not make my Tenement more compact to buy them in, if not already dispos'd of. They seem by the rental to be of trifling Value, but may however make my land more convenient.

Much of this activity in exchange and consolidation of land may be associated with the surveying of the estate. In England estate surveys were originally written documents describing the owner's holdings, so that he might know what lands he held and how they were used. Gradually maps were added, usually including a map of the demesne and a series of farm maps. During the late seventeenth and eighteenth centuries these maps became works of great skill and considerable artistic merit, and their compilation was in itself a claim to high socio-economic status. The earliest Cardiganshire map of this kind known to me is the Grogwynion map of 1741 already referred to; its main purpose was not agricultural, but to show who owned which of the complex lead-ore workings in the area.[25]

The Trawsgoed demesne map of 1756 by W.W.Matthews may perhaps have been part of a wider survey made at the time, but if so, only the one map remains. Unfortunately it has been exposed to sunlight and the colours have faded, but it is still an invaluable source for local topography. It shows a large fenced park full of trees north of the mansion, of which no trace remains. In 1763 the Nanteos estate was surveyed by Thomas Lewis, one of the most active of a large band of estate surveyors of his period. He had so much work in Cardiganshire that he lived in Aberystwyth for many years. His earlier work is two-dimensional and plain, but later he was to produce a long series of beautiful maps, as we shall see. The 1771 Mercier map of the demesne and Probert's survey and suggestions for change have already been mentioned in the previous chapter in the context of the remodelling or rebuilding of the house. Probert made other suggestions, for example that the nearby farms of Tan-yr-allt, Penpompren and Llannerch-yr-oen should be amalgamated. Whether his detailed recommendations for dunging, liming and turnip-cropping were taken up is uncertain, though quite likely.

The survey of 1781 was carried out by Thomas Lewis, and survives in three splendid volumes; two large ones for the main body of the estate lands, and a slimmer one for the Court grange, i.e. the belt of land in the Penrhyncoch area running from Bron-castellan to

Troedrhiwseiri. Lewis charged fourpence an acre for surveying and mapping 21,546 acres; his bill fortunately survives in one of the volumes, as do his complaints about the months of time he had to wait for 'Mr Probert's coming into the Country to give his opinion of the Survey'. It was about this time that William Young of London became Wilmot's most trusted agent, and he had severe problems with Thomas Lewis. The maps are dated 1781, but in 1783 Young was actually complaining to his employer that they were useless and incomplete.

However, Thomas Lewis's work in this survey, using colour far more skilfully than in his early maps, is a pleasure to the eye. The maps naturally throw more light than written documents on the appearance of the Cardiganshire landscape in the late eighteenth century, just before an intensive period of dynamic change, when slangs, fields and whole farms were exchanged between owners, when field-division, enclosure, hedging and boundary-making were still in progress, and before the creation of turnpike roads. As in the Tithe Maps of the 1840s, we can see that much land was devoted to corn; even Tŷ-llwyd, in high Cwmystwyth, was producing arable crops from its tiny riverside enclosures, while Llwynpren-teg and Wenallt in Llanafan, like other lowland farms, were between one third and one half arable. However, since the maps freeze the landscape in a single snapshot, it is difficult to work out any details of crop rotation. The little Tŷ-llwyd fields must have grown oats and barley (and perhaps rye) year in, year out on the infield-outfield pattern, using winter dung to maintain fertility. The lowland farms need not have been confined to this practice. That the farmland was frequently exhausted is confirmed by Probert's 1771 survey of the demesne, with its frequent criticism of over-cropping and under-manuring.

There is also indirect evidence for the agricultural backwardness of the estate in the Lloyd/Turnor report on Cardiganshire for the Board of Agriculture in 1794. They comment acidly on the great landowners of the county:

> these occupying proprietors are, in general, as backward in their improvements, as any of the tenantry. They are more solicitous to add acre to acre, than to improve what they already occupy.[26]

It will become apparent below that change was slow.

Problems of debt, and the difficulties with squatters described below, as well as his political life in London, did not prevent the fourth

Viscount from buying new land, particularly in order to consolidate the estate; farms were bought in Lledrod in 1770 and 1772, and in the latter year three more farms were bought in Llanfihangel-y-Creuddyn. 1772 also saw the purchase of tallies in the newly formed Turnpike Trusts which were to change the face of the country by providing the first good roads since Roman times.[27] In 1783 Wilmot, now first Earl of Lisburne, bought tithe portions in twelve parishes (ten in Cardiganshire, two in Carmarthenshire); he paid £7,560 for an income reckoned to be £413 per annum.[28] Tithes were however notoriously difficult to collect, and he may have been disappointed by the true yield; the subject is dealt with in more detail below.

The buying of more farms during the 1780s included the acquisition of the small Cwmnewidion estate in 1786. The name of Cwmnewidion occurs frequently in the archive long before that year; the Vaughans had already acquired Cwmnewidion Ganol farm in the early seventeenth century. However, in the mid-eighteenth century the main estate was owned by a widow, Elizabeth Lloyd. It consisted of Cwmnewidion Isaf and Mill, Lluest-y-bwlch, Gilwern, the two Rhos-rhudd farms, Cynon Uchaf, Cynon Fach, half of Cynon Isaf and two houses in Llanfihangel-y-Creuddyn village. Elizabeth Lloyd's touching will, originally made in 1744, left all to her grandchild Ann Lloyd, illegitimate daughter of her son Charles.[29] Ann was her only surviving relative, and Elizabeth had taken her in and brought her up. Later, Ann married one Cornelius Griffiths, but after his death in 1785, although she had three children, she sold the estate to Wilmot Vaughan, who expressed his savage opinion of the worthlessness of Cornelius Griffiths to his friend James Lloyd of Mabws. Griffiths had built up a considerable pile of debts, and in 1777 Wilmot had lent him money in the form of a mortgage for £400.

In 1787 Wilmot bought out the annual Crown rents of £112 and the triennial commortha of £38 due on the Cwmystwyth grange lands purchased in 1630. An Act of Parliament of 1786 had permitted the sale of Crown assets of this kind, and Wilmot moved quickly; the deal cost him £3,047, which seems a large sum compared with the £7,000 purchase of tithes worth £400 a year. Tithes were revalued from time to time, which gave some protection against inflation, while the Crown rent was unchanging, so that buying it back seems therefore to be a small return for such an investment, though the saving in trouble must have been valuable. More important, almost certainly, was the acquisition of mineral rights under the former Crown lands.

As well as buying lands and making other investments,[30] Wilmot did a good deal of exchanging lands with other owners in order to remove anomalies and consolidate local holdings. Much the largest of these exchanges was that effected with Thomas Johnes of Hafod in 1790, which had been under discussion since 1786.[30] Wilmot gave up a block of lands in Cwmystwyth (Lledwennau, Prignant, Cefnyresgair, Gwar-y-rallt, Peiran Mill and Nant-y-Cau) in exchange for lands in the lower vale of Ystwyth (Dolfor, Ty'n-y-berth, Gwarygeulan, Ty'n-y-bedw, Dolgwybedig, Lluest Fach) and lands in Gwnnws and Ysbyty Ystwyth (Pen-y-bont, Penlanwen, Tai-yn-y-rhydiau, Dolgwsfach and Tŷ Mawr). He had to pay £240 in equalisation, but the deal was a good one. Johnes clung to the valuable farm of Glanystwyth in the lower Ystwyth valley, which was not included in the deal, and only came into the Trawsgoed estate after 1830.[32]

With the first Earl's increasing age, constructive activity on the estate slowed down after 1790, but the debt problem was still a burden, and indeed was increased by the gambling propensities of his younger son, John Vaughan. In 1792 the Earl had to raise £6,000 by mortgage of the estate for the benefit of his children by his second marriage, John, Dorothy and Mallet Vaughan; £5,000 of the sum was for Dorothy. In 1793, when a debt of £5,000 was called in, he simply borrowed £5,000 elsewhere to clear the first debt; that this was his usual practice is quite clear from other cases. In 1794 he was unable to pay off a debt of £1,000 without borrowing from his brother Sir John Vaughan, who provided more cash in 1795. Shortly afterwards Sir John died, leaving his brother all his property (including the Llangoedmore estate) and a cash legacy of £10,025, a welcome accession. In 1796 the Earl's gambling son John was in serious difficulties, borrowing a sum of £1,000 against a bond of £4,000. Readers of Trollope's *Framley Parsonage* will remember the nightmares that such bonds brought to the conscientious; John Vaughan eventually had that debt cleared for him at a cost of £2,000 to his mother and sister; in 1797 he also had his annuity reduced and then stopped altogether, though his marriage in 1798 to Lucy Courtenay rearranged his affairs to his temporary benefit.

Mention has been made of several agents whose names and correspondence survive in the archive. There were of course many other employees whose names are lost, but that of the estate steward, Morris Hopkins, survives. William Young recruited him in 1783. He explained to Wilmot that Hopkins had been brought up a farmer, but had 'greatly displeased his Father by Marrying'. The letter tells us what qualities were deemed necessary in an under-steward:

> [He] writes a very decent hand, & seems a tolerable good Accountant, he also spells very well and speaks pretty good English . . . and is a good Judge of Cattle. This last Qualification I think a very necessary one in an Under Steward of Your Lordship's property in Wales.[33]

Hopkins' wages in 1797 were £30 a year; his wife earned £7 a year for looking after the mansion.[34]

The survival in private hands of a small notebook kept by Morris Hopkins from 1801 to 1809 gives a brief view of the myriad tasks which had to be undertaken daily on the Trawsgoed estate and many like it. The lower part of the garden had to be ploughed, women had to be paid for clearing hay, sawyers, labourers, carpenters needed their wages. Peat had to be dug, a gutter made for the dairy, which then needed flagging, the hayricks had to be thatched, Coetcae field needed ditching, seven oxen had to be bought for £98 at Cilgerran fair, and a poor sailor had to be paid a shilling at the request of Mrs Vaughan. Calves had to be castrated, weeds burnt, lime brought from Aberystwyth and Aberaeron and distributed to farms, squatters had to be persecuted and farmhouses rebuilt. Estate work was never done.

The death in 1800 of Wilmot, the first Earl, created a new situation. Wilmot the second Earl was declared unfit to manage his affairs on account of insanity, and a Chancery settlement made his half-brother John trustee and administrator of the estate, while John's sisters Lady Palk (née Dorothy Vaughan) and Lady Mallet Vaughan were made Wilmot's supervisors. There was a reassessment of the estate's debts, which totalled £29,070.[35] Some £9,000 of this was owed to Sir Lawrence Palk, who had married Dorothy Vaughan and was therefore brother-in-law to the second (insane) Earl and to John Vaughan the trustee. John Vaughan had tried to meet many of his debts by paying annuities to his creditors; a list drawn up about 1805 shows 21 separate annuities. These were fortunately not all concurrent, but the largest was for £147 a year, and there were seven others, each of £100 a year.[36] The total capital commitment was £10,800. A settlement in 1805 staved off difficulties for a few years, but the debts were recycled rather than paid off, and by 1812 the estate was in crisis. A trust was formed by the creditors, but on the same day John Vaughan created additional debts by borrowing £2,210! There was a court case for debt in Great Sessions (1814) and after his accession to the title in 1820 there were at least two cases in the King's Bench court, one of which involved the imprisonment for debt in the Marshalsea of his son Lord Vaughan, a fate shared by many of the quality.[37] Chronic indebtedness was a way of life for the wealthy; Thomas Johnes of Hafod was always short of cash, and ended his life bankrupt, while the Powells of Nanteos, the Pryses of Gogerddan and the Richardes family of Penglais were similarly burdened, as Richard Moore-Colyer has shown.[38] It did not prevent them from living in comfort (even though in Continental exile) at the expense of local tradesmen.

The trustees did their best, after a fashion, to look after the estate. They asked Adam Murray of Edinburgh to survey the whole Welsh estate, and he produced a stinging report.[39] After commenting that many of the boundaries had never been properly surveyed, and describing the squatter problem (for which see below), he remarked on the potential of the rivers and streams for working machinery and for fishing, and the need for preventing damage by flash flooding.

> The woods on this Estate have been intirely neglected for want of proper training and fencing in from Cattle and Sheep there are many Valuable Coppices of Oak . . . which if proper attention had been paid to them would now have constituted a very great additional yearly revenue to this Estate.

Like many of his fellow-Scots, and like Thomas Johnes of Hafod, Murray was an enthusiast for turnips, 'that invaluable Root':

> but I have not observed a Single Turnip sown on all this Estate except by the Hon. Col. Vaughan himself who raises from 20 to 30 Acres in drills every year.

He recommended that the tenants be given free turnip seed, because if generally grown they 'would enhance the Value of the Estate more than doublefold.' He was wrong, since the conditions in Cardiganshire were unsuited to turnip cultivation, being too wet and too stony. The land seemed to Murray to be in poor condition:

> on many parts of this Estate a great deal of draining is required also Inclosing, and the whole buildings on the Estate are nearly in a State of Ruin ill situated for the occupation of the Lands and a great many of them dangerous to inhabit . . . The Sheep walks . . . are very ill managed

and Stocked with a bad Kind of Sheep. The Best of the Estate is under the worst system of Cultivation of any Estate I ever witnessed, the arable Land intirely racked out by Successive Cropping the inclosures all down and the buildings generally in a Complete state of ruin.

Murray's recommendation was that the tenants should only pay half the cost of draining, enclosing and building; the whole cost of the programme he recommended would be £20,000. He suggested that an 'active Steward' should be appointed. His survey is additionally valuable in distinguishing between the primary and the secondary estate; in the previous generation General Sir John Vaughan had farmed the secondary estate, now it was in the hands of Colonel John Vaughan. Murray valued the primary estate as worth £12,089 in rent per annum in 1813-4, but showed that it was only yielding £7,347. His report is sobering reading for anyone who might be tempted to accept Samuel Rush Meyrick's opinion that 'the Hon. Colonel Vaughan is reckoned the best farmer in the county'.[40] In fact Meyrick's description is qualified by his subsequent statement that 'whatever improvements have been made in this district are certainly to be attributed to the liberal exertions of Mr (Thomas) Johnes.'

Trawsgoed park under snow.

In any case, the debt crisis at Trawsgoed meant that land had to be sold, and since the Welsh estate was entailed, lands in England had to go. In 1822 the trustees disposed of some lands in Alnwick, Northumberland, for £5,100, and in 1823 the whole Devon estate was sold for £106,000, though not transferred to its new owner until 1828. This enabled large debt repayments to be made in 1828 and 1829; apart from the major creditors, there was need to satisfy a wide range of tradesmen. Sales of more of the Northern estate brought in £35,320 before the death of the third Earl in 1831. At this point there was still a debt of at least £9,900 on the estate, but the worst seemed to be over, and although the Northern and Devon estates had virtually disappeared, the Welsh estate remained intact.

With the accession in 1831 of Ernest Augustus, the fourth Earl, a new trust was created to manage the estate and the Earl's financial affairs, and some old debts were repaid. In 1834 the Earl and his trustees were sufficiently confident to invest; they bought Glanystwyth farm, one of the largest in the Ystwyth valley, for £8,995. As we have seen, it had belonged to Thomas Johnes of Hafod Uchdryd, who had obviously been unwilling to include it in the exchange of lands in 1790. Four Tregaron farms were bought in 1837 for £3,730, and in 1840 the Aber-mad estate of 1,360 acres (in the parishes of Llanychaearn and Llanilar) was bought for an unknown sum. Between 1833 and 1841 mortgages worth £25,800 were redeemed. All these purchases were part of a policy of consolidation manifested in the land exchanges of the 1790s.

However, the confidence suggested by these investments is belied by the new burden of debt which the fourth Earl inevitably built up. Large sums were borrowed in 1833, 1834, 1839 and 1842; by 1844 there were debts of £67,875. Debts of £22,700 were repaid, but ominously there was for the first time talk of selling parts of the Welsh estate (the binding nature of the strict settlement system had by now been seriously undermined), and in 1852 the Aber-mad estate, an obvious case of overreach, was sold to Lewis Pugh. However, purchases of land continued despite the debts; in 1854 Llwyn-llwyd (Gwnnws) was bought for £1,400 and in 1858 Tan-y-bwlch (Llanafan) for £220.

The Earl's second marriage in 1853 involved another family settlement, and in 1857 another trust became necessary. Annuities were sold to pay debts, and 5,893 acres of land were mortgaged for

Robert Gardiner, the estate's agent, and his family, at Wenallt.

£14,751 to ensure an income of £800 for the heir, Ernest Augustus Mallet, on his twenty-first birthday;[41] this mortgage was still unredeemed in 1880. The heir's marriage in 1858 brought a dowry of £5,000 with his wife, but like so many of his ancestors, young Ernest found he could not live within his income. He borrowed £4,000 in 1866, and incurred a succession of further serious debts.[42] Despite these commitments, investment by the trustees continued. In 1864 the Earl bought Crown rights in Gwnnws, Rhosdie, Llanafan and Llanfihangel-y-Creuddyn for £5,000. Additionally, to redeem a fixed Crown rent of £16.17.2 a year, he was willing to pay £550; these two sums might well have been better invested elsewhere, but there may have been a hope of benefitting by lead-mining on the redeemed land. Between 1864 and 1868 the Earl paid out £5,335 for additional lands in Caron, Gwnnws and Llanilar parishes. He was able to recoup a certain amount, selling in 1867 some land to the Manchester and Milford Railway, which linked Aberystwyth to Carmarthen via Trawsgoed station, for £3,591. A valuation of the whole Welsh estate in 1870 totalled £340,600; four hundred properties were included, with values ranging from £12,800 (for Lodge Farm and for Morfa Mawr, Llan-non) to eight shillings.[43]

The fourth Earl spent generously on good causes. He founded and for several years maintained Llanafan School, rebuilt Llanafan church, and other churches benefited from his generosity. His death in 1873 brought a new drain on the estate which his heirs could not avoid, namely Gladstone's Succession Duty, which cost the estate £2,006. Fortunately for his heir, the duty did not yet apply to land, only to other wealth. His successor, the fifth Earl, attempted to clear some debts in 1874, but found himself obliged to raise loans of £26,000, partly as a result of provision for his brother and sister. His most interesting borrowing at this time was from the Lands Improvement Company, which provided an initial loan of £20,000 and a later loan of £17,000, against rents for specified farms. The money was originally intended for drainage, embanking, enclosing, improving roads and buildings and for planting trees. However, the Earl gained the Company's permission to use a great deal of the money to improve Trawsgoed mansion, which the Company should not have allowed.[44] Improvements were certainly needed according to the standards of the day for great houses, but the addition of the new wing in 1891 was an aesthetic disaster, and was soon to prove an encumbrance. However, six thousand pounds was spent on farm improvements.

By 1876 the estate's debts stood at £39,000, and a debt was incurred with the Eagle Insurance Company for £26,000 to meet the most urgent demands. When the Earl married for the second time in 1878, yet another family settlement was called for. In the meantime, the Earl and his long-serving agent, Robert Gardiner, had determined on a more vigorous policy of consolidation—of selling off the most distant farms, and buying farms close to Trawsgoed. Between 1875 and 1878 they spent £12,990 on additional land, while £15,360 worth of land was sold during 1877/78 alone. There were also exchanges of land with Nanteos and Hafod estates. The pace of buying and selling increased in the 1880s. Between 1878-1888 £40,610 was spent buying land and £24,430 earned by sales. The largest single purchase was the Ffosybleiddiaid estate, much of which, ironically, had been sold by Sir John Vaughan 250 years earlier.

Another financial settlement was needed in 1884 when the fifth Earl's son, Arthur George Henry Vaughan, came of age; like his predecessors, he then started borrowing on his own account. When the fifth Earl died in 1888 and A.G.H. Vaughan became the sixth Earl, the pace of selling increased again. The whole of Court Grange, once part

of the Strata Florida lands, was sold in 1890 to Pryse of Gogerddan for
£20,350. Pryse in his turn was following a policy of consolidation
which he could ill afford, but it is hardly surprising that he coveted the
Court grange, since Broncastellan farm, the westernmost in the
grange, overlooks Gogerddan mansion. It is unsurprising that the
estate was in need of money; the fifth Earl's will sought to augment
the provision of sums of £5,000 for each of his younger children to an
ambitious £16,000, though it is doubtful whether the trustees
succeeded in carrying this through.[45]

The policy of trusts, mortgages and loans, allied to continued
expenditure on too lavish a scale, could only have ensured survival if
income had increased to keep pace. But in the second half of the
nineteenth century several processes were at work all over Britain and
Ireland. The forces of democracy were undermining the traditional
confidence of the aristocracy and gentry on almost every side. At the
same time, while the incomes of industrialists, entrepreneurs and
merchants rose, income from land froze or declined. Britain's markets
were open to cheap wheat from abroad; prices fell, and with them
rents and the value of land. Whether an individual aristocrat attempted
to stem the tide by marrying an American heiress, or was swept along
in a tide of irresponsible hedonism, there was (after the passage of the
Settled Land Act of 1882) only one answer to the problem of land—
sell.[46] True, the problem was less serious in areas which relied more on
pastoral than arable farming, but the Vaughans of Trawsgoed were not
strongly placed to resist the forces of change.

Unfortunately the splendid collection of estate sales catalogues in
the National Library of Wales does not include the earlier Trawsgoed
sales, but documents are available for several. In 1890, as we have
seen, the Court Grange (2,551 acres) was sold to Gogerddan, and nine
farms in Aberarth, Llanrhystud and Gwnnws were disposed of. In 1900
twelve farms in the parish of Caron were sold, and in 1921 six farms in
Ysbyty Ystwyth, Gwnnws and Llanfihangel-y-Creuddyn came under
the hammer. In 1924 there were two large sales; only the cover and two
pages of the May sale survive in the National Library's copy, but farms
were knocked down in the parishes of Lledrod, Caron, Gwnnws,
Ystrad Meurig, Llanafan, Llanilar, Llanfihangel-y-Creuddyn and
Ysbyty Ystwyth. In September fifteen farms and smallholdings in
Lledrod, Caron, Llanfihangel and Llanafan went, as well as sheepwalks, many parcels of accommodation lands, and the 167 acres of

Maenarthur wood, near Pontrhydygroes. Many farms went to sitting tenants, who may not have been anxious to buy, since they benefitted by the annual tenancies which placed the responsibility for upkeep of buildings on the landlord. They were, however, highly suspicious of the possibility of purchase by London Welshmen, whom they did not trust.

The whole process must have involved the most extraordinary mixture of feelings; the family must surely have deeply regretted the break-up of so large and centralised an estate, assembled over so long a period at so great a cost. Yet, as we have already seen, the Vaughans had already lost the political and much of the social power which once accompanied the ownership of a great estate. Whatever their own feelings, others certainly rejoiced to see the control of so much land taken out of the hands of one man and put into the hands of many. Ironically, though, several generations later it can already be seen that energetic and successful farmers who once owned a single Cardiganshire farm have managed to acquire several, a process reminiscent of the earliest days of Trawsgoed in centuries past.

*   *   *

The management of the Trawsgoed estate has been dealt with in great detail by J.M.Howells in his unpublished thesis, and is part of the wider picture painted by D.M.Howell in *Patriarchs and Parasites*,[47] and by Richard Moore-Colyer in a number of valuable essays.[48] During the seventeenth century the general impression is of a successful, thriving estate, but the weight of debt becomes increasingly apparent during the eighteenth century. As we have seen, rents were often in kind and in services as well as cash; leases were for twenty-one years or shorter periods; only during the nineteenth century did annual leases become common, enabling the landlord to raise rent according to circumstances. Complications must have been caused by the irregular distribution of land; the demesne map of 1756 shows a strip belonging to Thomas Johnes in the middle of Palu meadow, and the splendid series of individual farm maps of 1781 also show such relict strips of intermingled lands, especially in the remarkable map of Ysbyty Ystwyth. These anomalies were almost entirely dealt with in the period of adjustments from 1770 already described above, and by the time of the Tithe Maps of the 1840s they had all but disappeared.

We have already seen that there were efforts made in the late seventeenth and early eighteenth centuries to ensure some small land-improvement by tenants. It was, however, only during the last third of the eighteenth century that serious efforts were made to improve the estate, coinciding of course with the countrywide drive towards improving stock and crop-yields in order to achieve greater profits (and feed a growing population). At Trawsgoed a number of surveys were commissioned, but the surviving evidence tells us more about drastic changes made to the house and demesne than to farming on the estate. In 1771 a beautiful map of the demesne itself was drawn, and a report made on the mansion itself, already discussed above. This was followed by the re-shaping of the mansion in typical classical form, by the creation of the woodland between the house and the road, and eventually by the re-making of almost the entire garden in Victorian and Edwardian times. Only hints of this process are to be found in the surviving documents. In his *Memorandum*, Wilmot the fourth Viscount prescribes:

> Hedges on the Demesne to be all made up, Banks repair'd, Water Courses opened in Palu & elsewhere, the Hedges on each side the Avenue fronting the House to be levelled & taken away so that the whole may look like one great Lawn from the Avenue of Oaks to Palu.

The planting of the roadside woodland must have been stimulated by the creation of the turnpike road (the present B4340), probably between 1785 and 1800.[49] The late eighteenth century saw a growing tendency among the gentry towards privacy, a tendency which in England occasionally led even to the relocation of whole villages. As we have seen in a previous chapter, Wilmot the fourth Viscount invested in the Turnpike Trust.

The fate of Maesdwyffrwd farm was dramatic. This had once been the freehold property of one Henry Lloyd. In his will of 1687 he left his little estate of six properties to his wife, with reversion to his kinsman Edward Vaughan (a seventh property went to Thomas Lloyd of Rhiwarthen and Abertrinant). Maesdwyffrwd was mapped in 1781, but soon afterwards it was emparked; house and buildings disappeared, to be replaced by tree-pasture and plantations, and there is no trace of its existence on the 1848 Tithe Map. This too was probably the work of the fourth Viscount.

As in so many aspects of this study, the overall management of the

Trawsgoed estate through the centuries is obviously typical rather than exceptional. When estates were growing, Trawsgoed grew. When dowries and spendthrift heirs became a burden on many estates, Trawsgocd also suffered. When agricultural improvement came in, Trawsgoed took some part in it, though without great enthusiasm. When mansions were rebuilt, Trawsgoed was recreated. When landscaping was the rage, Trawsgoed park was created. When game seemed more important than rents, Trawsgoed preserved and shot. And when selling was widespread, Trawsgoed sold.

NOTES

[1] J.V.Beckett, *The Aristocracy in England 1660-1914* (Blackwell, 19860.
[2] NLW CD II, 122.
[3] NLW CD I, 348, 360, 360-3.
[4] NLW CD II, 33.
[5] NLW CD I, 402.
[6] NLW CD I, 401, unnumbered pages. The document lists the mills of Peiran, Dolfor, Llanafan, Maenarthur, Glennydd, Court, Morfa, Hafodwen and Fulbrook. The bond was of course a promise to pay in the event of default, not an actual payment.
[7] Ibid. 'Couples' are the pairs of great timbers forming the frame of the house. A further clue to building methods comes in another lease from the same source, where Thomas Evan leased part of Castell Flemish, with the obligation to repair the mansion house and out-houses, 'and is to have liberty for cutting of soe much turffes as Shalbe spent upon the said premises'.
[8] NLW CD I, 489.
[9] D.W.Howells, *Patriarchs and Parasites* (Cardiff, 1986), p.75.
[10] NLW CD I, 798. Twenty-one years was the usual term of lease at this time.
[11] NLW CD I, 765, 767, 770.
[12] Report of the Royal Commission on Land in Wales and Monmouthshire, *Evidence*, Vol.III, 1895, p.564.
[13] NLW CD III, 61. Henceforth simply Memorandum. For commutation see also NLW CD I, 1021, cited in D.W.Howells, *op.cit.*, p.74.
[14] Like many senior Trawsgoed employees, Robson (of Dalkeith in East Lothian) was a Scot. See R. Moore-Colyer, 'The Land Agent in nineteenth-century Wales', *WHR*, vol.8, no.4 (1977), p.404.
[15] Eiluned Rees, 'The Sales-Book of Samuel Williams, Aberystwyth Printer', *Ceredigion* X, 4 (1987), p.363. The details suggest a comparatively enlightened attitude towards the Welsh language.
[16] NLW CD I, 130-143.
[17] NLW Lisburne-Northumberland papers, bundle 5, unnumbered.
[18] NLW CD I, 620.

[19]NLW CD II, 236.

[20]NLW CD II, 324; I, 977; II, 333; II, 365; II, 416; II, 523-526.

[21]NLW CD I, 768.

[22]NLW CD I, 960 and 989.

[23]NLW CD I, 980; II, 951.

[24]NLW CD II, 314.

[25]See Gerald Morgan, 'Local History in some 18th century Cardiganshire Estate Maps', *Journal of the University of Wales Agricultural Society*, 72 (1992/3), pp.48-77.

[26]Thomas Lloyd & the Rev. Mr. Turnor, *General View of the Agriculture of the County of Cardigan* (London, 1794) p.20.

[27]NLW CD II, 553.

[28]NLW CD II, 606.

[29]NLW CD I, 847.

[30]Wilmot Vaughan provided capital for the county Turnpike Trust. The minutes for 3 January 1788 show that he was paid £37.10.0 as a year's interest on five hundred and fifty pound. NLW Cardiganshire County Roads Board, A1.

[31]NLW CD I, 1131; II, 510.

[32]NLW CD II, 968.

[33]NLW Lisburne-Northern papers, bundle 5, unscheduled.

[34]NLW CD I, 1191.

[35]Dyfed (Ceredigion) Record Office, ADX 15/1/13.

[36]Dyfed (Ceredigion) Record Office, ADX 15/1/11.

[37]NLW CD I, 720

[38]See articles by Richard [Moore]-Colyer in *Ceredigion*, VII, 2 (1973), pp.170-88 (Gogerddan); VIII, 3 (1980), pp.58-77 (Nanteos); X, 1 (1984), pp.97-103 (Penglais).

[39]NLW CD II, 660.

[40]S.R.Meyrick, *The History and Antiquities of the County of Cardigan* (3rd edn., Brecon, 1907) p.117.

[41]NLW CD II, 1267.

[42]See e.g. NLW CD II.1290, II.1300, I.1780, I.1787, etc.

[43]NLW CD I, 1778.

[44]NLW CD I, 1869.

[45]NLW CD I, 2120.

[46]See chapter 3, 'The decline and dispersal of territorial wealth' in David Cannadine, *The Decline and Fall of the British Aristocracy*, (Oxford, 1990).

[47]Cardiff, University of Wales Press, 1986.

[48]See e.g. 'Some aspects of land occupation in nineteenth century Cardiganshire', *THSC*, 1981, pp.79-97.

[49]There is a crux here. The NLW Cardiganshire Turnpike Trust Minutes for 8 September 1773 show that Thomas Lloyd of Abertrinant and Edward Hughes of Aberllolwyn contracted for a road from Pen-y-wern (New Cross) via Abermagwr to Llanafan Bridge. However there is no trace of it on the 1781 estate maps of Thomas Lewis. I guess that it was not built until later; the minutes have serious gaps, and often show more in the way of intention than achievement.

VIII. MANAGING THE ESTATE: SOME ISSUES

This chapter is given over to particular issues in the affairs of the Trawsgoed estate which are best dealt with under subheadings. Most of these deal with the various sources of estate income, but the first issue, and perhaps the most lively and interesting, is a problem that all estates faced as the population inexorably rose, while land ownership was concentrated in fewer and fewer hands.

Squatters

As well as coping with problems of income and agricultural management, landowners had to face a growing problem of encroachment or squatting from the mid-eighteenth century onwards. Gateward's case of 1603 had determined that common lands were the property of lords of manors (which often meant the Crown) and their tenants, not of the common people.[1] That made easier the enclosure of common land for the benefit of landowners and tenant-farmers, and made it more difficult for the increasing population to find plots of land on which to settle, or even grazing and firewood. Common land is therefore not land in general public ownership; it is land over which a limited number of individuals other than the owner (whether the owner be the Crown, the lord of the manor or other freeholders) may have certain rights, such as grazing, the digging of peat and collection of wood. The rising population in the eighteenth-century countryside was not being wholly drained off into the new industrial communities, nor was there yet much emigration overseas.[1] There was hunger not just for land to farm, but simply for accommodation. It is hardly surprising that a popular view contrasted unfavourably the official attitude to enclosure and to encroachment; power was in the hands of the landed folk, and they used it to their own advantage, stealing the common from the goose.

Although squatting in the hope of gaining possession was an ancient practice, there was an apparent increase in the custom of building *tai unnos*, one-night houses, a phenomenon lucidly described by a London lawyer whose advice had been sought by Wilmot

Vaughan during the 1790s—the lawyer appears to be quoting from a lost letter from Wilmot himself:

> The Party Incroaching assembles his relations & Friends to his Assistance & they run up a Structure & inclose a small Quantity of Ground between sunset & sunrising the next morning. In this Structure without any Alteration they must reside a year & if in that time he has met with no interruption he claims such ground & Structure as his freehold property, pulls down his first rude Edifice & constructs another of more permanence & encroaches gradually on his Enclosures.[2]

There was no jot of legal justification for popular belief in the legality of *tai unnos*, but it was held fiercely, attributed in popular belief to Hywel Dda (ironically, he is claimed as a Vaughan ancestor), and it caused some dramatic incidents. The pattern of *tai unnos* on the hills east of Ysbyty Ystwyth can be clearly seen in a National Library of Wales map of the parish drawn in 1839. Many houses and ruins which began as *tai unnos* can still be seen on Rhos-y-gell north of Pont-rhyd-y-groes, and round Brynafan.

Wilmot the fourth Viscount had serious difficulties with squatters. In his Memorandum he set himself:

> To inquire into the Encroachments at Penrhiw in Morva Grange, Brongwin in Havodwen Grange . . . the Boundarys to be ascertain'd & these Tenements to be survey'd if necessary . . .

In 1797 Thomas Morgan, still the steward after more than thirty years' service, wrote to William Worrall, a London lawyer, describing the problem at Cnwch Coch, between Abermagwr and Llanfihangel-y-Creuddyn. On the Tan-yr-allt, Abermagwr, map of 1781, Cnwch Coch is shown as a vacant area of brushwood; but a village began to come into existence, created by squatters. Morgan describes the background:

> Cnwch Coch . . . was always considered as a joint property attached to Rhydycochied (a part of the Crosswood estate) and Cwmnewidion lately purchased by Lord Lisburne, together with some of the Abertrinant and Nanteos Estates. The said Land was lately divided by the proprietors of the adjoining estates, half to Lord Lisburne in right of his two farms and the other half divided between the proprietors of the Nanteos and Abertrinant properties. About the beginning of last May one David Morgan (in one night) erected a Cott on that part of Cnwch Coch allotted to Lord Lisburne and during the building sold such Cott to one William Mason for the price of the timber, and early the next

morning Mason was in possession and kept possession ever since. About the same time Margaret the wife of one William Rees who had left her and had gone to live in London assisted by others, erected another Cott on Cnwch Coch which she is in possession of, but neither of them have enclosed any lands with their Cotts . . .

Morgan had served notice on the two parties to quit possession and pull down the cottages, or face prosecution. The lawyers havered, however, pointing out the problems of ownership, obviously concerned that a flawed action could lead to serious difficulties, while straightforward eviction could lead to violent protest.

A generation later, in 1814, the squatters of Cnwch Coch and other areas were still causing problems. Mr Beynon, a family legal representative, wrote to Messrs Lambert & Son, lawyers, in London to describe current difficulties.[4] He noted that Trawsgoed, Nanteos and Abertrinant estates had by then divided up the Cnwch Coch common land between them, but three cottages had been built on the Trawsgoed portion, and the builders:

> had for years committed considerable depredations on the Woods on the property, besides being miserable looking Huts, to be seen from the Windows in front of the House.[5]

Beynon obtained writs of possession, and went with Colonel John Vaughan (the insane Earl's younger brother and heir) to carry them out:

> when one of the party acted with great Violence, and afterwards desired Colonel Vaughan to order the Cottage to be taken down which was accordingly done. The others thereupon submitted and entreated Colonel Vaughan to permit them to occupy their Houses until Michaelmas on paying a Nominal Rent, when they would give them up peaceably, which from principles of humanity he consented to . . . The limits of a Letter will not admit of my going into detail on the Subject of the general incroachments on Lord Lisburnes Estates, but Mr Murray assured me they would now let for 700£ per annum at a very moderate Calculation.

There were also squatters on Trawsgoed land in Ystradmeurig, but Beynon's efforts to get them expelled by six bailiffs and two clerks met with stiff opposition, and they were repelled. Beynon commented:

> that part of the Country is become so lawless, that no Sheriffs officer dare appear there without running the risk of loosing his Life, but if it

were possible to get a troop of Horse I would undertake to unkennel every Caitiff of them.

Cnwch Coch was eventually to become a lost cause; in the tithe map schedule of 1845 the occupiers of the village are described as freeholders.

Lord Lisburne's agents used what little influence they had in the court leet of Blaenaeron to campaign against encroachment:

> 11.11.1824 We Do Present that all Encrotchments being tacken in by buildings or Inclosure to be Prevented or taken Down within the said Lordships according to the antient Custom.[6]

From the landlord's viewpoint, the best way to cope with squatters was to enclose the common lands. Admittedly this had not been very successful in Cnwch Coch, but during the period 1820-65 large areas of Cardiganshire, in some of which the Trawsgoed estate had interests, were enclosed by Acts of Parliament. Meanwhile migration to the ironworks and coalfields of the South, and across the Atlantic, helped siphon off the bulging rural population, reducing the pressure on overcrowded lands. In Ysbyty Ystwyth, where the mountain slopes above the village were full of *tai unnos*, the fourth Earl abandoned efforts at eviction and came to agreement with the squatters in 1846. They were granted their holdings, but the estate retained mineral rights, which seemed likely to prove more profitable than efforts to extract miniscule rents on marginal land.

During the eighteenth and nineteenth centuries the Crown made intermittent efforts to enforce its claim to rent on mountain land in Cardiganshire, including much of the high land once belonging to Strata Florida. The Crown's principal obstacles were not the petty squatters who so exasperated successive Earls of Lisburne, but the great landowners themselves. One surviving document of 1864 shows that the Trawsgoed estate itself had encroached on several hundred acres of Crown land in Mefenydd and Llanafan.[7] Trawsgoed, like Gogerddan and Nanteos, had involved itself in large-scale unofficial enclosures.

Encroachments were to be found almost everywhere, and they modified the Welsh landscape considerably. The largest were those of the squires themselves, seeking timber, game and mineral rights. The most obvious in the landscape today are the moorland cottages and fields, now mostly abandoned, in places like Ffair-rhos and Rhos-y-gell. A modern eye may not perceive that many roadside houses and cottages, often providing beer for travellers, were also the creations of squatters settling on the roadside waste at a time when the road-verges were more extensive and less sharply defined than they are today. Many of the surviving cottages in villages like Ysbyty Ystwyth were originally built on common land by squatters, and the whole of Cnwch Coch was originally a squatters' camp.

Some squatters' settlements have virtually disappeared. A traveller from Aberystwyth to Trawsgoed passes through New Cross and down Allt-y-wern past the junction to Llanfihangel-y-Creuddyn and then crosses, perhaps without noticing, a small river-bridge. In the last century there was a hamlet at this point, Pentre-du. It probably came into existence in the eighteenth century; the parish register for Llanfihangel records several deaths there for smallpox in the first decade of the nineteenth century. The houses would have been of cob, and were inhabited into the twentieth century; once abandoned, the farmers of Glanystwyth, Pyllau Isaf and Pyllau Uchaf could easily have ploughed them back into the earth; one small stone building survives in use as a store. The Crown conducted its campaigns against the landowners by correspondence; the landowners in their turn pressured the squatters, who responded with the techniques of the oppressed: vigilance, silence and cunning. Whatever their impact on his Lordship's view from the mansion, they had to live.

Income: Introduction

The income of the Vaughan family over the centuries, as with any major landowning family, is a complex subject which could itself fill a volume. Rents, food and service renders, estate produce, mining royalties, dowries, investment income, tithes and earned income all played a part in fuelling a machine which consumed income as rapidly, usually more rapidly, than it was generated. Some of these subjects are discussed concisely below, with the intention of conveying something of the complexity of understanding this aspect of the Trawsgoed estate. Not enough evidence survives, however, to make it possible to discuss investment income, or the sale of estate produce other than timber, though we know that, for example, bricks were produced on the estate. Dowries have already been mentioned in previous chapters; although they brought financial credit, they also brought obligations, since if as often happened the bride eventually became a dowager, then her jointure was a drain on the estate. It seems impossible to gauge for any given year exactly what the estate's income was; indeed, it is most unlikely that anyone knew at the time, given the difficulties of ensuring prompt payment and the collection of arrears.

Rents

The Trawsgoed estate has a splendid run of surviving rentals in the archive; J.M.Howells published lists of the rent figures for 94 separate years between 1670 and 1944.[8] However, Howells pointed out the impossibility of reckoning the Vaughans' true rental income at any given time. Some rent figures survive for the Northumberland, Enfield and Devon estates, which for some periods must have contributed a good deal to the family income. The Enfield property in Middlesex brought in £2,117 in 1821; by 1881 it yielded £2,540.[9] The Northumberland estate in 1829, immediately before its sale, had a rental of £2,230.[10] In 1827 the Devon estate, on the brink of its sale, actually yielded £1,876 of the £2,096 due in rent. The figure for rents due and for actual payment did not always coincide, sometimes due to invidual hardship, at other times to more general difficulties. Rent-collecting problems were obviously linked to market difficulties caused by harvest failures and cheaper food imports, which caused market prices to vary, sometimes wildly.

There were certainly fluctuations in the rental of the Vaughans' Welsh estate. Of twenty-seven rent totals between 1670 and 1763, only one figure is above £1,200—the year 1690, which returned rents of £1,548, for no reason now apparent. After 1763 there was a slow but steady increase, and the rents reached £2,000 for the first time in 1779; by 1794 they were £3,200, and in 1814 they reached £11,634. This startling rise is a well-known result of the agricultural prosperity engendered during the Napoleonic Wars, and was repeated on estates throughout the country. 1822 was a good year, at £10,200, but then the figures fell rapidly with the onset of overseas agricultural competition; £4,077 was the total in 1823. This followed threats by tenants to withold their rents, since they felt they were not being compensated for improvements.[11] There was a rise in the late 1820s, but in the 1830s income fell again.

Howells' figures for 1870 and 1874 present violent contrasts: £10,590 for the former year, £5,722 for the latter, followed by £12,878 in 1880! That was a belated *annus mirabilis*; the Welsh estate would never again yield so much. By 1890, when some land sales had already taken place, and when rebates of between 10% and 15% were being given because of agricultural depression, the rental was £9,966. It remained above £9,000 for most years till 1909, and actually rose above £10,000 for the period 1910-1914. Then it slid, slowly and inexorably, following sale after sale and affected by the severe agricultural depression between the World Wars: £9,046 in 1920, £3,055 in 1929, £2,422 in 1939 and £2,514 in 1944 from the remaining farms. In 1947 the seventh Earl abandoned the struggle and sold up though retaining several farms and a good deal of shooting land.

Tithes

It is essential, in view of common misunderstandings, to explain the background to tithes in general. Tithe was a tax on the produce of the land and the sea, an annual tenth payable by farmers and fishermen. It was originally levied as an income for the Church, but the tithes of many parishes, especially in the diocese of St David's, were impropriated at an early stage, along with the parishes themselves; i.e. they became the property of the Crown, of monasteries, of Oxford and Cambridge colleges or of laymen, all known as impropriators. It is safe to say, for example, that the tithes of the original parish area of Llanbadarn Fawr (the whole of north Cardiganshire from Llanilar to the river Dyfi) were *never* paid to the local church. They became Crown property by right of conquest in 1277, and were given in 1359 by the Black Prince to the Abbey of Vale Royal, then confiscated by the Crown at the dissolution of the monasteries, and finally sold off to laymen. Almost the whole tithe income of the area eventually became the property of the Chichester family of Arlington in Devon, who for the whole of the eighteenth and nineteenth centuries drew thousands of pounds a year from north Cardiganshire, which kept that family in great comfort. Their only return was grudgingly to contribute on occasion to the maintenance of the chancels of the parish churches, and the payment of pittances to their priests, obligations which seem often to have been avoided. In Wales, tithe became a scandal to nineteenth-century nonconformist farmers who were unwilling to pay tithe to a church they did not support, and there were vigorous protests, mainly in North Wales. Protest in Cardiganshire was presumably diluted by the fact that much tithe money did not go to the church, but to lay owners, who bought and sold tithes exactly like stock market investments.

By 1670 the Vaughans had managed to accumulate small shares in the tithes of Gwnnws and Ystradmeurig parishes, and in Court grange (Penrhyncoch) which brought in £37.11.8, and they derived another £75.16.0 from Llanfihangel Ystrad in the Aeron valley.[12] They also succeeded at some stage in gaining some small parts of the Chichester tithes in Llanfihangel-y-Creuddyn, though I cannot discover how. Tithes were actual returns of produce—hay, corn, livestock—but the Tithe Commutation Act of 1836 valued all areas which had not already done so by local agreement for payment by cash. Consequently the tithes of the Ystwyth valley parishes were divided as follows, to the nearest pound:[13]

	Chichester	Vaughan	Other	Vicar
Llanfihangel-y-Creuddyn	£453	£38	-	£181
Llanilar	£302	-	£13	£136
Llanafan	£136	-	-	-
Llanychaiarn	£354	-	£3	-
Ysbyty Ystwyth	-	£45	-	-
Gwnnws	£170	£61	-	-

The first Earl had invested in the tithes of eleven more Cardiganshire parishes to create an income for his second son. Thus George Lawrence Vaughan (1802-79), second son of the third earl, was entitled to £1,186 a year of tithe income. In addition, by 1840 the fourth Earl drew £189 from the tithes of at least seven other Cardiganshire parishes.

In the seventeenth century the usual practice had been for the owner of the tithe to farm it out to a collector for the best price he could get; thus the tithes of Hafodwen Grange were leased in 1680 by Edward

Vaughan to John Haberley of Llanafan, and Vaughan's widow Letitia leased the tithes of Ysbyty Ystwyth and Ystradmeurig to Edward Morgan of Llanfihangel-y-Creuddyn for £19 rent, Morgan paying Crown rent and the curate's salary.[14] The family owned other tithes in the Strata Florida granges, including some in the parishes of Llanfihangel Genau'r-glyn, Caron and Llanfihangel-y-Creuddyn Uchaf, and the parishes of the Aeron valley. The Llanfihangel-y-Creuddyn Uchaf tithes were let in 1734 to the Reverend William Williams, rector of Llangynllo in Carmarthenshire, on condition that he resided at Trawsgoed, acted as chaplain to Lord Lisburne and served the church of Llanafan.[15] In 1783, as we have seen previously, Wilmot the first Earl bought the tithes of ten additional parishes in Cardiganshire and two in Carmarthenshire.

By the end of the 18th century the Cardiganshire and Carmarthenshire tithes owned by the estate were a minor but useful source of income. In theory the tithe income for 1796 should have been £445; in fact, while the Carmarthenshire tithes were paid in full (£123), the Cardiganshire parishes were £100 in arrears. By 1815 the income should have been £908; in fact it was £513. Sometimes arrears were recovered; in 1879 £889 was due in tithes, and £922 was actually paid. In the early years of the twentieth century the average income from tithes was £450 p.a. between 1907 and 1916, but thereafter it dropped away rapidly; for example, it was £218 in 1925, but by 1933 it was only £27. In 1936 tithes were abolished by the Tithe Act of that year.

Lead Mining

While we have a fairly good idea of estate rental income from the mid-eighteenth-century onwards, details of the mineral royalties are only available in detail from 1835. However, Mr Howells in his thesis and Mr W.J.Lewis in his *Lead Mining in Wales* have gathered together some threads of the earlier history of the Trawsgoed involvement in mining.

Lead ore is a widely distributed mineral in Wales, which is often found associated with zinc and, especially in Cardiganshire, with silver. Metal-mining and smelting were ancient industries in Wales; lead, copper and gold were probably exploited before, and certainly by, the Romans. North-eastern Cardiganshire has a number of veins bearing lead, silver and zinc, which could once be found outcropping on hill-tops and slopes. However, the veins are capricious; sometimes they swell into rich deposits, only to disappear entirely, making their exploitation financially risky. Large fortunes were made and great sums lost in the Cardiganshire mines before world market prices eventually finished the industry off in the first decades of the twentieth century.

Mediaeval mining in Cwmystwyth is known from surviving Strata Florida documents, and John Leland recorded the devastation wrought by mining when he visited Cwmystwyth in the 1530s. In 1568 the Society of Mines Royal was incorporated to work metal reserves in England and Wales, which were all claimed by the Crown. It seems that the early success of the Society's licensees was largely north of the Rheidol, in Cwmsymlog, Cwmerfin, Goginan and Tal-y-bont; it was resented by local landowners under whose lands the ore lay. We know that south of the Rheidol, mines in Cwmystwyth were leased and worked, but the land had not yet come into the ownership of Trawsgoed. Closer to home, the Grogwynion mine, in its spectacular setting high on the ridge above the Ystwyth between Pont-rhyd-y-groes and Llanafan Bridge, was leased to Sir John Bankes in the 1630s, against the opposition of John Vaughan of Trawsgoed.[16] However, John Vaughan was supportive enough when almost at the same time Thomas Bushell successfully proposed the establishment of a mint in Aberystwyth Castle.[17] Protests against mining continued, however, and Sir Richard Pryse, John Vaughan and others were summoned to the bar of the House of Lords to answer for the vandalising of mining equipment and harassment of the workers, even of the Lords' messenger. They were detained for a while, but released on a bond for good behaviour, which they did not observe.[18] Little is known of the Cardiganshire mines between 1650 and 1690, when the discovery of rich lead ore on the Gogerddan estate at Esgair-hir led to the important decision of the House of Lords to allow landlords to develop their own mineral rights without the interference of the Society of Mines Royal. The first Viscount Lisburne acted quickly; he leased mineral rights under two farms in Llanfihangel Genau'r-glyn to a Cornishman in 1695,[19] and in 1721 his son leased all the mineral rights of the estate for fifty guineas and a one-seventh royalty on the ore to a West Country consortium, but no results are known. The only early reference I have so far found to direct mining income is in Edward Vaughan's rentbook of the 1660s, already cited above:

I also haue £20 more to compleate the £500 receivd from the mines.

If that figure was the mineral income for a single year, then it was providing a substantial proportion of the estate's income.

Despite their victory against the Crown over Esgair-hir, the Pryses of Gogerddan did not profit quickly from it, although they floated a mining company and retaining half the shares. Sir Humphrey Mackworth and William Waller took over the enterprise, but with no better success for many years, despite the further takeover of a number of other mines. The Cardiganshire lead industry did not revive until the 1740s, at which time Wilmot the third Viscount Lisburne and Walter Pryse of Gogerddan were at loggerheads over the Goginan mine. We know that Wilmot Vaughan had made a new mineral lease in 1742, this time only of the ores under Grogwynion, Blaen-ddol and Berth-lwyd, to the Mine Adventurers of England. The farm of Ty'n-rhyd (now Pengrogwynion) was Pryse property, but surrounded by Lisburne land, and the two eventually went to law on the matter, since the mining works were under both men's lands. There were further leases on Grogwynion, and on Logau-las above Ysbyty Ystwyth in the 1750s and 1760s.

The House of Lords' decision in the case of Esgair-hir did not prevent long-running struggles between local landowners and the Crown, which still owned many tracts of waste and therefore claimed mineral rights. The increase in illegal Cardiganshire mining on lands claimed by the Crown soon came to the attention of the authorities, and a Steward of the Crown Manors of Cardiganshire, William Corbett, was appointed in 1746, with the Anglesey polymath Lewis Morris as his deputy. In 1752 Morris was appointed Agent and Superintendent of His Majesty's Mines in Cardigan and Merioneth. He immediately began to develop the old works at Esgair-mwyn, on the high moorland slopes between Ffair-rhos and Ysbyty Ystwyth, with such success that Wilmot Vaughan and the Powell brothers of Nanteos, Thomas and William, who owned land bordering on the waste, were soon involved in a fierce quarrel with the prickly Morris. In 1753, on the order of the Court of Exchequer, the area between the Marchnant and the Teifi was beautifully mapped by Edward John Eyre. It shows that the common or waste land was bordered to the west and south-west by a string of freehold farms, four belonging to Lord Lisburne, two each to Thomas Johnes Dolaucothi, to David

Lloyd, and to the Rev. William Powell of Nanteos, with one each to David Williams, Lewis Williams, John Williams and Queen Anne's Bounty. The Lordships of Ysbyty Ystwyth to the north and of Uwch Clawdd to the south both belonged to Lord Lisburne. The landowners disputed the right of the Crown, which was being upheld by Lewis Morris, to exploit lead ores under their lands, and in 1753 the notorious arrest of Lewis Morris and his jailing in Cardigan took place at the hands of Herbert Lloyd of Peterwell, John Ball (local agent to the Mine Adventurers) and hundreds of Powell's followers. A troop of soldiers had to be called in to re-establish peace. Lord Lisburne, himself Lord Lieutenant of Cardiganshire, did not take part in the arrest and imprisonment, nor do his tenants appear to have done so, but he was certainly no friend to Lewis Morris, as the latter's correspondence with his brothers shows.[20]

It is hardly surprising that Wilmot Vaughan was not prominent in the Esgair-mwyn fracas. He had consulted counsel, and received a shrivelling response:

> I . . . cannot see the least appearance of any right in his Lordship to those Mines, for there is no grant of any Mines to his family, nor of the Land where these Mines lie, nor is the Manor granted him, which might entitle him to the Waste or Commons.[21]

The Esgair-mwyn affair was settled by compromise; Herbert Lloyd and Powell of Nanteos were not prosecuted for riot, but had to sell their 'pretended title to the mine' to Chauncey Townsend, who resold it to the Treasury. Townsend was an M.P. and City of London alderman, owning a lead smeltery at Swansea and coal mines near Neath. He then bid for a lease of Esgair-mwyn, but Lord Powis succeeded in outbidding him, so he turned to Lord Lisburne's mines, and acquired the lease of Grogwynion, which produced an average of 300 tons a year before the end of the 1760s, but only 247 tons in total between 1768 and 1775. A report on the Grogwynion mine in 1754, written by Lewis Morris for the Company of Mine Adventurers, shows considerable malpractice there.[22]

Townsend also leased Logau-las from Lord Lisburne, producing 847 tons of ore between 1768 and 1775. By 1785 Townsend's interests were being managed by Thomas Bonsall, a Derbyshire man whose success was so great that the Bonsalls became a gentry family in the Aberystwyth area, with a seat at Fronfraith, near Comins Coch;

Thomas Bonsall was knighted on the occasion when, as mayor of Aberystwyth, he presented a loyal Address from the town to George III. Another man who leased and exploited Lord Lisburne's mineral rights was John Probert; he opened the Fairchance mine near Ffair-rhos in 1769, and his company had acquired many of the most important mines by 1790. Other evidence of the importance of mineral rights to the estate is to be found in a letter of Thomas Morgan, the Trawsgoed agent, writing to Wilmot Vaughan on 22 November 1763:

> There is very good ore now at Grogwinion, Logelas and Cwmmawr, which obliges me to spent most part of my time at one or other of them daily to see the ore weighed and have now very little (i.e. time) to do anything else.[23]

After Wilmot the younger became the fourth Viscount, he gave some of his energies to the issue of the mines. In 1770 he leased two properties in Gwnnws parish, Nant-y-fynaches and Pen-y-wern Hir, to his brother John, Edward Hughes of Aberllolwyn and John Probert of Shrewsbury, at a royalty of 30s per ton of ore. The three formed the Fair Chance Mine Company, which included not only the three lessees but Wilmot Vaughan, William Powell of Nanteos and Stephen Saunders of Perth-y-berllan, Carmarthenshire. A quarter of the company's profits was to go to Wilmot himself.[24] This is the only example of direct commercial involvement of any of the titled Vaughans in lead mining. Wilmot withdrew from the company in 1784.

A few figures of royalties from some of the family's mining leases survive. We know that between 1768 and 1775 Logau-las produced £976 in royalties, and Grogwynion a mere £78. A new lease of the Llanfihangel Genau'r-glyn mines in 1772 does not appear to have been very profitable—nothing remotely like the £11,500 royalties which Cwmsymlog produced for the Powells of Nanteos between 1751 and 1772.[25] Nor did Wilmot do better from the Fairchance mine near Ffair-rhos, which between 1769 and 1791 was exploited by John Probert, once steward to Lord Powis. He developed other mines on Lisburne land, notably Llwynwnwch and Fron-goch. The latter had been leased in 1759 without much success, but under Probert some lead was raised from 1792 onwards despite flooding, and he took over the Grogwynion and Logau-las leases as well. Probert was never as successful as the ruthless Thomas Bonsall, whose profitable exploitation of the Nanteos-owned mines drew attention away from his vandal-methods and his exploitation of 'truck' at the miners' expense. Such was Bonsall's success that he founded a local dynasty complete with mansion (Fronfraith). However, the falling price of lead during the last twenty years of the eighteenth century brought the closure of many mines and a period of comparative inactivity.

The nineteenth century saw the last long burst of activity in the Cardiganshire lead (and zinc) mines. During the early years the most successful exploiters were Sir Thomas Bonsall (who died in 1808) and Job Sheldon, who took over the Probert mines. In the 1820s matters began to improve. Nanteos benefited from the revived Cwmystwyth mine, and the Lisburne mines were leased to the Cornish family of Williams and their partners in 1824. This was again a failure, and the Williams company had to surrender their lease in 1833, having lost £20,000. However, one of the Williams's partners had seen possibilities in the Lisburne mines. This was the remarkable John Taylor, the most intelligent and successful of all the engineers who worked in the county's lead industry during the nineteenth century.[26]

Where others attempted to get rich in the shortest space of time and with minimum investment, John Taylor surveyed his mines carefully, drained them properly, provided better water-supplies to drive the water-wheels, made new roads and invested in new machinery. After more than a century of poor or no returns, the Trawsgoed estate reaped a royalty bonanza. Between 1834 and 1893 the Lisburne mines produced 107,000 tons of lead ore, 50,000 tons of zinc ore and a little copper, the total valued at £1,338,793. J.M.Howells gives a marginally different total for the ores produced 1839-1893, and gives a total of £119,727 royalties received by the Trawsgoed estate. The best years were 1844-1877, when apart from one poor year in 1873, the royalties never dropped below £2000 a year. In 1850 a £75 share in the Lisburne company had been quoted at £600![27]

However, the poor return for 1873 was a warning that the great days of Cardiganshire lead-mining were drawing to an end. In 1877 there was a sudden drop from £2049 to £1169, and after 1881 royalties fell away rapidly. The Taylor family company, which in the latter decades of the period had taken over the running of all the major mine companies in addition to the Lisburne Mining Company, began to make losses; £20,000 was lost in the Powell Cwmystwyth mine alone. In 1878 the company surrendered the Fron-goch lease to the fifth Earl of Lisburne, who paid £5,000 for the machinery and gave the company a new lease on Ysbyty Ystwyth and Llanafan mines. He leased Fron-goch, one of the most successful of all the county's mines, to John Kitto, selling the machinery to him for £6,500, but receiving a much-reduced royalty, only one-twentieth per ton.[28]

In 1892 the Lisburne Mining Company, still managed by the Taylor family company, asked the sixth Earl for a reduction of royalties to help them meet the company's loss of £863. Lord Lisburne refused, writing to his agent Robert Gardiner:

> I must decline to forego the royalties, unless you were strongly to recommend me to do so—neither can I see that my doing so would benefit them much, as looking at the report their loss is £861.1s while the Royalties amount to £141.17.7, while the damage done to the river means a very large sum to me.[29]

His arithmetic was reasonable but his comprehension poor; the Taylors withdrew, and the Lisburne Mining Company was to all intents at an end. However, following the withdrawal of the Taylors, the Earl applied the lesson they had taught him, and reduced the Fron-goch royalty to one-thirtieth.

The reference to river damage is most unusual and interesting; it must certainly refer to the lovely part of the river between Pontrhydygroes and Llanafan Bridge. By the end of the nineteenth century both the Rheidol and Ystwyth were drastically polluted by lead-mining which killed all fish and made some water-sources a more subtle menace to life than the many abandoned and unprotected shafts, some of which still dot the hills. The Ystwyth suffered particularly badly; Cwmystwyth, the Pont-rhyd-y-groes mines, Grogwynion and Gwaith Goch polluted it directly, while the Fron-goch and Wemyss mines still poison the Newidion tributary to this day.

In 1898 the Fron-goch lease was given to the Societé Anonyme Minière at a rent of £230 and a complicated sliding-scale royalty; the company paid royalties of between £70 and £243 until 1903. A new lease was made in 1907 to the Lisburne Development Syndicate, and further leases followed between 1910 and 1919 until the the company was disbanded in 1923. The final period of exploitation of lead resources between 1907 and 1923 was mainly surface work. There were huge waste-dumps at Fron-goch which held enough lead to be worth re-working, but there was too little water for a washery. An aerial ropeway was therefore built from Fron-goch over the hill and down to Gwaith-goch, on the banks of the Ystwyth. To provide a sufficient head of water, a wood and concrete dam was built at a narrow point in the beautiful canyon above Grogwynion. Not far from the falcon-haunted Craigycolomennod, the ugly remains of this edifice still rear up like the ruins of a jungle temple between mossy cliffs; the iron sluice-gate is still in place, and one can walk along the leat bed, perhaps disturbing the goosander family that inhabits the river in summer. Further down, at Grogwynion itself, a huge bank of waste still lies along the river bank. Further downstream again, the last remains of a bridge to Gwaith-goch, in use during the 1920s can still be seen. By 1930 activity had virtually ceased, and in 1937 the seventh Earl sold all his mining rights for £6,000.

Income: Some Conclusions

The New Domesday report on land ownership in England and Wales in 1873 offers a unique opportunity to compare estates and their incomes. The following are figures for some Cardiganshire landowners, and for several major landowners in the rest of Wales:

Landowner	Estate	Acreage	Gross Estimated Rental
Lisburne	Trawsgoed	42,666	10,579
Pryse	Gogerddan	28,684	10,623
Powell WTR	Nanteos	21,933	9,024
Richardes	Penglais	1,610	1,149
Waddingham	Hafod	10,963	1,638
Williams	Wallog	1,473	827
J.E.Rogers	Abermeurig	3,263	896
James Loxdale	Castle Hill	4,915	2,458
Mrs M.A.Lewis	Llanerchaeron	4,397	2,591
Lloyd	Bronwydd	1,519	1,287
Bulkeley	Baronhill	16,516	17,997
Marquess of Anglesey	Plasnewydd	8,485	9,132
Meyrick	Bodorgan	16,918	13,283
Wynne (Denb)	Wynnstay	33,998	25,741
(Montgomery)		32,963	10,341
(Merioneth)		20,295	6,800
Lord Tredegar	Tredegar	6,157	29,843
Bute	Cardiff	21,402	180,286
Cawdor	Golden Grove	33,782	20,780
Lord Dynevor	Dynevor	7,208	7,253

The Tredegar and Bute figures show how much larger were incomes from urban property, coal-mining and industry, while comparison of the figures for Hafod and Plasnewydd show how much poorer is hill country. The county totals in the 1873 report show that whereas land in Anglesey brought in almost £1 per acre, Cardiganshire yielded only half that sum, making it the poorest of all the Welsh counties. The incomes are simply rental figures, of course, taking no account of debt and other charges, nor of investment and other sources.

The 1873 figure for Trawsgoed gives us a clear rental income figure, but for much of its history the estate's total income is not easily arrived at. Despite the many deficiencies in the sources, it may be possible to guess at an income figure for, say, the year 1827. In that year the Welsh estate was bringing in some £7,000; the Devon estate yielded £1,800; the Enfield estate some £2,000; the Northern estate had been yielding some £2,000; tithes brought in at least several hundred pounds. There may in addition have been other offices and fees of which I have found no account. Lead-mining royalty figures are not available for the year, and may or may not have contributed. The income was certainly over £11,000, and may well have been a good deal more. Yet of course much, perhaps most, of the income went elsewhere, to meet the mortgage and loan interest and repayment costs, and to pay annuities and allowances. Legal fees must have been considerable; there was land tax to pay. By the end of the nineteenth century the Welsh estate, still bolstered by tithes but lacking any support from elsewhere following the collapse of the lead market and the sale of the English estates, was still yielding about ten thousand a year—after a century of slow inflation.

A jesting phrase attributes true aristocratic wealth to patrimony, matrimony and parsimony. The later generations of Vaughans inherited a questionable patrimony, since the great estate had been encumbered with debts. In matrimony, three Vaughans married heiresses (the first, third and fourth Viscounts), but others married women with dowries, and these were cancelled out by provision for daughters and dowagers. On parsimony, like so many aristocratic families, the Vaughans failed comprehensively. The demands of 'the port of a gentleman', the endless needs of children and annuitants, the expected conspicuous consumption, the tempting sins of gambling, legal fees, the maintenance of mistresses, even (as we shall see in the next chapter) the precedence given to game over farming—all sucked greedily at the milch cow of inherited income.

NOTES

[1] See J.L. & Barbara Hammond, *The Bleak Age*, (London, 1934), chapter VI.
[2] See A.E.Davies, 'Enclosures in Cardiganshire', *Ceredigion*, VIII, i (1976), pp.103-7.
[3] NLW CD I, 1174.
[4] NLW CD II, 663.
[5] NLW CD II, 663.
[6] NLW CD II, 1255.
[7] NLW CD I, 1740.
[8] J.M.Howells, *article*, pp.83-84.
[9] NLW CD I, 2052.
[10] NLW CD IV, 16.
[11] NLW CD I, 1028, cited by Richard [Moore]-Colyer, 'Aspects of land occupation in nineteenth century Cardiganshire', *Transactions of the Honourable Society of Cymmrodorion* (1981), p. 85n.
[12] NLW CD I, 401.
[13] These figures are to be found in the schedules attached to each parish map in NLW.
[14] NLW CD I, 484, 528.
[15] NLW CD I, 762.
[16] W.J.Lewis, *Lead Mining in Wales*, (Cardiff, 1967), p.45. Henceforth Lewis.
[17] Lewis, p.48.
[18] Lewis, p.50.
[19] NLW CD I, 597.
[20] E.g. *The Morris Letters*, ed. J.H.Davies, (Aberystwyth, 1903), Vol. II, p.153; *Additional Letters of the Morrises of Anglesey*, ed. Hugh Owen, (London, 1949), Vol. I, p.211, pp.259-60. But Wilmot Vaughan was fairly low on the list of Lewis Morris's targets.
[21] NLW CD I, 879.
[22] Lewis, pp.105/6.
[23] Cited in D.W.Howell, *Patriarchs and Parasites*, p.55.
[24] NLW CD I, 1034, 1037.
[25] Lewis, p.110.
[26] For his career see R.Burt, *John Taylor, mining entrepreneur and engineer 1779-1863*, (Buxton, 1977).
[27] Lewis, p.180.
[28] David Bick, *Frongoch Lead and Zinc Mine* (Sheffield, 1986). This admirable booklet contains a supplement (pp.48-53) by Dr Stephen Briggs on the visit of the French engineer Leon-Vivant Moissenet to Fron-goch; Moissenet 'expressed surprise that the owners of the mineral rights (i.e. Lord Lisburne) extracted such huge royalties'.
[29] J.M.Howells, *thesis*, citing the unscheduled NLW Ivor Evans MSS, but actually intending, not the Ivor Evans MSS, but a separate group of Crosswood documents deposited by Lord Lisburne through Ivor Evans. See NLW *Annual Report* 1949/50, p.40.

IX. PHEASANTS AND POACHERS

In folk-memory there can be few more vivid scenes from the gentry life of the past than game-shooting. For several months every year the squire, his sons (and frequently his daughters), often with neighbours, friends and visitors, attended by keepers and beaters, would set out daily, guns ready and dogs at heel. In the days of muzzle-loaders they must have returned with blackened faces, and on a good day they must have been half-deaf as well. For pheasant-shooting, beaters would be employed to drive the birds over the guns, but a sportsman would be just as happy quietly seeking out river-edge snipe or duck. As in other fields, so in this, the Vaughan family and the Trawsgoed estate were typical; shooting was an essential part of the annual round. By contrast, fox-hunting is barely represented in the family archive.

It may seem odd to devote a whole chapter of this book to a study of game and shooting, especially as evidence for the Trawsgoed estate barely exists before the early nineteenth century. Some of the most important published studies of the landed aristocracy and gentry pay little attention to the matter of game and the game laws.[1] Yet the mass of game legislation should alert every student of the history of land in Britain to the significance of the subject. Hunting, shooting and fishing were not an aristocratic joke, nor mere hobbies for those fortunate enough to have the means to enjoy them; for centuries they were central to the way of life of British landowners. Never was this more true than in the second half of the nineteenth century. Indeed, it might even be suggested that many men, disappointed at their declining political and social influence, turned ever more to the pursuit of pleasure, and especially of game. At a time when many took their agricultural pursuits seriously, others seem to have put game first, whatever the damage to their tenants' farms (and their home farms too).[2]

Entertaining evidence for this in west Wales is to be found in Captain Newton Wynne Apperley's *A Hunting Diary*, published in 1926 but relating his hunting feats during the 1870s with the Gogerddan foxhounds and otterhounds, and with other packs in Merionethshire and Cardiganshire. Apperley and his fellow gentry revelled in the slaughter of the very animals whose courage and endurance they admired so much; the diary betrays a veritable obsession with mud and blood. These activities were protected by numerous Acts of Parliament, largely the product of a centuries' old war between poachers and landowners. Two principles were in opposition, the liberty of the subject and the right to property of the landowner. On the popular side, wild creatures were seen as the property of all or none, whereas the landowner regarded them as his property, and unauthorised access on his land as trespass. This conflict saw murder committed on the Trawsgoed estate in 1868.

The Crown had largely lost control of its once overwhelming hunting rights by the mid-seventeenth century; by an Act of 1671 the right to hunt game was allowed to four classes of men:-

owners of land worth £100 a year
99-year-leaseholders of land worth £150 a year
eldest sons of Esquires and men of higher rank
holders of franchises.[3]

The Act authorised the employment of gamekeepers with powers of confiscation, search of property and night arrest of poachers. To achieve conviction it was only necessary to hail the accused before a single J.P. and for one witness (e.g. a gamekeeper) to swear against the accused on oath. The J.P. could imprison and/or fine the guilty party on the spot. Such a hearing could take place at the justice's home, with no formal records kept. Inability to pay a fine could mean automatic imprisonment, often with dire consequences for the prisoner's family, though not every landed Justice took advantage of the full and savage rigour of the law. The sale of game was made illegal—though not its purchase. During the 18th and early 19th centuries Game Laws became more and more numerous. The so-called Black Act of 1723 made death the penalty for disguising oneself to kill deer illegally. An Act of 1770 punished killing game at night with 3-6 months' imprisonment and a public whipping.

Although some of these Acts were made less stringent in subsequent years (from 1773 public whipping could only be administered for a third offence, and fines could be imposed instead of imprisonment, if the poacher could pay), the game-hunting classes fought fiercely to guard their privileges and their pheasants. In 1752 the Society of Noblemen and Gentlemen for the Preservation of Game was formed, which specialised in prosecuting butchers who sold game. In 1827 spring guns (which may have killed more innocent parties than poachers) and man-traps, used for much of the eighteenth century, were made illegal, but in 1828 the Night Poaching Act imposed sentences of fourteen years' transportation on gangs of three or more who poached at night, and gave powers to keepers of searching travellers on the high road.

Fierce, bloody and sometimes fatal clashes between keepers and poachers blighted the countryside for two centuries. The keepers were their masters' servants; the poachers were often poor labourers for whom their prey could be the means of avoiding starvation, though they could include a wider social range of men. They would justify their practice with the doctrine that wild creatures could not possibly be the property of any man. There was certainly a feeling among many that poaching was a justifiable revenge on the landowning class, in a society where so few owned so much. There was also huge resentment of the Game Laws by tenant-farmers and small property-owners who were unable, after the 1671 Act, to shoot on their own land either to preserve their crops or to fill their pots. Nineteenth-century radicalism was hostile to the game-preserving interest; the first wave of parliamentary reform also saw the Game Reform Act of 1831, which made the sale of game legal but was otherwise toothless. In spite of the fierce campaigning of John Bright in the 1840s, an Act of 1844 increased the severity of the game laws once again, and parliamentary select committees of the 1840s and 1870s achieved little, despite the weight of evidence in favour of reform.

It is difficult to study individual cases of petty poaching or to deal in statistics, since so much of the justice meted out by J.P.s was summary and unrecorded. True, it was considered bad form for a J.P. to try to convict a man who had poached on his own land, but he expected the neighbouring J.P. to keep the side up, if necessary sweetening him with gifts of game. It is easier to follow the outbreaks of murderous warfare between the keepers and the poachers, and the evidence is overwhelming that ordinary country people were on the side of the poachers. A poacher convicted of murdering a keeper could expect a huge outburst of sympathy on his behalf, though it rarely saved him from the rope once arrested. The landed interest regarded game as property and property as sacred; logically therefore game was sacred.

I have as yet discovered only the barest of references to game in the Trawsgoed archive before 1800. Nevertheless, it is fair to assume that the heads of the family had long been involved in the traditional pursuit of their class, and that only lack of records prevents any description of their involvement. The very earliest references come as early as 1633, when John Vaughan, in making grants of land, reserved to himself the fowling and fishing rights.[4] There is also a series of pre-1800 references in the court leet papers for Pennardd and Blaenaeron. The Vaughans had held the lordships of several Cardiganshire manors since the Restoration, and one of the principal rights and duties was to hold the manorial courts. Local landholders and tenants were assembled in court, usually a public house, under the rule of the Lord of the Manor's appointee, usually his agent or steward. On 24 October, 1783, the Pennardd court leet passed:

> that we present all Persons that keep Greyhounds Guns and Nets or other Arms for to destroy the Game within this Lordship . . . in the Sum of Seven Shilling and Six pence each.[5]

The court went on passing this or similar motions annually year after year, sometimes referring specifically to fowling, to killing hares, and to the need to protect salmon spawning grounds.

Further evidence comes from the files of Samuel Williams, the Aberystwyth printer, during the early decades of the nineteenth century; he was asked to print '100 Notices not to kill Game on the Crosswood Estate', '60 Notices not to shoot on Earl of Lisburne's Demesne' and '100 Notices not to kill Game on the Manors of Yspytty, Ystradmeirig'.[6] Much more direct evidence suddenly appears in 1825, as the following story tells.

Ernest Augustus Vaughan was known (after his father's accession to the earldom in 1820) as Lord Augustus Vaughan, and under that title he figured in an unfortunate court case in 1825. He and his brother George had been shooting, apparently on open land somewhere south of the Ystwyth. They encountered another would-be sportsman, John Parry, one of the Llidiardau family. There was a quarrel; the Vaughan brothers claimed (incorrectly) that their father owned the shooting rights over the land in question; Parry would not accept their word that he could not shoot on the land, but carried on trying to kill grouse. The Vaughan brothers annoyed and tormented him until, in exasperation, he raised his stick and tapped Lord Augustus on the shoulder in warning manner. Lord Augustus raised his gun threateningly, but was restrained by his brother.

The enraged young Lord Vaughan brought a case of assault against John Parry in the Court of Great Sessions at Cardigan, but when Parry arrived at the court determined to plead guilty, since he had technically committed assault by raising his stick and tapping his lordship, he found that Lord Vaughan had moved the case to the King's Bench in London without giving him notice; this was a common abuse of procedure. Lord Vaughan was reproved in court both for his behaviour in the shooting incident and for not advising John Parry that he had moved the case to London. Parry was fined £5, the smallness of the sum obviously reflecting the judge's opinion of the prosecution, and of the arrogance of the young aristocrat who had brought it.

This discreditable incident, disinterestedly preserved in the Trawsgoed archive, smacks of farce, but the application of the Game Laws (perfectly legally) on the Trawsgoed estate was to lead to severe suffering. The war between keepers and poachers was fought without quarter over the estates of England and Wales, and reached savage depths during the period 1820-1880, by the end of which there were more gamekeepers than policemen in the country. For example, a keeper was killed near Chelmsford in 1856 and a poacher was hanged for the crime; in 1859 a poacher and a keeper were shot dead at Bishop Burton, and another keeper was killed near Rotherham in 1865. There were many more incidents than these. Nearer home, for example, there was a serious encounter near Ruthin in 1820. John, Richard and Robert Roberts, three brothers, were charged at Denbigh Great Sessions on the capital charge of the attempted murder of a keeper; the keeper had received four pellets in the face, and others in his clothes and hat. The good Welsh jury, obviously unwilling to be responsible for the hanging of three brothers, acquitted them, but they were afterwards tried by a special jury on the lesser charge of being armed, in enclosed grounds, with the intention of killing game, and this was sufficient to see them transported for seven years.

A typical result of such conflicts was the death near Trawsgoed of Joseph Butler in 1868, an event still vividly alive in local tradition, and obviously related to the game-preserving practices of the Trawsgoed estate. Butler was one of six gamekeepers employed by the fourth Earl of Lisburne. The incident happened close to Dolfor, a large farm at the east end of Llanilar parish, beside the little road that crosses from Trawsgoed Bridge to Llangwyryfon; Ty'n-y-berth is between Dolfor and the river Ystwyth. The incident is best described in the words of

James Morgan, one of the keepers, speaking at the inquest held a few days later:

> On the 28th ult I was out with Richard Jones, Morgan Evans and Joseph Butler the deceased, watching the coverts. About 1 o'clock in the morning I heard a shot on Dolfawr ground, and we all left Ty'n y Berth wood, where we were standing, to go and see who was shooting. We were not much more than a hundred yards off, as we were going away, when we heard the report and saw the flash of another shot. We were in advance of Richard Jones (the head-keeper), as we could go faster. I saw more than one person starting away from where I saw the flash. I followed them as well as I could, according as I heard their noise. I ran them out of the wood into a field called Cae Gwyn. I called to the other keepers: 'Forward, here they are.' I was on the point of laying hold of one of the men I was pursuing when one of them turned round, with his gun to his shoulder, and pointing it at me said: 'D-n you, stand back, or I will shoot you.' I said, 'Oh, don't shoot me.' The three men were together, and one of them, a short man, had also a gun, but he neither threatened nor did anything offensive with it. They then ran away again, and I followed them, and overtook them, on which the tall man turned round again, pointing his gun at me, saying, 'Stand back.' He also told the other two in Welsh to shoot, but they stood quiet and did nothing. I dared not lay hold of one of them, as I all along expected the other keepers to come to my assistance. They started off again, and when I got up to them the tall one again held up his gun at me until his two companions got into a garden, and from there they ran up a hill towards Lledrod. I closely followed them, and suddenly Joseph Butler came across to them. I said, 'Hurrah, Joe,' and laid hold of the one now in custody, at the same moment the tall one fired, and Joseph Butler fell. The third man had a stick, with which he struck at me. He and the tall man ran away then, and escaped. Morgan Evans, another keeper, then came up, and we took the man I had caught to the cottage where Richard Jones, the head keeper, was. We then returned to fetch the body of Butler. He was quite dead. It was a dark morning, in consequence of clouds, otherwise it was a moonlit night. The man in custody had nothing to do with the shot that killed Joseph Butler.[7]

The following week Morgan Jones, the captured poacher, was charged by the magistrates of Llanilar with being concerned in the murder and with night poaching. During the hearing a solicitor arrived with an offer from the prisoner's brother, Henry Jones, to surrender if he were granted bail. The bench naturally refused, and the police soon captured Jones and thrust him into the dock with his brother, but he

The grave of the murdered gamekeeper, Joseph Butler.

had to be removed as he had not been formally charged. In his evidence to the magistrates James Morgan added a detail of the conversation between him and Morgan Jones after Butler's death:

> 'You villain, you have killed the man.'
> 'I did not shoot him, it was bachgen Cefn coch.'

Cefncoch was a thirteen-acre holding in the parish of Llangwyryfon; the walls of the house still stand, but it is unoccupied. At the census of 1861 William Richards, aged 21, was living there with his father. Morgan and Henry Jones lived at Ty'n Llwyn, Llangwyryfon, and in

1861 were aged 23 and 14 respectively. William Richards' description may best be read in the poster which was swiftly brought from the press. For months he was on the run in the locality, sheltered in various homes.

According to lively local tradition the renegade was hidden on one occasion in the bed of a newly-delivered mother, on another in the foaming bed of the water-mill wheel at Cwmnewidion, (with a variant that he hid in the machinery). The £100 reward proved fruitless; the local community was mute. Nothing indicates so well the gulf between the wealthy, anglicised, Anglican landlord and the poorer Welsh farmers and labourers as that wall of silence, though doubtless some would-be informers were only deterred by fear of ostracism by their neighbours. Hostility to the privileged classes even extended to respectable but radical members of the Aberystwyth town community

Ernest Edmund Vaughan, 7th earl of Lisburne, with one of his gamekeepers.

like John Jones (known as Ivon, 1821-1898). Ivon was an Aberystwyth grocer, Sunday School superintendant and man of letters, who had been the driving force behind the Aberystwyth Eisteddfod of 1865. According to one Edward Morgan, writing in the *Welsh Gazette* in 1945, Ivon and a Tregaron watchmaker, David Joseph, helped organise Wil Cefn Coch's escape, dressed as a woman, to Liverpool in the spring of 1869, and thence to the U.S.A.[8] Morgan heard Ivon telling his father the story on more than one occasion. In the U.S.A. Wil is said to have lived with a loaded gun at hand, and there his Welsh sweetheart Bet Morgan joined him and married him in 1872. He died in 1921 at Oak Hill, Jackson County, Ohio, where his grave is still to be seen.

In the meantime Morgan Jones was brought to trial at the Cardigan Quarter Sessions of March, 1869. The judge threw out the charge of assisting in the murder, since he was in the keeper's power at the time. Despite the statement on the reward-poster and the previously-quoted evidence, the crime was said at the trial to have happened on the night of 26-27 November. Jones was sentenced to twelve months' hard labour. I have not been able to find any account of his brother Henry's trial. Of William Richards, the judge said: 'It is a discredit to the county that the murderer is still at large.'[9] The whole incident must have upset Ernest Augustus Vaughan, the fourth Earl; the family's penultimate effort to capture the county seat in Parliament (through his nephew Edmund Vaughan) had newly failed. Remarkably, Joseph Butler's granddaughter was still alive at the time of drafting this chapter in 1993.

*   *   *

Far more detail of the Trawsgoed estate's involvement in game preservation and shooting becomes available at the time of the fourth Earl's death in 1873. The Game Book of his son George, the fifth Earl of Lisburne survives, as do two successive volumes which bring the story up to the present day.[10] As we have seen, Ernest Augustus the fourth Earl employed six gamekeepers; his estate was extensive, and no one or two men could have patrolled it all. A well-detailed Game Book gives the date, the names of those shooting, the place shot, the numbers of game in columns by species, and gives space for notes. For 1872 and 1873 Ernest Augustus did not bother to name the guns, nor to add any notes, but the dates, places and species-numbers are all carefully entered in his neat writing. The early entries in 1872 are one for a day in July, when he shot eight hares, one for the 12th of August, when he shot ten grouse, and then a string of entries for October. In that month his prey was not so much pheasants (17) as partridges (97), hares (32) and rabbits (45). The substantial pheasant shooting at that time was not on the farms but on the land north of Trawsgoed mansion, particularly the plantations, which were not then rhododendron-ridden as some are now. On December 3rd 144 pheasants were bagged, with 56 hares, nineteen rabbits and two woodcocks. During December the Earl was out shooting virtually every day until the 20th, but then there was a ten-day pause for Christmas. January was busy, February less so, and then there is no entry until he started again shooting hares in July. There was never shooting on Sundays.

The Earl's annual totals, drawn up at the end of each February, show that more rabbits were killed than all other game put together. The totals can be tabulated by years, with the understanding that a year, e.g. 1872, is really the period July 1872—February 1873.

	1872	1873	1874	1875	1876	1877	1878	1879	1880	1881
Pheasant	347	332	815	902	1300	1312	1547	572	1420	1688
Partridge	161	137	295	114	509	200	484	44	240	428
Hares	195	163	198	159	252	254	349	349	485	336
Rabbits	961	1473	3674	3184	2616	4412	4043	6253	9814	8737
Grouse	20	32	31	-	7	24	10	17	26	19
Woodcock	99	63	48	-	44	40	42	45	26	11
Snipe	5	10	66	-	21	34	28	12	18	39
Landrails	-	2	-	-	-	1	-	-	2	3
Mallard	1	-	23	-	-	10	77	37	18	33
Teal	-	-	10	-	-	5	21	13	26	7

The figures make interesting reading. Partridges have disappeared from Ceredigion in the late twentieth century; they cannot be reared by hand like pheasants, and they only flourish where there is arable farming. The Trawsgoed estate maps, and the Tithe Maps of the 1840s, show that there was plenty of arable in the county, and it survived on some farms into the 1940s. The figures for rabbits killed in this period are also interesting; from 1876 for several years there is an additional figure for rabbits killed by the gamekeepers—2,616 in 1876. However, there is no separate figure for 1880, suggesting that the large total includes the keepers' work. The figures suggest that rabbits, once carefully preserved in mediaeval warrens, were a mounting plague during the last decades of the century; we shall see that the annual cull rose to more than fifteen thousand. 1878 is interesting for revealing that hare-coursing was part of the estate's sport—95 were killed in addition to the number shot, and figures are noted for several subsequent years.

The fifth Earl put a rare comment at the end of the 1877-78 season's figures: 'The worst Partridge year ever known, and to what cause I know not.' Certainly it was poorer than the previous year, but not worse than earlier seasons. However, when he set down another despairing comment at the end of the 1879-80 season:

> The worst year known for Pheasant and Partridges unless better next shall give up rearing by hand.

we know that he was in good company; the season was a disastrous one in many areas of Wales and England, caused by heavy rain and a cold breeding season.[11] Just as other local squires like Vaughan Davies and landed in-laws like the Probyns came to shoot on the Trawsgoed estate, it must be presumed that the Earl spent periods shooting on their lands, and could speak from wider experience than that of his own estate alone.

At the end of the 1880-81 season, the Earl commented enigmatically:

> On the whole satisfactory, but think Jem took credit for more Pheasants than really existed, and should have done better with Rabbits had. Tom's Hill better shot earlier as the Snow destroyed so many.

Perhaps the most revealing comment is the one he made at the end of the 1881-82 season, when in spite of killing the largest-ever number of pheasants, he noted:

> Not as good as I expected, must have more Pheasants.

Much wants more. The pheasant figure for that year included shooting 326 on November 15th and 348 on November 17th. In fact, the following year showed another slump in pheasants (639) and partridges (212) shot, followed by the comment:

> Worst year ever known for Pheasants and Partridges—Hatched out well but gradually died off from I suppose the wet & cold.

Pheasant shooting revived in 1883, but the Earl still expressed his dissatisfaction. During the season of 1884, 5,417 rabbits were shot, while the keepers disposed of another 9,403. The season of 1885 was a poor one, which the Earl blamed on 'wretched weather and late harvest'; 1886, with very similar figures, produced the unusual comment 'Satisfied, but should have done better had I not been obliged to keep down the rabbits', a task which of course his tenants had been forbidden by law to perform, though the Ground Game Act of 1881 had alleviated their position. In 1874 the Earl began including the names of his shooting companions—sometimes visitors, sometimes local friends, his tenants, keepers, and of course members of the family, including his wife Alice. Unfortunately it is not always easy to decide who is who in the lists of names, since so often, knowing his own companions well, he gives either first-names or surnames but not both.

We know a little about the fifth Earl's material requirements for shooting. The inventory of his goods drawn up in 1890 as part of the evaluation of the succession tax (death duties) lists, in the kennel:

> one pointer, three retrievers, one mastiff, fifteen ferrets, six dozen traps, five breech loaders, four muzzle loaders.[12]

The sixth Earl's 1899 inventory includes the following as the responsibility of the gamekeeper:

> 200 pheasant coops, 150 yards of rabbit netting, six dozen purse nets, six dozen traps, twelve guns, four dogs.

The fifth Earl's successor, Arthur George Henry, had bought a new and larger game-book well-suited to his bold handwriting. He was an even more zealous sportsman than his father. The record for his first year, 1888-89, includes 1,761 pheasant, 442 partridge, 140 snipe, 57 mallard, 67 teal, 6 wigeon, 4 golden plover and 3 wild geese. He also gives figures for unnamed 'various' game. The following year he doubled the number of partridge killed to 885 and increased the number of snipe to 189. His comments are rare, and laconic in the extreme; on September 27th, 1890, he noted:

> Poor old Derry Shot. Recovering.

'Derry' may be the Earl's cousin of Derry Ormond; his aunt Elizabeth Malet Vaughan had married John Jones of Derry Ormond (d.1879).

The year 1890 is the first in which he began to record the number of pigeons shot, suggesting a natural increase of the birds. At the end of that year he shot a wild swan on Cors Caron, followed by a goosander in the New Year. On August 8th 1891 he noted that the two partridges picked up on Cors Caron were 'killed by train'.

The distress any modern ornithologist must feel on reading that a bittern was shot on Cors Caron in January 1892 is natural but anachronistic. This was not an age of scientific ornithology. Rarities were only recorded by shooting, as is clear from such an authority as the Witherby-Jourdain *Handbook of British Birds*. At least the record of the Caron bittern survives. On September 6th, 1893, a quail was shot at Cefn-gaer, and on January 18th 1894 a shoveller duck on Cors Caron, and from then on there are occasional shootings of both species. A scaup was shot on Cors Caron on February 2nd, 1894.

Rabbits were increasing rapidly all over the country, and on the Trawsgoed estate they were the commonest prey.[13] On November 6th, 1894, a party of six men shot 2,823 rabbits on Talfan hill; the next day they went out and bagged 504 pheasants on the Home shoot, only 44 on the following day, but on the 9th another 264 pheasants were killed. What did they do with so many corpses? Despite those two large bags of pheasants, only 1,075 were shot in that season, but the number of pigeons rose to 427, many more than in previous years. In the following season the Earl and his friends went out far less often than usual during the winter; the partridges killed (563) actually outnumbered the pheasants (459); only 5,785 rabbits were shot, compared with more than twelve thousand in 1894-95. In 1896-97, however, the totals were back to normal, including 2,367 pheasants, 441 partridges and 15,035 rabbits. The totals of pheasants shot at Trawsgoed can be set in proportion by comparison with the figures of 19,180 pheasants and 2,627 partridges shot at the famous Elveden estate in Suffolk during the 1895-96 season.[14]

Although Trawsgoed did not aspire to such huge quarries, these were the great days of Trawsgoed shooting, for those privileged enough to enjoy it. That privilege was not necessarily confined to family, friends and keepers. Sometimes the names of farmers are noted, suggesting that the Earl may have called to see how the game was, and invited the farmer out with him, an obvious way of maintaining good personal relations with his tenants. Other occasions were the high holidays of the time, the December shoots near the mansion, bringing out many of the local men as beaters while gunfire filled the air and birds thumped to the ground. These would be fetched in by the dogs reared and trained by the keeper at Dolgelynen, where the kennels and the apparatus for boiling the dogs' food are still to be seen.

1898-99 was another highly successful season, and at the beginning of the next season, in the August of 1899, the Earl began shooting grouse and duck confidently enough on Cors Caron. On August 18th he went to Tom's Hill, killing three grouse and one duck—his last shoot, and the last entry in the Game Book for six years. The sixth Earl had died, his son and heir, Ernest Edmund (born 1892) the seventh Earl was only a child, and the shooting was let, and unrecorded, until 1906. In that year the young Earl noted, in schoolboy copperplate, his shooting of rabbits and pigeons in small numbers in April, and he continued during the school summer holidays, restricted to rabbits, a hare and a few pigeons. In January of 1907 he was out again, killing a few pheasants, rabbits, hares and woodcock.

By December 1909 the young Earl was able to go out with a party of six others who killed 205 pheasants in a day on the Home shoot. He recorded:

> Excellent day. New drives tried very successful, especially River drive.

During subsequent seasons he was readier than his father or grandfather to add notes, e.g.:

> Very bad day. Heavy rain & birds though fairly plentiful very wild. (23.8.1910)

> Drake (a friend) shot hare from car going 30 m.p.h.!!!

> 1911 was a year remarkable for its dry summer. From May 1st to early September there was no real spell of wet weather except Coronation week. Temp. often recorded 100 in the shade.

However, the great days of Trawsgoed shooting had passed; the season's total for 1911-12 including only 314 pheasants, 189 partridge and 3,448 rabbits, while the following season saw a crash in the number of partridge (26) and a rise in the total of rabbits to 5,437, but only 706 of those were shot by the Earl and his parties; the rest were culled by the keepers. The Earl changed his counting method in 1913, adding up the totals for August-December, and starting anew in January 1914 through till February 1915. Naturally the totals for 1913 were small, and even the count for the longer subsequent period was poor: 245 pheasant, 38 partridge and 3,907 rabbits, nearly all the latter killed by the keepers.

The Earl's handwriting ceases in March 1915; in that year he transferred to the Welsh Guards, and did not shoot again at Trawsgoed until January 1918, when he recorded a month's shooting before returning to the Army. In the intervals the shooting record was maintained in a neat hand, presumably of a lessee, and Lord Lisburne is recorded in that hand as being present for two days in November 1915, presumably when on leave. In August 1919 the Earl once more began recording his shoots; he went out frequently, but the bags were small, and the record stops at the end of October. He began again in August 1920 and maintained the record until the first week in January—recording that he had seen a bittern on Cors Caron in December. On November 17th he notes that a keeper shot a bittern by mistake, it being a misty day. Attitudes had already changed.

During the 1920s the Earl shot regularly, but the numbers of birds and animals killed is only a fifth of those shot in the late-Victorian heyday. In 1925-26 600 pheasants, 17 partridges, 24 hares, 963 rabbits, 15 grouse, 44 pigeon, 117 duck of several species made up most of the bag; only snipe (177) compare in numbers with the earlier period. The estate of course had been drastically reduced in size, but the numbers of pheasants shot around the mansion, where the largest kills had always been made thanks to the plantations and the special rearing efforts of the keepers, was greatly reduced. Partridges disappear from the record altogether.

The impact of the Wall Street Crash of 1929-30 seems to have impinged even on the Game Book. Totals of pheasants shot during the later 1920s averaged about 500 a season, and in 1929 the Earl noted that 2,000 pheasant eggs had been bought and 1,691 hatchlings had been taken to the rearing field. However, in the season of 1930-31 only seven shoots are recorded, and the victims were mostly rabbits (44), pigeons (21) and grouse (21). Only four pheasants were killed.

Nothing daunted, the Earl began shooting again in August 1931, but rented out the Cors Caron shoot to one Colonel Cosens for two months, and the numbers shot are still small. The book closes with the

242   The Vaughans of Trawsgoed

records for August-September 1932. On August 8th he notes that his son John (the present Earl) went out for his first shoot, and that on August 13th John shot his first grouse. Ever since that August, for more than sixty years, the present Earl has been a keen sportsman, who until recently shot regularly on a much-reduced range, and employed a keeper who reared pheasants and mallard for release.

Some readers may express surprise at the amount of space I have given to this side of the family's activity on the estate for the brief period during which records are available. What the position was before the nineteenth century it seems impossible to know in any detail. However, its importance in the later history of the estate is obvious. There is, certainly, a darker side visible in the two recorded cases of eviction of tenants for killing rabbits in 1875 and 1893 which have already been discussed. Preservation of game affected farming adversely not only by the potential for friction between tenant and landlord, but by the very activity of the game and its impact on crops and grazing. A final justification of this chapter is the shooting of Joseph Butler, one of the most dramatic Welsh incidents in the centuries-long struggle over game.

On the positive side, preservation gave local employment to keepers, who in the later period at least seem usually to have been Welshmen, rather than the Scots and Englishmen previously preferred. Casual payment must have been made to beaters. There was also an environmental pay-off. Woodlands and hedgerows were maintained and coverts planted. Crows, magpies and jays were kept down, which must have benefitted the small birds, though the slaughter of falcons, hawks and owls was short-sighted.

Families like the Vaughans were not, however, directly concerned with such a balance-sheet. The Trawsgoed family simply did what almost everybody else in their position did. Shooting was a proper, almost an obligatory, pastime for a wealthy gentleman of leisure. It was part of the social activity of the head of a family to invite his relatives and friends to shoot over his lands, and to visit them for the same reason. It was also expected that he would bring up his sons to share his enjoyment. Should anyone doubt this view, Captain Apperley's *A Hunter's Diary* will soon enlighten them. And though most of us may not wish for the return of those days, it would be good to see as many partridge and snipe in the area today as thronged it then.

NOTES

[1]18th and 19th century hunting and shooting are only very briefly described in D.W.Howell, *Patriarchs and Parasites: the gentry of south-west Wales in the eighteenth century* (Cardiff, 1986) pp.185-7, and the same author's *Land and People in Nineteenth-century Wales* (London, 1977) pp.77-79.

[2]The background information is derived from the following sources: articles by Chester Kirby, 'The English Game Law System', in the *American Historical Review* (1933) pp.240-262; 'The Attack on the English Game Laws in the Forties', in the Journal of Modern History, 1932, pp.18-37, and by Douglas Hay: 'Poaching and the Game Laws on Cannock Chase' in Hay et.al., *Albion's Fatal Tree* (Peregrine Books, 1977) pp.189-254. For lively full-length accounts see Harry Hopkins, *The Long Affray*, (London, 1985) and E.P.Thompson, *Whigs and Hunters*, (London, 1975).

[3]22 & 23 Chas II c.25.

[4]NLW CD II, 36, 37.

[5]NLW CD II, 1255.

[6]Eiluned Rees, 'The Sales-Book of Samuel Williams, Aberystwyth Printer', *Ceredigion*, X, 4 (1987), p.364.

[7]*Aberystwyth Observer*, 5.12.1868.

[8]*Welsh Gazette*, May 24, 1945.

[9]*Aberystwyth Observer*, 13.3.1869. There are less detailed references in the *Carmarthen Journal*, but only a paragraph in the *Cambrian News*.

[10]I am most grateful to the present Earl for the opportunity to examine these books at leisure.

[11]See Colin Matheson: 'Gamebook Records of Pheasants and Partridges in Wales', NLWJ, IX, 287-94.

[12]NLW CD II, 1549.

[13]See 'The Rabbit and the Hare in Wales', *Antiquity* (1941) pp.371-81.

[14]Matheson, op.cit., p.292.

Afterword

by

The Hon. John Vaughan

When Gerald Morgan first started researching this book in 1989, the only published account of the Vaughan family was J.M.Howells's article in *Ceredigion*, 'The Crosswood Estate 1547-1947, a four hundred year survey of a Cardiganshire family and its estates', based on his University of Wales M.A. thesis. Howells described his article 'as a window through which the reader can view the last four hundred years of what may justifiably be termed the Lisburne era'.

Gerald Morgan has now made a much wider opening, and he invites us to step through it into the world of the Vaughans as major representatives of the Cardiganshire landed class, of their properties and those over whom they held sway. He has, I know, worked tirelessly in his research to provide some fascinating insights into that world, and not least to show how the Vaughans rose from insignificant squiredom in the Ystwyth valley to become members of the aristocracy as well as major landlords wielding political influence and economic power. But the book is more than a study of rank ambition and self-advancement. This study of the strategies and alliances which the early Vaughans used in amassing their estate and fortune are of particular interest, both in a personal and historical sense. The business acumen and sheer verve of Sir John Vaughan, the great lawyer, could be textbook reading on any MBA syllabus.

Of course on a national scale the family were simply emulating their peers, and they managed, through dogged resourcefulness, shrewdness and undoubtedly some low cunning, to set themselves apart from all but one or two of Cardiganshire's gentry families. At the same time, I like to think, they never lost touch with and consideration of their Cardiganshire origins. Despite much living in London and elsewhere, the family always regarded the Crosswood estate as its principal asset, and were always concerned to continue making an imprint on the landscape whenever funds were available. The appearance of much of Ystwyth valley is essentially their creation, from the design of the woodlands to that of the farmhouses and cottages.

It is difficult to read a history of one's own family without feeling a combination of admiration for their human achievement and reservations about some of the characters involved, and some aspects of the pursuits of land-ownership. Gerald Morgan, following J.M.Howells, notes a cyclical proclivity in the family towards extravagance, indebtedness and dissipation. Pride too is clearly there in full measure, although it seems that on balance the Vaughans were more driven than handicapped by that particular sin.

It is not hard to detect, in Howells's account, a touch of triumphalism over the demise of the Crosswood estate as a major social and economic entity which was clearly considered by many at that time to represent an inequitable and unwarranted amount of wealth and privilege. The landed classes were in truth a soft target for those seeking political change—and how the world has changed since 1956. I am grateful to Gerald Morgan for distancing himself from a too politicised assessment of my family which would, I think, have been open to criticism not least because one generation cannot entirely be judged by the standards of another. The family's business and private correspondence, much of it used here as source material, reveals the family's genuine concern for the welfare of their tenants and employees.

Over several decades of this century my grandfather went out of his way to assist his agricultural tenants during the extremely difficult years of the agricultural depression, and to set an example himself by ensuring that the estate's revenues were reinvested in the property and not the family's indulgences. My grandfather was a man who counted his pennies, and he was ever anxious to avoid any comparison with that Lloyd of Bronwydd of whom Dr D.R.Jones, whose family were Bronwydd tenants, said at the Welsh Land Commission (1895) that all the rent they paid for their farm went 'on one night's feasting at the palace'.

Why did my grandfather sell the mansion and most of the estate in 1947? Unlike many other landowners at that time, he was certainly not in any serious debt. Throughout his ownership, he made sales of Crosswood property, of land which was at best a poor investment. It was only through these sales that he could afford to continue to run the estate. He always referred to himself as being 'land poor', that is, without any cash, because the property absorbed so much of his income. That said, he certainly had the resources necessary to have remained longer at Crosswood had he so wished.

As to why he sold, the answer is down to several factors. One must be because of the increasing burden of taxation introduced by the post-war Labour government, and another was the personal concern he felt about the future welfare of the family as a whole. He was also concerned about his ability to keep running the estate as a widower, as his experiences in the Welsh Guards during the First World War had left him a little nervous of being without the company of family and friends nearby. Had my grandmother lived beyond the Second World War, things might well have turned out differently; she loved Crosswood and the local community there. My grandfather was unable to foresee the enormous increases in agricultural land values which began in the early 1960's and have broadly continued apace since then. However, he did ensure that all the Crosswood tenants were offered the purchase of their farms, which in most cases they were able to buy on reasonable terms. Also, by selling the mansion and the park to the Ministry of Agriculture, he believed the estate would always remain as the centre for employment in the locality.

That the sale of Crosswood in 1947 signalled a complete withdrawal of the family from Cardiganshire and concluded the family's history there is something I have always been keen to contradict. The estate was too large and complex to sell at a stroke, and in any event my grandfather was determined to retain a part of it, not least because he wanted to remain as Lord Lieutenant of the county, a position he held until 1952.

That part of the Crosswood estate which was made over to my father in 1963 is what I am most familiar with. It has very much shaped my life and career and instilled in me a great sense of rootedness and an affection for the Cardiganshire countryside, its culture and its people, many of whom I consider as my friends. Those are convictions and friendships that I hope can be built upon in the future. One Lisburne era ended in 1947, but, quietly, another one continued.

I know that all my family wish to express their appreciation of Gerald Morgan's efforts in writing a history of the Vaughans of Trawsgoed; it is an unusual compliment and we wish this publication every success.

The Hon. John Vaughan
July, 1996

BIBLIOGRAPHY

A. Collections of Deeds and Manuscripts

National Library of Wales collections of manuscripts:-

Alcwyn Evans genealogies (NLW MS 12,359D)
Cardiganshire County Council Records (Roads)
Church in Wales Probate Records
Courts of Great Sessions, Gaol Files, Cardiganshire
Crosswood Deeds
Crosswood Maps Vols I, II & III
Cwrtmawr Deeds
David Thomas Papers
Llidiardau MSS
Morgan Richardson MSS
NLW MSS
Nanteos MSS
Plas Llangoedmore MSS
Tithe Maps and Schedules for N.Cardiganshire
H.M.Vaughan MSS

Public Record Office:-

Archdiocese of Canterbury Probate Records
Chancery C2
Hearth Tax
Lay Subsidy Rolls E/179/219

Ceredigion Record Office, Aberystwyth:-

ADX 15/1/11-13

In private ownership:

The Lisburne Pedigree, unique copy by York Herald of Arms (1921)

B. Unpublished Dissertations

Howells, J.M. 'The Crosswood Estate, its Growth and Economic Development 1683-1899', University of Wales M.A.thesis, 1956 (cited as Howells, Thesis)

Roberts, H.D. 'Noddwyr y Beirdd yn Sir Aberteifi', University of Wales M.A. thesis, 1969

Williams, J.Gwynn. 'Sir John Vaughan, Chief Justice of the Common Pleas', University of Wales M.A. thesis, 1952

C. Books

Apperley, N.W. *A Hunting Diary* (London, 1926)

Bartrum, P.C. *Welsh Genealogies A.D. 300-1400* (Cardiff, 1974)

Bick, David. *Frongoch Lead and Zinc Mine* (Sheffield, 1986)

Burt, R. *John Taylor, mining entrepreneur and engineer 1779-1863* (Buxton, 1977)

Cannadine, David. *The Decline and Fall of the British Aristocracy* (London, 1990)

Clay, C. *Rural society: landowners, peasants and labourers 1500-1750* (Cambridge, 1990)

Davies, J.C. *The Life, Travels, and Reminiscences of Jonathan Ceredig Davies* (Llanddewibrefi, 1926)

Davies, J.H. *The Letters of Lewis, Richard, William and John Morris* (Aberystwyth, 1907)

Davies, K.G. *Documents of the American Revolution 1770-1783 XV* (Dublin, 1976)

Dinely, Thomas. *The Account of the Official Progress of His Grace Henry the First Duke of Beaufort Through Wales in 1684* (ed. R.W.Banks, London, 1888).

Dwnn, Lewis. *Heraldic Visitations of Wales*, I (Llandovery, 1846)

Edwards, Ifan ab Owen. *A Catalogue of Star Chamber Proceedings relating to Wales* (Cardiff, 1929)

Evans, H.T. *Wales and the Wars of the Roses* (Stroud, 1995)

Evans, J.T. The Church Plate of Cardiganshire (Stow-on-the-Wold, 1914)

Girouard, M. *Life in the English Country House* (New Haven & London, 1978)

Glassey, L.K.J. *Politics and the appointment of Justices of the Peace 1685-1720* (Oxford, 1979)

Green, F. *Calendar of Deeds and Documents, Vol.II, The Crosswood Deeds* (Aberystwyth, 1927)

Green, Mary (ed) *A Calendar of State Papers Domestic*: Charles II, 1661-1662)London, 1861)

Griffiths, Ralph A. *The Principality of Wales in the Later Middle Ages, I* (Cardiff, 1972)

Hay, D. et.al, *Albion's Fatal Tree: Crime and Society in Eighteenth- Century England* (London, 1975)

Heal, F. & Holmes, C. *The Gentry in England and Wales 1500-1700* (London, 1994)

Henning, B.D. (ed.) *The History of the House of Commons, 1660-1690* (London, 1983)

Hope, Evelyn. *Llangranog and the Pigeonsford Family* (Cardigan, 1931)

Historic Manuscripts Commission, *Diary of the First Earl of Egmont*, vol.II, ed. R.A.Roberts

Historic Manuscripts Commission, *The Manuscripts of the Marquess of Ormonde*, ed. F.Elrington Ball

Historic Manuscripts Commission, T*he Manuscripts of the House of Lords 1692-3*, ed. E.F.Taylor & F.Skene

Historic Manuscripts Commission, *The Manuscripts of the Duke of Portland*, vol.V, ed. S.C.Lomas

Historic Manuscripts Commission, *Manuscripts in Various Collections*, VI (MSS of Capt. H.V.Knox) ed. S.C.Lomas (London, 1909)

Historic Manuscripts Commission, *The Manuscripts of the Earl of Carlisle*, ed. R.E.G.Kirk (London, 1897)

Historic Manuscripts Commission, *The Manuscripts of Mrs Stopford-Sackville*, I, ed. R.B.Knowles, W.O.Hewlett & S.C.Lomas (London, 1904)

Hopkins, Harry. *The Long Affray* (London, 1985)

Howell, D.W. *Land and People in Nineteenth-century Wales* (London, 1977)

Howell, D.W. *Patriarchs and Parasites: the gentry of south-west Wales in the eighteenth century* (Cardiff, 1986)

Hughes, J. *A history of the parliamentary representation of the county of Cardigan* (Aberystwyth, 1849)

Hughes, J. *Bywyd y Parch. Isaac Jones* (Liverpool, 1898)

Hyde, H.A. & Harrison, S.G. *Welsh Timber Trees* (Cardiff, 1977)

Jenkins, Philip. *The Making of a Ruling Class: the Glamorgan Gentry 1640-1790* (Cambridge, 1983)

Latham, R. *The Shorter Pepys* (London, 1987)

Lewis, W.J. *Lead Mining in Wales* (Cardiff, 1967)

Lloyd, H.A. *The Gentry of South-West Wales* (Cardiff, 1968)

Mackesy, Piers. *The War for America 1775-1783* (London, 1963)

Meyricke, S.R. *A History of Cardiganshire* (1910, 3rd edn.)

Mingay, G.E. *English Landed Society in the Eighteenth Century* (London, 1963)

Mingay, G.E. *The Gentry: the Rise and Fall of a Ruling Class* (London, 1976)

Mingay, G.E. *Land and Society in England 1750-1980* (London, 1994)

Namier, Lewis. *The Structure of Politics at the Accession of George III* (London, 2nd edition 1957)

Owen, G.D. *Wales in the Reign of James I* (London, 1988)

Owen, Hugh (ed.). *Additional Letters of the Morrises of Anglesey I & II*, (London, 1947-9).

Phillips, Bethan. *Peterwell* (Llandysul, 1983)

Phillips, J.R. *A List of the Sheriffs of Cardiganshire* (1868)

Phillips, J.R. *Memoirs of the Civil War in Wales and the Marches* (London, 1874)

Phillips, J.R.S. *The Justices of the Peace in Wales and Monmouthshire 1541 to 1689* (Cardiff, 1975)

Roberts, Glyn. *Aspects of Welsh History* (Cardiff, 1969)

Royal Commission on Land in Wales and Monmouthshire, *Evidence*, vol.III (London, 1896)

Sedgwick, Romney (ed.). *The History of Parliament: the House of Commons 1715-1754*, II (London, 1970)

Selden, John. *The Table Talk of John Selden*, ed. Sir Frederick Pollock (London, 1927)

Stone, L. *The Crisis of the Aristocracy* (London, 1967)

Stone, L. & Stone, J.C.F. *An Open Elite? England 1540-1880* (Oxford, 1984)

Stone, L. *The Road to Divorce: England 1530-1987* (Oxford, 1990)

Stroud, Dorothy. *Capability Brown* (London, 1975)

Theakston, L.E.Ll. & Davies, J. *Some Family Records and Pedigrees of the Lloyd Family of Allt yr Odyn . . .* (Oxford, 1912)

Thompson, E.P. *Whigs and Hunters* (London, 1975)

Thompson, F.M.L. *English Landed Society in the Nineteenth Century* (London, 1963)

Thorne, R.G. *The History of Parliament: the House of Commons 1790-1820* (London, 1986)

Lloyd, T. & Rev.Turnor, *General View of the Agriculture of the County of Cardigan* (London, 1794)

Valentine, Alan. *Lord North* (University of Oklahoma Press, 1967)

Valentine, Alan. *The British Establishment 1760-1784* (University of Oklahoma Press, 1969/70)

Vaughan, Edward (ed.). *The Reports of Sir John Vaughan, Lord Chief Justice of the Court of Common Pleas*, (London, 1677)

Williams, D.H. *Atlas of Cistercian Lands in Wales* (Cardiff, 1990)

D. Periodicals

Barber, Jill. 'The Problem of Debt: the papers of Charles Parry Solicitor 1844-1855', *NLWJ* XXVIII, 2 (1993), pp. 197-217.

Colyer, R.J. 'A Breconshire Gentleman in Europe 1737-8', *NLWJ* XXI (1979-80), pp. 265-97.

Colyer, R.J. 'The Land Agent in nineteenth-century Wales', *WHR* 8, 4 (1977)

Colyer, R.J. 'Aspects of land occupation in nineteenth century Cardiganshire', *THSC* (1981), pp. 79-97.

Colyer, R.J. 'The Gentry and the County in nineteenth century Cardiganshire', *WHR* X, 4 (1981), pp. 497-535.

Colyer, R.J. The Pryse Family of Gogerddan and the decline of a great estate, 1800-1960', *WHR* IX, 4 (1979) pp. 407-31.

Davies, J.F. 'Excavations at Trawscoed Roman Fort, Dyfed', *Bulletin of the Board of Celtic Studies*, XXI (1984), pp. 259-92.

Davies, T.I. 'The Vale of Aeron in the Making', *Ceredigion* II, 3 (1958) pp.194-206

Howells, J.M.'The Crosswood Estate, 1547-1947', *Ceredigion* III, 1 (1956), pp. 70-88

Jenkins, David 'The Pryse Family of Gogerddan, II', *NLWJ* VIII, pp.176-98.

Jones, Francis. 'The Old Families of South-West Wales' *Ceredigion* IV, 1 (1960) pp.1-18

Jones, Ieuan Gwynedd. 'Cardiganshire Politics in the Mid-Nineteenth Century', *Ceredigion* V, 1 (1964), pp. 14-41.

Kirby, Chester. 'The Attack on the English Game Laws in the Forties', *Journal of Modern History* (1932) pp. 18-37.

Kirby, Chester. 'The English Game Law System', *American Historical Review* (1933), pp. 240-62.

Lloyd-Jones, H. 'The Lesser Country Houses of Cardiganshire', *Ceredigion* II, 3 (1953)

Matheson, Colin. 'The Rabbit and Hare in Wales', *Antiquity*, XV (1941), pp. 371-81.

Matheson, Colin. 'Gamebook records of Pheasants and Partridges in Wales', *NLWJ* IX, 3 (1956) pp.287-94.

Morgan, Gerald. 'Local History in some 18th century Cardiganshire Estate Maps', *Journal of the University of Wales Agricultural Society*, 1992/93, pp. 48-77.

Morgan, Gerald. 'The Trawsgoed Inheritance', *Ceredigion* XII, 1 (1993) pp. 9-40.

Morgan, K.O. 'Cardiganshire Politics: the Liberal Ascendancy, 1885-1923', *Ceredigion*, V, 4 (1967) pp. 311-46

Rees, Eiluned. 'The Sales-Book of Samuel Williams, Aberystwyth Printer' *Ceredigion* X, 4 (1987) pp. 357-72.

Thomas, P.D.G. 'Eighteenth-century elections in the Cardigan Boroughs constituency', *Ceredigion* V, 4 (1967), pp.402-23.

Thomas, P.D.G. 'County Elections in Eighteenth-Century Cardiganshire', *Ceredigion* XI, 3 (1991) pp. 239-58

Vaughan, H.M. 'Household Accounts of a Welsh Peeress in the XVIIIth Century', *West Wales Historical Records*, V (1915), pp.293-6.

Williams, David. 'Cardiganshire Politics in the Mid-eighteenth Century', *Ceredigion*, III, 4 (1959), pp. 303-18.

Williams, J.Gwynn. 'Sir John Vaughan of Trawscoed, 1603-1674', *NLWJ* VIII (1953-4), pp. 33-48, 121-145, 225-243.

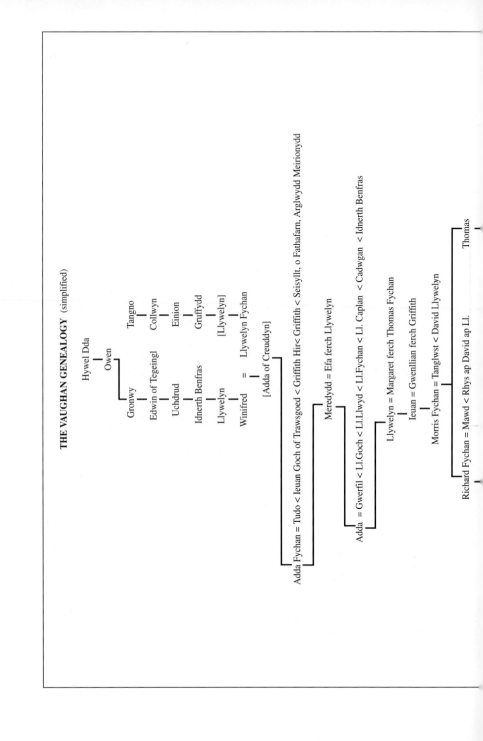

THE VAUGHAN GENEALOGY (simplified)

Hywel Dda
|
Owen
|
Gronwy   Tangno
| |
Edwin of Tegeingl   Collwyn
| |
Uchdrud   Einion
| |
Idnerth Benfras   Gruffydd
| |
Llywelyn   [Llywelyn]
| |
Winifred   =   Llywelyn Fychan
|
[Adda of Creuddyn]
|
Adda Fychan = Tudo < Ieuan Goch of Trawsgoed < Griffith Hir < Griffith < Seisyllt, o Fathafarn, Arglwydd Meirionydd
|
Meredydd = Efa ferch Llywelyn
|
Adda = Gwerfil < Ll.Goch < Ll.Llwyd < Ll.Fychan < Ll. Caplan < Cadwgan < Idnerth Benfras
|
Llywelyn = Margaret ferch Thomas Fychan
|
Ieuan = Gwenllian ferch Griffith
|
Morris Fychan = Tanglwst < David Llywelyn
|
Richard Fychan = Mawd < Rhys ap David ap Ll.   Thomas

Sir John Vaughan (1603-1674) = Jane Stedman

Mary Stedman = Henry (d.1666)

Edward Vaughan (d.1683) = Letitia Hooker

3 daughters

(2) Elizabeth (d.1716) = John Vaughan (first Viscount Lisburne) (c.1670-1721) = (1) Malet (Lady Malet Wilmot) (1676-1709)

George

John (2nd Vis: 1695-1741)=Dorothy Hill

Wilmot (3rd Vis:d.1764)

Sir John Vaughan Lt.Gen. (?1748-1795)

Elizabeth m. T.Lloyd Abertrinant

Elizabeth Nightingale 1

Dorothy Shafto 2 = Wilmot (4th Vis) (1st Earl 1776) (d.1800) (twice married)

Wilmot (2nd Earl) (1755-1820)

3 daughters

Col John Vaughan (twice m.) (3rd Earl 1769-1831)

Ernest Augustus Vaughan (twice m.) (4th Earl 1800-1873)

3 other sons, 1 daughter

John 1799-1818

Ernest Augustus Malet Vaughan (thrice m.) (5th Earl 1836-1888)

3 sons, 2 daughters

Arthur George Henry Vaughan (6th Earl 1862-1899)

three daughters

Ernest Edmund Vaughan (twice m.) (7th Earl 1892-1965)

Enid Evelyn

John David (8th Earl b.1918) m. Shelagh McCauley

Gloria   Honor   Auriel

David b.1945   Michael b. 1948   John b.1952

Appendix: The Trawsgoed Portraits

A collection of portraits was a usual part of the apparatus of aristocratic and gentry houses. Walls had to be decorated, but much more importantly, portraits are a statement of genealogical tradition, and even of involvement in history. Their value in sustaining the identity, the *esprit de corps* of an aristocratic family is worth reflecting on; children grew up surrounded by pictures of men and women who were their ancestors, about whom their parents could tell anecdotes. Visitors to the house could be impressed by the variety, quality and antiquity of such pictures, which could distinguished old blood from new. Crudely put, they supported the *amour propre* of the family. Sale of family portraits is regrettable, since even when they are the work of major artists, a thread is broken, and when they lose their identity in passage and become simply `Portrait of a Gentleman, 18C', they are simply fashion plates. Even the removal of portraits from their original settings is sad, however inevitable; a family collection was an essential part of the statement made by the whole house.

Even the largest Welsh houses could not remotely compete with the great English art collections in quality or scale, though some are of particular interest, especially the well-known collection of portraits of servants at Erddig, Wrexham. The Trawsgoed collection, however, is of much more than average Welsh interest. Scattered references have been made through the text to portraits in the collection, which was displayed throughout Trawsgoed mansion until the 1940s. After the sale of mansion and estate in 1947, the pictures remained in family ownership, though a few have been sold.

A list of Trawsgoed pictures was made in 1900, perhaps in connection with the inventory made at that time after the death of the sixth earl. Unfortunately the list was not a complete one; a number of other pictures are known to have been in the family's possession at that time, though they may possibly have been held at Birch Grove, the dower house, or elsewhere. Another list was made by John Steegman, but that too is incomplete.[1] The first head of the family whose portrait survives was Sir John Vaughan (1603-74) the Chief Justice of the Common Pleas; other portraits of him were at Derry Ormond and Gwysaney, Flintshire. A number of pictures represent Sir John's personal loyalties and social interests: there are portraits of his mentor, friend and benefactor, John Selden, of Thomas Wentworth, earl of Strafford, of Barbara Villiers, Duchess of Portsmouth, and of Charles I's children and of his sister Elizabeth, Queen of Bohemia. All save the Queen of Bohemia and Barbara Villiers remain in family ownership.

[1]John Steegman, *Portraits from Welsh houses*, II (Cardiff, 1962)

Sir John's son Edward and grandson John, the first viscount Lisburne, both survive in portrait. The viscount's marriage to Lady Malet Wilmot, daughter of the earl of Rochester, brought in a number of Rochester pictures, most of which still belong to the family. These include the earl himself and his childless son, as well as several pictures of Malet herself; the portraits of her sisters listed by Steegman have been sold. John Vaughan the second viscount is not portrayed; he may never have bothered to have himself painted, and as the black sheep of the family he would not have been a candidate for public display by his heirs. Wilmot Vaughan his brother likewise does not survive in the collection, but Wilmot's sons Wilmot II (the first earl) and General Sir John Vaughan are each the subjects of two portraits. Mr Peter Lord suggests to me that the image of General Vaughan reproduced in this volume may be the work of Benjamin West, Sir Joshua Reynolds's successor as President of the Royal Academy. The General served in the United States, and West was an American, so the two may have become acquainted either in America or Britain. The two of the first earl may both be by Sir Joshua Reynolds himself, and not simply `studio of'. Several portraits survive of associated family members, notably Dorothy Vaughan, the earl's daughter, who married Sir Laurence Palk. Palk was a family trustee, and he too is portrayed.

Neither Wilmot III the insane second earl, nor his half-brother John the third earl, seem to have been added to the collection, but there is an energetic portrait of the fourth earl, Ernest Augustus Mallet Vaughan. Neither his son nor his grandson survive in the collection, but the seventh and eighth earls have both been painted. Most notable of the twentieth century pictures, however, are those by Sir Gerald Kelly and Sir William Orpen of Regina, countess of Lisburne, wife of the seventh earl.

The portraits have been well cared for, and are in good condition. A detailed study of their attributions and history is beyond my ability, but would be an interesting research project.

INDEX

Titled members of the Vaughan family are noted under Lisburne, and are ordered chronologically.